PRISON LITERATURE IN AMERICA

PRISON LITERATURE In America

The Victim As Criminal and Artist

H. Bruce Franklin

LAWRENCE HILL & COMPANY

Westport, Connecticut

Paperback edition published 1982 by Lawrence Hill & Co., Inc., 520 Riverside Avenue, Westport, Connecticut 06880 by permission of the Oxford University Press. Originally published by Oxford University Press 1978 hardcover under the title *The Victim as Criminal and Artist: Literature from the American Prison.*

Library of Congress Cataloging in Publication Data

Franklin, H. Bruce (Howard Bruce), 1934-
   Prison Literature in America.
   Rev. ed. of: The victim as criminal and artist. 1978.
   1. American literature — History and criticism. 2. Prisoners' writings, American — History and criticism. 3. American literature — Afro-American authors — History and criticism. 4. Prisons in literature. 5. Slavery in the United States in literature. I. Title
PS153.P74F7   1982   810'.9'920692   82-2929
ISBN 0-88208-146-2 (pbk.)

No person held to service or labor in one state, under the laws thereof, escaping into another, shall, in consequence of any law or regulation therein, be discharged from such service or labor, but shall be delivered up on claim of the party to whom such service or labor may be due.

from Article 4, Section 2,
of the Constitution of the United States

Repealed by Article 13, Section 1 (1865):

Neither slavery nor involuntary servitude, except as a punishment for crime whereof the party shall have been duly convicted, shall exist within the United States, or any place subject to their jurisdiction.

Acknowledgments

Many people have helped me create this book. I am especially grateful to Hayden White, Carolyn Karcher, Ed Huberman, Joan Hedrick, Heyward Ehrlich, the late Richard Robey, Irwin Primer, Ellen Royer, and the late Charles T. Davis, all of whom made important suggestions and criticisms. I have received various kinds of aid from Joan Farrell and Jeanette Truscott of the Center for the Humanities at Wesleyan, James Brown of the Newark Public Library, Joe Bruchac, Knox Burger, Jane Card of Humming Bird Press, Louie Crew, Louis Cuneo of Mother's Hen, Paul Foreman of Thorp Springs Press, Len Fulton of Dustbooks, Kathryn King of King Publications, Sheldon Meyer of Oxford University Press, Robert Pierce, A. D. Winans of Second Coming Press, and Jeff Youdleman. I owe more than I can acknowledge to the constant unselfishness and comradeship of Karen, Gretchen, and Robert Franklin.

My greatest debts are, as always, to my dearest friend, Jane Morgan Franklin. The major ideas of this book all come from the interplay of our two minds and experience, and are as much her creations as mine. She has also helped in the actual compostion of every part of the book, read proofs, and prepared the index. And without her inspiration and love none of it would have been possible.

The research for this book was aided immeasurably by the generous support of a Visiting Fellowship at the Center for the Humanities at Wesleyan and a Humanities Fellowship from the Rockefeller Foundation.

Substantial sections of Chapter 6 have been published as "The Literature of the American Prison" in *The Massachusetts Review* 18 (Spring, 1977), 51-78. The section of Chapter 5 on Malcolm Braly has been published, in substantially the same form, as "Malcolm Braly: Novelist of the American Prison" in *Contemporary Literature* 18 (Spring 1977), 217-40. A portion of Chapter 1 has been published, in substantially the same form, as "Animal Farm Unbound" in *New Letters* 43 (Spring 1977), 25-46. An earlier and much abbreviated version of Chapter 2 was published as "Herman Melville: Artist of the Worker's World" in *Weapons of Criticism*, ed. Norman Rudich (Palo Alto, Calif.: Ramparts Press, 1976), 287-310. A much earlier version of some parts of Chapter 1 was published as "'A' Is for Afro-American: A Primer on the Study of American Literature" in *The Minnesota Review* n.s. 5 (Fall 1975), 53-64.

Contents

Introduction to the New Edition

In the four years that have passed since the first edition of this book, approximately forty million arrests have taken place in the United States. The population of America's prisons has grown by 20 percent. America has now attained recognition as locking a larger proportion of its population in cages than any other country.

This ratio is based only on those in state and federal prisons, not those in juvenile "correctional" facilities, institutions for the criminally insane, nor the local jails, which now receive well over five million persons a year, twenty-five times the admissions to all state and federal prisons. In these local jails, where those legally innocent but too poor to afford bail are caged for months or even years awaiting trial, suicide has become a common escape. For example, the *New York Times* of October 26, 1981, reported that seventeen suspects, mostly young first-time offenders, committed suicide by hanging in Chicago's police district lock-ups in twenty-two months, while sixteen such suicides by hanging were reported by New York City and sixteen more by Los Angeles in the same period.

Many prisoners are murdered by guards or other prisoners, or are burned to death in their locked cages, as in the July 1977 fire in the federal prison in Danbury, Connecticut, or the December 1979 fire in a South Carolina county jail. In the last several years we have discovered that the use of prisoners as guinea pigs exceeds even the horrors reported in Jessica Mitford's 1971 *Kind and Usual Punishment:* scores of Black prisoners were given syphilis so that the progress of the untreated disease could be recorded; the Atomic Energy Commission beamed X-rays into the testicles of 131 prisoners to see whether this would make them sterile; the U.S. Army used prisoners to conduct tests for its chemical warfare program; Dow Chemical tested Dioxin, one of the most dangerous known substances, on prisoners while preparing its use in Agent Orange for chemical warfare in Vietnam.

Tens of thousands of Vietnam veterans are in state prisons. (A 1978 General Accounting Office report had put the current number at 125,000, but a 1981 Justice Department report claims that the state prisons as of 1979 housed "only" 39,500 Vietnam era veterans.) Riots and rebellions have become so commonplace in the jails and prisons that they make headlines only when they approach the dimensions of the 1980 New Mexico bloodbath in which 33 convicts were killed.

As the economic crisis of our society deepens, unemployment and inflation drive more and more people into crime. The social crisis involves the steady spread of drugs, with addicts now looting the suburbs as well as the cities. Harsh new sentencing laws are passed, further swelling the prison population. Constitutional liberties are attacked in the name of "law and order." People lock themselves in their homes and grow accustomed to electronic surveillance outside. Some note the growing similarities between prisons and the rest of society.

So it is no surprise that literature by American prisoners has become an even more vital part of our culture than it was when the first edition of this book was published four years ago. That edition contained an annotated bibliography of literature by American convicts, which I intended to revise and expand for this present edition. But in those four years, so many new books by American convicts have been published that it has become necessary to publish the expanded bibliography as a separate companion volume (also available from Lawrence Hill & Co.).

Much attention in the press and the popular imagination has been given to one book, Jack Abbott's *In the Belly of the Beast*, which quickly went through five printings in a few months of 1981, even before the author became the center of national controversy for killing a man just after his release from prison. Jack Abbott has presented himself to tens of thousands of relatively affluent and sheltered readers as an example of the people created by our system of "corrections."

First incarcerated when he was nine years old, Abbott was sent to a juvenile penal institution at the age of twelve for the "crime" of "failure to adjust to foster homes." There he was imprisoned, except for six months, until he was eighteen. After being free for five months, he was next given an indeterminate sentence of up to five years in the Utah State Penitentiary for the crime of "issuing a check for insufficient funds." Three years later, he killed another convict in a fight. Between the ages of twelve and thirty-seven, when he wrote the letters to Norman Mailer collected as *In the Belly of the Beast*, he had been free less than one year.

Abbott's revelations about his decades of torture—beatings, starvation, forced injections of dangerous drugs, and a total of ten years spent in solitary confinement, sometimes in total darkness, almost always in cells awash in feces and urine—have produced mixed reactions in the literary world: shock, sympathy, admiration, and contempt. Abbott argues that our penal institutions force each prisoner to become either a broken, cringing animal, fawning before all authority, or a resister, clinging to human dignity through defiance and rebellion.

This is a central theme of much recent prison literature. It is dramatized poignantly in the 1981 semiautobiographical novel *Little Boy Blue* by another child of the state, Edward Bunker. *Little Boy Blue* shows precisely how our "correctional" institutions convert a love-starved little boy into an implacable enemy of society who perceives the police and guards who torture him as merely the "surrogates" of his real oppressor, the respectable people he robs. Bunker and Abbott, like most white contemporary convict authors, ridicule the myth that prisons teach their inmates *how* to commit crimes. What prisoners do acquire, in Abbott's words, is "the *will* to commit crimes."

Edward Bunker's 1977 novel *The Animal Factory* uses an ideal point-of-view character to bridge the chasm between the author and most of his readers: an educated, liberal, first-time convict. He, like Abbott, discovers that the modern American prison is a racist nightmare where racial hatred, inflamed by the guards and officials, is used to keep the prisoners fighting among themselves. Although Bunker's liberal young convict sympathizes with the Blacks, he sees no way to avoid "catching" the "endemic disease" of consuming racism.

As I argue in the final chapter, the experience of white convicts is somewhat different from that of the Black and other nonwhite peoples who now make up the majority of America's prison population. Most of the nonwhites already perceive the dominant white society as the enemy, and they already recognize that they are in prison not for what they have done as individuals but for what they are collectively. White convicts like Jack Abbott, who advance to a revolutionary understanding of their own lives, are thus especially dangerous, for they begin to challenge those racial conflicts so essential to the functioning of the modern American prison.

White convicts are threatened with the stick of being reduced to the level of nonwhites while being offered the carrot of reintegration into the domi-

nant white society—represented immediately by the prison officials, ultimately by the nation outside—if they only acknowledge that the problem
lies within them, that they themselves are responsible for their living in
cages. As Abbott puts it: "I have never accepted that I did this to myself. I
have never been successfully indoctrinated with that belief. That is the only
reason I have been in prison so long." Abbott is then able to make the extraordinary leap from his own individual experience of oppression into a comprehension of the Black response to their oppression as a people:

> When I think of the *profundity* of the injustices done to black people in
> America, I feel a horror I cannot easily describe.
> I would not be a man if I believed that blacks are not *justified socially*
> in treating any and all white people in this society with violence and
> hatred.

Throughout much of this book I have tried to show how and why the
prison system, designed largely to replace the earlier form of Black chattel
slavery, lies at the very center of the oppression of Black people since the
1860s. Today nonwhite people—the so-called "minorities" in America—constitute a majority of the prison population in all regions of the country.
(Only in the West do the official figures seem to indicate a white majority,
but that is only because California, where Chicano prisoners are the largest
group, officially reports them all as "white.") According to a 1980 U.S.
Department of Justice report, *American Prisons and Jails*, the official 1978
rate of incarceration per 100,000 was 59.3 for the white population, 467.3
for the Black population. Two 1977 studies, one by criminologist Eugene
Doleschal, the other by former deputy warden William G. Nagel, both
prove conclusively that the prison rate in various states and regions is not at
all determined by the crime rate but strictly by the size of the nonwhite population. Areas with very low crime rates and very high Black populations
(Mississippi, for example) have very high rates of imprisonment, with
Blacks sometimes forming two thirds or more of the prison population.
In New Jersey, the arrest rate for violent offenses among nonwhites is 11
times the comparable rate among whites. Even more revealing is the fact
that among nonwhites the commitment rate for those convicted of violent offenses is 22 times the commitment rate among whites. Various studies have demonstrated that Blacks convicted of the same offense as
whites, with the same or better records, consistently receive sentences far

more harsh. In the District of Columbia, the nation's capital, where one third of the population is white, recent records show 2,184 Black prisoners and 26 white prisoners. A retired New York judge, investigating the application of the 1978 Juvenile Offenders Section of the Omnibus Crime Bill, discovered that in New York City only 3.1 percent of the children arrested, charged as felons, and sent to Rikers Island were white.

Most white Americans, unlike most Blacks, refuse to believe that America's prisons are primarily concentration camps for nonwhite peoples. This is, however, the underlying assumption that generally governs sentencing. Of course this is rarely admitted. But recently a Manhattan Criminal Court judge actually declared that he was refusing to imprison a convicted white criminal because of his "color and ethnic background," which would make him "immediately subject to homosexual rape and sodomy and to brutalities from fellow prisoners such as make the imagination recoil in horror" (*New York Times*, April 9, 1981).

These concentration camps for nonwhites and for the relatively small percentage of whites deemed so recalcitrant that they must be treated like nonwhites have produced an astounding body of literature in the last two decades alone. Unknown to most of the readers of the books by Bunker and Abbott, which are put out by major publishers, is the bulk of literature by Black convicts, most of which is put out by small presses and Black publishers. This literature now forms a major subterranean current in modern American culture.

Studies of popular American culture recognize the importance of such literary genres as science fiction, westerns, detective stories, and gothic romances. If you were today to walk into the principal paperback bookstore in Newark, New Jersey, a predominantly Black city, you would indeed find sections devoted to each of these well-known popular categories along with such other staples as cookbooks, dictionaries, science, and so on. But you would also find that one of the largest sections in the store is devoted exclusively to the publications of Holloway House, a Black publisher specializing in "Black experience" books and largely supported by the works of Black convict authors, particularly Donald Goines and Robert Beck, better known as Iceberg Slim. On display here are twenty-three books by these two authors alone.

Donald Goines's meteoric career began in 1971, with the publication of his first two novels, both written in prison. By 1974, he had written a total of sixteen novels. All are still in print, and the women who work in that

Newark bookstore tell me that all are in constant demand, along with a biography of Goines, also published by Holloway House. Goines's career came to an end in late 1974 when two white men entered his apartment in Detroit and gunned down him and his wife before the eyes of their two young daughters.

His sixteen novels are an impressive, though very uneven, achievement. At their core is an unflinching revelation of the horrors of life in the Black underworld, especially the devastating physical and psychological effects of drugs, and the consuming fantasies of power among people daily robbed by the capitalist economic structure and ground down under the iron heel of the white state.

The first two novels, *Whoreson* (1971) and *Dopefiend* (1971), are social naturalism. Then emerges a nascent revolutionary imagination in *Black Gangster* (1972), the tale of a ruthless ex-convict who builds a minor criminal empire, partly by creating a phony organization ostensibly dedicated to the liberation of nonwhite people, only to be drowned in bloody struggle against the Mafia, the police, and an authentic revolutionary organization modeled on the Black Panther Party. *White Man's Justice, Black Man's Grief* (1973) presents one of the most horrifying visions of prison, even within prison literature.

Four out of Goines's last seven books constitute an epic tetralogy of the rise and fall of the ambiguous Black revolutionary Kenyatta, a giant of a man with enormous passions, who builds a personal army of Black fighters dedicated to wiping out the drug trade in the ghettos. Counterpointed to Kenyatta's messianic imagination are the contradictory views of a pair of detectives, one white and one black, hunting him down.

Although Goines has sometimes been branded as a "reverse racist" whose fiction shows unrelenting hatred of whites, probably the most consistently admirable character in his work is Paul Pawloski in *Never Die Alone* (1974), a down-and-out writer, the son and grandson of Jews killed by the Nazis. When Paul takes a dying Black con man, notorious in the ghetto for his viciousness, to a hospital, he is rewarded by the dead man's illicit fortune and autobiographical manuscript. In a sometimes dazzling display of shifting points of view, the manuscript and Paul's reactions form a contrapuntal commentary on Goines's own writings, many other "Black Experience" narratives, and the responses of their readers. Paul has trouble deciding whether the manuscript is primarily a diary or a novel: "The poor sonofabitch was really trying to write a book! Now I wonder just how much of this shit in here is real, or just parts of an over-worked imagination."

The distinction between fantasy and reality is perhaps the main theme in a subgenre of Black experience literature, the fictional and nonfictional narratives of pimps. Although the shape of this literature is foreshadowed in the section of *The Autobiography of Malcolm X* describing his life as a pimp, the archetypal work is the 1967 *Pimp: The Story of My Life* by Iceberg Slim.

This autobiography chronicles the pimp culture—the world of "players" at the "game" of "cop and blow" (capturing and losing whores)—especially during the Depression and the years just after World War II. The even earlier legendary history comes from Slim's master teacher, who tells him that the "game" was invented by ex-slaves who migrated to the Northern cities only to discover that these were replicas of "the plantations down South." These first pimps were "black geniuses" who wrote in their own minds the "skull book on pimping," a systematic way to turn affluent and powerful white men into mere "tricks" willing to pay a price to satisfy their most depraved urges with Black women. Just as these white men perceive these Black women as mere animals, their racism also leads them into incessant gullibility to a variety of con games, for each usually has a "complete inability to conceive that the 'black boy' before him was intelligent enough to fool him."

Of course, the other side of this game of naked power is the reenslavement of Black women, this time to the pimps. Unlike some other pimp books, which are little more than extended indulgences in sexual fantasies, Iceberg Slim's works all insist that pimping "ain't no sex game" but the most brutal exercise of cunning and punishment designed to turn women into instruments of wealth and power so that the Black pimp can become just "like a slick white boss."

The Naked Soul of Iceberg Slim (1971), a collection of autobiographical and political essays, goes even deeper in its exposé of the fantasies of pimps. Here the author expresses in a magnificent letter of reconciliation to his father his acceptance of both the strengths and weaknesses of the "straight" life of Black working people, and shows how the Black Panther Party helped him to understand both the self-deceptive brutality of the pimp's "game" and the revolutionary potential implicit in the confrontation with Black reality.

His 1977 novel *Death Wish* is a complex and fully wrought work of art that dramatizes a further stage in the dialectic. Here the Mafia is locked in struggle with a primarily Black but interracial revolutionary organization dedicated, like the army of Goines's Kenyatta, to smashing the organized apparatus of the most terrifying slavery, drug addiction. Although the

Mafia incarnates social and psychological evil, and their nemesis the Warriors embody a progressive force, we are gradually led to see that the Warriors are doomed to tragic failure because they have not purged themselves of many of the qualities of their enemy: egoism, lust for power, enjoyment of violence, self-delusion, and male supremacy. Scenes in the two camps alternate (almost as in the *Iliad*), and the turning point for each comes when the wife of its principal leader decides to leave him. In this novel by a Black ex-pimp, it is the wife of the Mafia chieftain who implies another level of struggle: "I'm glad women have declared war on men to force their humanity. I'm thrilled to join that war to save the world's sanity for our children."

The 1977 novel *A Right to Anger* by Karamoko Baye (once convicted of bank robbery, now Director of PACE, an organization for prisoners' art and education) imagines a multiracial revolutionary alliance in which both ex-prisoners and progressive women play leading roles. Here the revolutionary organization is betrayed by the appropriately named Willie Lumpen, who embodies the most trecherous qualities of the street hustler, just as the protagonist, a pimp known as Blood, gradually comes to embody the hustler's revolutionary potential. But the final words of the novel are spoken by one of Blood's Black prostitutes, who scorns the adventurist bomb-throwing shootout in which the would-be revolutionaries are cut down:

> "I can't be bothered with all that mess. Them niggas is goin' crazy. What they oughtta be about, is building a party."

The literature of female prisoners themselves gives insights not generally accessible in literature by men, whether convicts or not. This literature is not voluminous. Since only 4 percent of the population of federal and state prisons are women, most of the published works by female prisoners are found in anthologies gathered from the local and county jails where women are more often incarcerated.

Viewed from the women's side, the fantasies of the pimps' world look thin and ragged. These fantasies also serve as extremely clear projections of a capitalist culture that reduces all human relations to the relations between money and the things money can buy. Thus Carolyn Baxter's "Lower Court," a poem in her splendid chapbook, *Prison Solitary and Other Free*

Government Services (1979), displays a prostitute in a courtroom reduced to an assortment of objects:

> She opens her mouth wider, crumpled one dollar bills
> fall out, along with prophylactics, 10¢ perfume, lipstick,
> a newspaper clipping for a pair of $30 boots, a whip,
> an explanation for the forged driver's license/a
> picture of her favorite group, "The Shantells."

Her pimp makes her complete the showing by "activating" her with his fist, so that she projects for everyone's entertainment "last night's streetreel." Baxter describes in "To Gary Frase" the feelings of a woman losing her lover to the objects which make "apt. 52" her irresistible "competition":

> I sit in her wooden, corduroy couch embarrassed,
> as you kiss her police lock neck, stroking her denim,
>   and assorted flat paint. Playing with her brass clitoris
> Getting all excited over her darkroom, and
>   heavy air-conditioned breathing.
>
> Easing yourself in between her antique oak
> quadrophonic thighs. Enjoying the waterpic, terri cloth,
>   dripolator, screwing her cork.
> Finally coming in her stainless steel,
>   blue printed, multi-shelved, butcher block, nicon telephoto
> 88mm, mini-refrigerated cunt.

Kay Bynum, whose poems first appeared in the 1978 anthology *Kites* (published by the Women's Unit of the Arkansas Department of Corrections), dramatizes the most vicious—and ordinary—personal relationships as expressions of contemporary capitalist culture. Her poem "Hating omen is a CONTAGIOUS DISEASE REACHING EPIDEMIC PROPORTIONS IN AMERICA" begins:

> It is a national pass time, forever amber in a country
> of technicolor creatures, phallic pharaohs who worship
> the change in their pants pocket and never alter their pace

for the women who pant for change beneath their weight.
Why do you think Madison Avenue sells aspirin and iron fortified
vitamins like waters over Niagara Falls when the honeymoon
ended in "Not tonight, dear"?

After stanzas equating drug addiction and wife beating with spectator
ports, Bynum imagines "love" reduced to a sordid seduction that merges
into an addict shooting up:

> He pushes her against the dirty sink and enters, painlessly,
> into the virgin vein, collapsing against his weight,
> black tiles beneath his feet. She licks a final drop of love
> from his pointed stick and follows its shadow onto the street.

Redemption from this loveless world tends to appear in relations based on
a revolutionary commitment to replace it with a better one. Assata Shakur
(Joanne Chesimard), whose revolutionary leadership is not a fiction in a
novel, expresed it this way in a stanza of her poem "For Rema Olugbala
(Youngblood)," published in *Songs from a Free Space: Writings by Women
in Prison* in 1978:

> They think they killed you
> But I saw you yesterday
> With your back against the wall
> Muscles bulging against the chains
> Eyes absorbing truth
> Lips speaking it
> Heart learning how to love
> Head learning who to hate
> Blood ready to flow, towards freedom
> Youngblood!

The following year Assata Shakur was rescued from prison by her com-
rades, Black and white.

H. B. F.
Newark, New Jersey
January, 1982

Introduction to the First Edition

After two hundred years of existence as an independent nation-state, we still approach American literature as though it were a mere colonial implantation, no doubt modified by local conditions but in essence an offshoot of European culture. We teach "our" culture as a subcategory of "Western Civilization," something traced back through the various European national cultures to a common origin in the first European city-states. American literature is therefore consigned to an academic department named English, where it is presented as a relatively minor branch of a particular European national literary tradition stretching back through periods defined largely by the rise and fall of British monarchs—Victorian, Restoration, Jacobean, Elizabethan—or by the alleged preeminence of a handful 'of British literary geniuses—the Romantic Period, the Age of Milton, the Age of Chaucer, etc.—until it reaches its primal source in a few fragments written in, or translated into, a language spoken by the Germanic tribes that invaded the southeast corner of one of the British isles. These tribal origins merge into the mighty river of "Western" (a euphemism for white European) culture flowing in with the Romans, whose cultural history in turn is traced back to the first Greek tribes to become civilized (i.e., citified).

At first glance, the procedure used for defining American literature and culture seems analogous to that used for most national literatures and cultures. German or French literature is indeed the literature of the German or French people, extending back from the period of national unification through feudalism into the Ur-literature of the tribal groupings whose descendants were eventually to make a nation. But to apply this procedure to American literature is to construct a false analogy which radically distorts and misrepresents the history and culture of America. For "America" is not a single people formed from the territories and descendants of neighboring and marauding tribes, but a historical contradiction among peoples from three separate continents.

Begin with the primary, and what should be the most obvious, fact in the history of America: the conquest and virtual extermination of the people living here. If our procedure were really analogous to that used for the definition of English or German or French literature we would begin in the tribal past of America, not the tribal past of England or Athens. But from the point of view of those doing the defining, American literature is composed of works in the language of one of the peoples who destroyed the societies inhabiting the continent, so the oral and written literature in the native languages has been, by definition, excluded, though these languages (unlike the dialects of the Angles and Saxons) are still spoken and though the peoples who speak these languages are all supposedly citizens of the United States of America. I am not arguing that it is mere ethnocentricity that has excluded the native cultures of our territory from "our" culture or at best presents them as a tacked-on appendage. For the very existence of the "Indians" is a refutation of the concept "America," a land that came to exist only when it was discovered by Europeans, and one named for a Florentine merchant-navigator.

Having some other European language, even the one spoken by the main "discoverers" and claimants of America, does not qualify a people to have its oral and written culture included in American literature. When the northern half of Mexico was seized by the United States and converted into the southwestern quarter of the national territory (Arizona, California, western Colorado, Nevada, New Mexico, Texas, and Utah), the Spanish-speaking people of this vast area were guaranteed coequalty. Yet their culture has been dismissed as alien. In 1883, Walt Whitman, deploring the exclusion of both Spanish and Indian culture from what is deemed American, wrote: ". . . we tacitly abandon ourselves to the notion that our United States have been fashion'd from the British Islands only, and essentially form a second England only—which is a very great mistake." He predicted that the Spanish and Indian cultures would be integral to the "composite American identity of the future." Yet still the academy excludes both from "our" culture.

Certain unstated assumptions, rather than the question of language itself, are critical. After all, we teach as part of "our" culture, in translation from the ancient Greek, the collections of oral tales about warriors and heroes known as the Homeric epics. And linguistic homogeneity, the main overt argument used to exclude the cultural heritage of native Americans and Chicanos in defining American literature, certainly is not the assumption used to exclude the culture of Black Americans.

If the first great historical fact that defines and distinguishes "America" is the colonization of much of the continent, the second, and the dominant one since 1850, is the enslavement of Black Africans. The descendants of these Africans are in many senses the truest Americans, for the Afro-American people were created in the United States, their unpaid labor provided the capital base for the political economy of modern America, and their culture has, for more than a century, been central to American culture in general. Only in the academy, the last bastion of European colonialism in the United States, is it possible to pretend that our culture for over a century has not been primarily an expression of the interaction between two groups of peoples, one of European and the other of African descent. And even in the academy, as this book itself attests, all is no longer secure. Insofar as American literature is in fact a unique body of creative work, what defines its identity most unequivocally is the historical and cultural experience of the Afro-American people. At long last we have come to understand that this is obviously true for American music and dance, and we are on the verge of recovering our lost vision of the interrelations between music and poetry. When we grasp the significance of this truth for American literature as a whole, we will be forced to change radically our critical methodologies, our criteria for literary excellence, and our canon of great literature—or perhaps even the entire notion of a canon.

World War I through the 1930s was an exciting period of discovery for the literature produced by the peoples of America. These decades included: the Harlem Renaissance; the unearthing of a forgotten nineteenth-century author named Herman Melville; the publication in 1918 of a seminal collection, *The Path on the Rainbow: An Anthology of Songs and Chants from the Indians of North America,* which claimed about its contents that "none exhibit the slightest traces of European influence; they are genuine American Classics";[1] the development of proletarian theories of literature and conscious groups of working-class authors; the collection and study of many forms of oral folk literature; and, as we shall see in Chapters 3 and 4, a growing awareness of the importance of the songs of Black convicts and the written narratives of white convicts. By the early 1930s, anthologies of American literature often included generous selections of Negro spirituals and blues, Indian poetry, ballads and worksongs, folktales, and other forms of popular literature. The most widely used anthology of poetry, for example, was Louis Untermeyer's *American Poetry from the Beginning to Whitman* (New York: Harcourt, 1931) and *Modern American Poetry* (New York: Harcourt, various editions through the 5th, 1936). The first volume included poems by Phillis Wheatley together with an analysis of her achievement plus sections entitled American Indian Poetry; Spanish-Colonial Verse; Early American Ballads; Negro Spirituals; Negro Social, "Blues" and Work-Songs; "Negroid" Melodies; Cowboy Songs and Hobo Harmonies; Backwoods Ballads; City Gutturals. The second volume contained generous selections from such Black poets as James Weldon Johnson, Paul Laurence Dunbar, Claude McKay, Jean Toomer, Langston Hughes, and Countee Cullen.[2]

But during this same period there emerged a group of critics, originally coalescing at Vanderbilt University, who frankly proclaimed themselves "reactionaries" and who dedicated themselves to squelching all this. Their announced purpose, spelled out in *I'll Take My Stand* (1930) and *Reactionary Essays* (1936), was to separate literature from its social context and to combat the "vulgar" culture of industrial America, promulgating in its place the "finest" values of "the Old South," some precious, archaic literary forms (such as seventeenth-century metaphysical poetry), and a select handful of modern authors (notably themselves and such equally reactionary figures as T. S. Eliot). They immediately began churning out anthologies intended to make their values dominant in the teaching of literature.[3]

Then came World War II and its sequel, the sweeping repression of the late 1940s and early 1950s. During this period, New Criticism became the dominant critical methodology; and those anthologies the New Critics had produced were accomplishing their purposes quite well. Probably relatively few of the professors who had survived the 1947–53 purges thought of themselves as political ideologues. When they were choosing from within the canon the handful of "masterpieces" they were going to require their students to read, or when the most eminent among them were constructing even more up-to-date anthologies, they, unlike their confederates in the 1930s, probably did not think of themselves as making selections and rejections based on criteria congenial to their own social class. But by the mid 1950s, almost the entire body of literature created and widely enjoyed by the peoples of America had been rejected in favor of an infinitesimal canon of "great" works by literary "masters," mostly professional white gentlemen of the same race, sex, and social class as those selecting them.

This is most easily seen in the exclusion of Afro-American literature. The American literature taught in our colleges and universities, collected in our anthologies, and discussed in our literary histories was as lily-white as the faculty club at Johns Hopkins or Stanford.

For example, the 1959 edition of *Masters of American Literature,* edited by Leon Edel, Thomas H. Johnson, Sherman Paul, and Claude Simpson, includes not a single selection from a nonwhite author in its 1396 pages. The same is true for the 1119 pages of Perry Miller's 1962 edition of *Major Writers of America* and the 1246 pages of the 1965 edition of *American Poetry,* edited by Gay W. Allen, Walter B. Rideout, and James K. Robinson.[4] Of course these anthologies all professed to be based on literary excellence alone. The editors of *Masters of American Literature* asserted that they had been guided by the belief that the student "will profit more from regarding the works he reads to be studied and enjoyed on their own terms than he will from viewing them as illustrations of the course of literary or cultural history." Perry Miller claimed that his chosen writers were all "superior" because "the study of American literature—inside and outside the universities—is now systematic and mature" and "the canon of American literature" has now been established "on as broad a basis as possible." The editors of *American Poetry* went so far as to claim that it covered "the entire sweep of the American poetic achievement" with only one guiding criterion for selection: "literary excellence."[5] Nobody seemed to notice who and what was being rejected.

Then came the Black urban rebellions, those "long, hot summers" of 1964, 1965, 1966, 1967, culminating in April 1968, with simultaneous uprisings in 110 U.S. cities. At the same time came the mass movement against the Indochina War. Rebellion moved onto the campus, and even into the classroom. Blacks, students, women, Chicanos, Indians, workers, Puerto Ricans, even a few white male professors of literature—all sorts of people seemed to be demanding radical changes. The social upheaval of 1964-72 has had some effect on every institution, and almost every individual, in American society. Certainly it changed my own life and thinking profoundly. This book itself is a product of the changes forced upon my outlook on our literature, and it will end by attempting to show some of the ongoing—and deepening—cultural changes flowing from those events.

Within the academy, those rebellions produced some immediate, quite apparent, results. Afro-American studies were allowed to occupy one or two seats at the counter in the free academic marketplace of ideas, a few Black authors were given walk-on parts in some literature courses and anthologies, and English departments scrambled to hire their Black token. Programs for the study of Chicano, Indian, Puerto Rican, and other "ethnic" cultures (as if all cultures weren't ethnic) were established. Those "vulgar" theories of culture, supposedly refuted in the late 1930s and expunged in the late 1940s and early 1950s, once again raised their ugly heads. Courses began to proliferate in oral literature, science fiction, detective fiction, women's studies, film, children's literature; some courses were even labeled with those quaint old adjectives "proletarian" and "working-class."

But we should not fool ourselves. Under cover of an economic crisis, partly real, partly manipulated, a systematic assault has been mounted against all the academic changes and innovations, just like the assault on all those ghetto programs won by the mass rebellions of the 1960s. In fact, many of the young scholars and critics who had begun a radical reexamination of the study of literature and culture have been driven from the academic profession, under one pretext or another, in a purge more sweeping than that of 1947–53.

The fundamental definition of American literature remains what it was before 1964, with Afro-American literature safely ghettoized within the curriculum and represented by tokens in the anthologies. As an extreme example, take the standard history of American literature, *Literary History of the United States,* by Robert Spiller, Willard Thorp, Thomas H. Johnson, Henry Seidel Canby, Richard Ludwig, and William M. Gibson. In 1974, a greatly revised fourth edition was published, with 1555 pages of facts and analysis in small print. There are three chapters on the literature produced in the South through the Civil War; all this literature is by whites. The authors discussed include such literary giants and eminent apologists for slavery as Hugh Legaré, William Wirt, and George Fitzhugh, author of *Cannibals All! Or, Slaves without Masters.* Nowhere in the volume is there a discussion of the slave narrative or slave poetry. There is no mention of William Wells Brown, the nineteenth-century Black novelist, playwright, and historian. Not even the name of Frederick Douglass appears, though Stephen A. Douglas is cited four times. The *Bibliography Supplement,* published in 1972, includes bibliographies for 218 individual authors, including John C. Calhoun, Thomas Bailey Aldrich, James Lane Allen, and Allen Tate. Only four Black writers are included: Charles Waddell Chesnutt, Paul Laurence Dunbar, Langston Hughes, and Richard Wright.

This is no isolated example. The 1972 revised edition of *Eight American Authors,* the standard bibliographic volume on nineteenth-century American literature officially sponsored by the Modern Language Association, deals exclusively with white (and male) authors. The companion volume for twentieth-century American literature, *Sixteen Modern American Authors,* 1973 edition, consists of bibliographic surveys of fifteen male white authors plus one white woman (Willa Cather). The most influential anthology of American literature, *The American Tradition in Literature,* edited by Scully Bradley, Richmond Croom Beatty, and E. Hudson Long, begins to show the impact of modern historical events in its 1967 edition. At the very end of its 3500 pages of literature written exclusively by whites come two short poems by LeRoi Jones, thus introduced by the editors: "Jones is easily the most interesting of the young Negro poets, but race is not often at issue in his poetry and does not restrict its appeal." The 1974 edition feebly reflects some of the changing consciousness in the surrounding society. Now the editors include 16 pages of Afro-American literature among the 1843 of Volume 1, and devote the grand total of 104 pages out of the 3685 in the two-volume set to Afro-American authors and their biographies. So the entire Afro-American people are given as much space as Royall Tyler and Jonathan Edwards. The editors also revise that headnote about the sole Black author in the 1967 edition; it now concludes: "After having established a poetic reputation as LeRoi Jones, he adopted the name Imamu Amiri Baraka and became more militantly race conscious, active in politics as well as in literature. *The Toilet, Dutchman,* and *The Slave* treat black-white relationships explicitly and sometimes shockingly." They make no mention of his extensive literary and cultural criticism or his fiction, and their selections of his work are still limited to those two short 1964 poems. The utmost liberal effort is the tokenism of *Anthology of American Literature,* edited by George McMichael, Richard P. Adams, Frederick Crews, J. C. Levenson, Leo Marx, and David E. Smith in 1974. In the 3983 pages of its two volumes, 149 pages (3.7 percent) are devoted to Afro-American authors and their biographies. (This compares with 2.8 percent for the 1974 edition of *The American Tradition in Literature.*) Merely counting pages has its limitations, but at least it offers a quantifiable, literally palpable, demonstration that ethnic and class criteria are used to determine literary excellence and prominence. It also demonstrates that these criteria respond to historical change.

I am in no way suggesting that after the late 1940s Black literature was consciously excluded from the canon of American literature because of the skin color or physiognomy of its authors. It simply no longer matched up with the prevailing literary criteria. Certainly since 1964, those professors who edit the anthologies, survey the literary history, and decide the curriculum have been actively searching for Black authors who fit their notion of excellence. That is precisely the point, for the criteria they apply are determined by their own people and social class, and most Afro-American literature conforms to criteria determined by a different people and a different social class. And thus any large-scale inclusion of Afro-American literature within what we call American literature forces a fundamental redefinition and a complex process of revaluations.

Historical events have forced certain choices upon all of us students of American literature. Surely it is no longer possible to use the term "American literature" to encompass no more than belletristic writings by a select handful of white authors. Eventually we will probably have to grasp the fully multiethnic range of literature by "Americans," including the peoples native to the continent. My own procedure in this book is far more conservative, for I limit the field of study to the literature produced in the English language within the nation-state known as the United States of America. Furthermore, except for an essential chapter on the songs of slaves and Black convicts, I focus almost entirely on written and published literature, excluding oral and manuscript material. And I even adopt some of the prevailing formal criteria in choosing particular works for discussion. Nevertheless, even within these partly self-imposed limitations, I believe that this book leads inevitably to a fundamental redefinition of American literature, its history, and the criteria appropriate to evaluating all literary works produced within the United States.

My subject is literature created by those members of the oppressed classes who have become artists with words through their experience of being defined by the state as criminals. All the works studied in this book were produced by "criminals" who spent time physically incarcerated for their actions or beliefs or social status. I am not, of course, talking about the novels of Spiro Agnew and E. Howard Hunt, or the memoirs of Richard Nixon, men whose crimes are obviously more significant than their art, but of the art produced out of the sufferings inflicted by such men, their social class, and the political economy they defend. The authors' "crimes" are mostly those peculiar to the condition of poverty and forced labor: refusal to work; desertion and escape; mutiny and revolt; revolution. Their art expresses the experience of being legally kidnapped, plundered, raped, beaten, chained, and caged—and the understanding that results.

A few of these authors, very few indeed, have literary reputations. As my research for this book began to lead me off the beaten paths, I found myself stumbling on treasures far beyond my expectations, in both quantity and quality. The final three chapters and the Appendix, "An Annotated Bibliography of Literature by American Convicts: 1800-1976,"* merely hint of what lies out there. I am convinced that my own discoveries will eventually prove to be merely an introduction to the literature of the American prison. In the seven-year period during which I worked on this book, I gradually realized that I was not looking at some peripheral cultural phenomenon but something close to the center of our historical experience as a nation-state. At least from the viewpoint of the people creating these works, America is itself a prison, and the main lines of American literature can be traced from the plantation to the penitentiary.

---

*Now superseded by *American Prisoners and Ex-Prisoners: Their Writings: An Annotated Bibliography of Published Works, 1798-1981*, the companion volume to this new edition.

Part I

The Victim as Criminal and Artist in America

CHAPTER 1

The First Literary Genre of the United States: The Slave Narrative

A literature that was consciously "American" first came into being in the eight decades between the Revolution and the Civil War. During this period most white Americans thought of Blacks as anything from funny childlike creatures to animals of a distinct subhuman species. Fundamental to the outlook of most of the new Republic's writers, this view was implemented thoughout American society and was codified into the founding Constitution and subsequent legislation. Here is one widely disseminated expression of the dominant picture:

> The situation of the slave is, in every particular, incompatible with the cultivation of his mind. It would not only unfit him for his station in life, and prepare him for insurrection, but would be found wholly impracticable in the performance of the duties of a laborer....
>
> Inert and unintellectual, he exhibits no craving for knowledge; and prefers, in his hours of recreation, indulgence in his rustic pleasures to the pursuit of intellectual improvement... the negro never suffers from the thirst for knowledge. Voluptuous and indolent, he knows few but animal pleasures; is incapable of appreciating the pride and pleasure of conscious intellectual refinement.... The dance beneath the shade surpasses, for him, the groves of the academy.[1]

In the literature of the South, or rather in literature by white southerners, this view was virtually unanimous. William Gilmore Simms, still widely touted as the greatest writer produced by the "Old South," argued that "there are few people so very well satisfied with their conditions as the negroes,—so happy of mood, so jocund, and so generally healthy and cheerful."[2]

The New England writer now most venerated, Nathaniel Hawthorne, shared this view. In his fiction he simply pretended Black people did not exist, except as stereotyped faithful body servants, such as Caesar in "The White Old Maid," Scipio in "Egotism," or the other Scipio whose stock role provides comic relief in *The House of the Seven Gables* (just like Jupiter in Poe's "The Gold Bug," Scipio is scared of a ghost that comes to "frighten a poor nigga"). His only distinct Black character is also a stereotype, the stock "nigger" of "Mr. Higginbotham's Catastrophe," a mulatto who turns from "yellow" to "ghastly white" when confronted with a crime he was too cowardly to commit. In the sketch "Sunday at Home" he pictures the highest aspirations of Blacks in the persons of "two sable ladies and a sable gentleman" to whom "bliss in heaven" means "'There we shall be white!'" Twice Hawthorne explicitly stated his opinion of slavery. In "Old News" (1835), he characterizes "slave labor" in eighteenth-century New England as "a patriarchal, and almost a beautiful, peculiarity of the times":

> But the slaves, we suspect, were the merriest part of the population, since it was their gift to be merry in the worst of circumstances; and they endured, comparatively, few hardships, under the domestic sway of our fathers. . . . Sometimes the slaves assumed the property of their own persons, and made their escape; among many such instances, the governor raises a hue-and-cry after his negro Juba. But, without venturing a word in extenuation of the general system, we confess our opinion that Caesar, Pompey, Scipio, and all such great Roman namesakes, would have been better advised had they stayed at home, foddering the cattle, cleaning dishes,—in fine, performing their moderate shares of the labors of life, without being harassed by its cares.[3]

And nine years before the Civil War, Hawthorne lashed out at all antislavery "agitation," which, he asserted, threatened "the ruin of two races which now dwelt together in greater peace and affection . . . than had ever elsewhere existed between the taskmaster and the serf."[4]

In opposition to this view and to the system it defended, there emerged a literary genre whose form and content is uniquely American—the narrative of the escaped slave. The slave narrative is the literary. creation of those "inert and unintellectual" bodies without minds, those happy serfs, those "voluptuous and indolent" animals with no human aspirations. The racist mentality of William Gilmore Simms and Nathaniel Hawthorne, of Edgar Allan Poe and James Fenimore Cooper, is not unique to America; it was, and still is, generally characteristic of European societies and the colonialists exported from Europe to the Americas, Asia, and Africa. The slave narrative, however, is truly American. In fact, it was the first genre the United States contributed to the written literature of the world.

This event in literary history was recognized in print as early as 1849, by the Reverend Ephraim Peabody, who put it this way in his article "Narratives of Fugitive Slaves" in the *Christian Examiner and Religious Miscellany:* "America has the mournful honor of adding a new department to the literature of civilization—the autobiographies of escaped slaves."[5] In *Many Thousand Gone: The Ex-Slaves' Account of Their Bondage and Freedom,* the pioneering twentieth-century history of the genre, Charles H. Nichols demonstrated the vast popularity and influence of these autobiographies by Black Americans.[6] (This study was published in 1963, in Holland, revealingly enough; it was not until 1969 that it finally achieved publication in America.) The genre produced several of the greatest works of nineteenth-century American literature. In 1863 an escaped slave who had written one of these narratives, the man now once again being recognized as America's first Black novelist and playwright, William Wells Brown, included a history of the genre in his vanguard study, *The Black Man: His Antecedents, His Genius, and His Achievements.*

In less than a century, however, this literary achievement had been effectively expunged from the study of American literature, which, in the words of Perry Miller, was "now systematic and mature." By the time of the 1954 Supreme Court decision against apartheid in education, only one example of the slave narrative was in print.[7] But since then our history has prepared us to understand both the social and the artistic significance of these works.

The slave narrative was usually told by a fugitive slave, whose escape from slavery was perceived, quite accurately, as a threat to the entire system. Those who defended slavery argued, like Simms and Hawthorne, that Negroes were happy to be slaves. Every escaped slave was a living refutation of that argument. Another defense of slavery, one underlying the first, was that Negroes were not thinking human beings. Every author of a slave narrative was a refutation of that argument. And if the slave narrative could transcend the literature being published by the apologists for slavery, it would embody even more radical implications—about human potential, about the meaning of culture, about the relations among social classes.

The audience for the slave narrative was generally the reading public of the northern states, overwhelmingly white and relatively "cultured." An odd relationship existed between the authors and the readers, one exacerbated by the passage of the Fugitive Slave Act of 1850. The audience was part of the body of citizens whose lawful duty was to help ferret out the authors and return these runaway pieces of property to their rightful owners. The narratives were frankly polemical, and, whether actually written by the slaves themselves or, as in some cases, ghost-written by their abolitionist friends, generally used the polite literary language and style expected by their audience. But the experience being rendered was so brutal and sordid as to be almost beyond the imagination of most of these readers.

From Ephraim Peabody and William Wells Brown to the present, all students of the slave narrative have agreed that the masterpiece of the form is Frederick Douglass's first autobiography, published in 1845, *Narrative of the Life of Frederick Douglass, An American Slave: Written by Himself.* And even if the rest of the genre did not exist, the *Narrative* stands on its own as "a classic American autobiography."[8] Nevertheless, the book has received scandalously little critical attention as a work of literature, and Douglass himself, one of the most important authors in nineteenth-century America, has remained a virtual nonentity outside the academic ghetto of Afro-American studies. *Articles on American Literature, 1950–1967* (Duke University Press, 1970) includes not a single entry on Frederick Douglass, though it lists over fifty articles on Jonathan Edwards, James Kirke Paulding, and William Wirt. The omission cannot be explained by the fact that Douglass's works are mostly essays and autobiographical narratives, for there are 459 articles listed on Henry David Thoreau. Douglass's books are not even included in the standard *Bibliography of American Literature* compiled by Jacob Blanck, and, as noted in the Introduction, the standard history of American literature never mentions his name. The only extended discussions of the *Narrative* published in books have been in studies of Afro-American literature and the slave narrative.[9] There have been, to the best of my knowledge, only two published articles on the *Narrative,* and both appeared in *College Language Association Journal,* a publication devoted to Afro-American literature.[10] In other words, the white academic establishment still pretends that Frederick Douglass does not exist as a literary artist or that, like Satchel Paige, he is not good enough to play outside the Negro leagues.

I shall be exploring here the wider significance of one theme and set of images in the *Narrative,* using some methods we customarily deem appropriate to a short story by Poe or Hawthorne, a poem by Whitman or Dickinson, or an autobiographical narrative by Thoreau or Henry Adams. A subsidiary part of my intention is to show that individual early Afro-American works of literature merit the kind of close attention we usually reserve for works of the canon. It is curious that such a demonstration should be necessary for the slave narrative, for it, like most forms of early written Afro-American literature, thoroughly accepts the dominant European literary conventions.

Narrative of the Life of Frederick Douglass, An American Slave: Written by Himself is a book created by a being who was once considered an animal, even by himself, to an audience not quite convinced that he is in fact a fellow human being. So it should come as no surprise that animal imagery embodies Douglass's deepest meanings.

In *Long Black Song,* Houston Baker notes that animal metaphors "appear in most of the chapters of the *Narrative."* Baker offers several explanations. He observes that "Douglass is aware of American slavery's chattel principle, which equated slaves with livestock, and he is not reluctant to employ animal metaphors to capture the general inhumanity of the system." He makes an intriguing suggestion about overtones in the *Narrative* from the animal tales of Black slave culture. And he emphasizes the appropriateness of the animal imagery to "the agrarian settings and characters."[11] Albert Stone disagrees with Baker, arguing that Douglass's "images of ships and the sea" are far more central than animal imagery, forming a pattern which "connects and defines all stages of his personal history."[12] Stone's sensitive exploration of the nautical imagery is a valuable contribution to our appreciation of the artistic richness of this book. It is, however, the animal imagery that is crucial, and in ways more significant than even Baker perceived.

These images not only structure the development of the *Narrative,* but also locate the book on the front lines of a major ideological battleground of the 1840s and 1850s. Douglass makes one question central in the *Narrative:* What is a human being? That is, within his historical context, how is a human being different from animals (or machines) that can perform labor? This was also the central philosophical and scientific question of his time, a question that all our subsequent history has been trying to resolve. While Douglass wrote, Darwin and Marx were both wrestling with precisely the same question. And in America, natural science and its definition of what was human was in the process of coming to focus most narrowly on "the Negro."

Slavery, as we now recognize, went through a fundamental change around 1830, completing its evolution from a predominantly small-scale, quasi-domestic institution appended to hand-tool farming and manufacture into the productive base of an expanding agricultural economy, utilizing machinery to process the harvested crops and pouring vast quantities of agricultural raw materials, principally cotton, into developing capitalist industry in the northern states and England. Prior to the 1830s, open assertions of the "*permanent* inferiority" of Blacks "were exceedingly rare."[13] In fact, many eighteenth-century and early nineteenth-century apologists for slavery defended it as a means of "raising" and "civilizing" the poor, benighted, childlike Negro. But in the 1830s there emerged in America a world-view based on the belief that Blacks were inherently a race inferior to whites, and as part of this world-view there developed a scientific theory of Blacks as beings halfway, or even less than halfway, between animals and white people. This was part of the shift of Blacks from their role as children, appropriate to a professedly patriarchal society which offered them the opportunity of eventual development into adulthood, into their role as subhuman beasts of burden, the permanent mainstay of the labor force of expanding agribusiness.

By 1833 this world-view had been scientifically formulated in Richard Colfax's *Evidence Against the Views of the Abolitionists, Consisting of Physical and Moral Proofs of the Natural Inferiority of the Negroes* (New York, 1833). In his researches into the skulls and facial angles of Negroes, Colfax prefigured the developed science of the 1840s and 1850s known as the "American School of Ethnology." He argued that "the acknowledged meanness of the Negro's intellect only coincides with the shape of his head." This can be readily seen in the Negro's "facial angle," which was "almost to a level with that of a brute."[14] Colfax concludes that Negroes are halfway between animals and white people: "the Negroes, whether physically or morally considered, are so inferior as to resemble the brute creation as nearly as they do the white species."[15]

Colfax did not further develop the concept of Negroes as a distinct *species,* but by the late 1830s this next logical position was achieving its first systematic presentation in a body of scientific literature dedicated to demonstrating "that the black man was a member of a separate and permanently inferior species."[16] In the early 1840s came the theory of polygenesis. Dr. Samuel George Morton proved scientifically in *Crania Americana* (Philadelphia, 1839) and *Crania Aegyptiaca* (Philadelphia, 1844) that Negroes did not descend from Adam but were a distinct and subhuman species originating in southern Africa.[17]

Frederick Douglass had lived the social reality which these

scientific theories were adduced to perpetuate. He had begun life as a farm animal. Looking back, he traces the course of his development into a conscious human being, threatened all along the way by the danger of being reduced once again to a beast. Brilliantly manipulating his audience's literary conventions, Douglass is able to show what it means to be a human being in an age and society dominated by racist ideology and maintaining its basic productive activities through the use of one class of human beings as work animals by another class of human beings. For Douglass, as for Karl Marx, writing the previous year in what we now call the *Economic and Philosophic Manuscripts of 1844,* human beings are distinguished as a species by a creative consciousness which derives from the circumstances of their existence; this consciousness gives us the potential freedom to change those circumstances to meet human needs and desires, and it is in the struggle for that freedom that this consciousness evolves.

The first paragraph of the *Narrative of the Life of Frederick Douglass, An American Slave: Written by Himself* is concerned with the basic circumstances of his birth—place and date. Douglass has no problem locating the place and he does so, in the first sentence, establishing at once the artfully restrained, almost unemotional, matter-of-fact style which is to be the underlying norm for the entire narrative: "I was born in Tuckahoe, near Hillsborough, and about twelve miles from Easton, in Talbot county, Maryland."[18] But the second sentence poses a problem for this precise, no-nonsense narrator: "I have no accurate knowledge of my age, never having seen any authentic record containing it." In dryly explaining his predicament to the reader, Douglass can only compare himself and his fellow slaves to other farm animals: ". . . slaves know as little of their age as horses know of theirs." This is the starting point of his consciousness, something like a human, something like a beast.

Like most slaves, Douglass never knew his father. He learns, however, that his father was a white man, quite possibly his master, one of those who made the satisfaction of his "lusts" both "profitable as well as pleasurable" by increasing the number of his slaves (26). So Douglass himself apparently was created through the sexual union of the two "species" of beings defined by those scientists of the 1840s, and one of these—the loftier—would probably make a profit from the transaction when the little suckling became marketable. Following the "common custom," his mother was deliberately separated from him while he was a small baby: "I never saw my mother, to know her as such, more than four or five times in my life; and each of these times was very short in duration, and at night" (24).

The little boy's first consciousness of the meaning of slavery comes through the spectacle of his beautiful aunt being whipped by his master, apparently because of sexual jealousy. The master "stripped her from neck to waist," tied her hands to an overhead hook, and then proceeded to "whip upon her naked back till she was literally covered with blood":

> The louder she screamed, the harder he whipped; and where the blood ran fastest, there he whipped longest. He would whip her to make her scream, and whip her to make her hush; and not until overcome by fatigue, would he cease to swing the blood-clotted cowskin. I remember the first time I ever witnessed this horrible exhibition. I was quite a child, but I well remember it. I never shall forget it whilst I remember any thing. (28)

The words the master uses over and over again to define Douglass's aunt while he flagellates her cannot be repeated to the polite readers of the *Narrative*. Douglass has to record them as "'you d——d b——h'" (29–30). But their meaning is clear enough, for they signify the essence of the slaveowners' views of their Black slaves. The human master is merely punishing a female animal.

As for the little boy, he was but "seldom whipped," as Douglass tells us in a passage that I believe stands as one of the most brilliant achievements in style and content of nineteenth-century American prose:

> I was seldom whipped by my old master, and suffered little from any thing else than hunger and cold. I suffered much from hunger, but much more from cold. In hottest summer and coldest winter, I

was kept almost naked—no shoes, no stockings, no jacket, no trousers, nothing on but a coarse tow linen shirt, reaching only to my knees. I had no bed. I must have perished with cold, but that, the coldest nights, I used to steal a bag which was used for carrying corn to the mill. I would crawl into this bag, and there sleep on the cold, damp, clay floor, with my head in and feet out. My feet have been so cracked with the frost, that the pen with which I am writing might be laid in the gashes. (51–52)

After the first two sentences, simple but meticulously balanced, the style becomes stripped and stark, almost as bare as the little boy it describes living, or rather existing, on the level of brute survival. On the surface almost laconic, the passage virtually explodes with artfully arranged, volatile tensions. The first great disparity is between the little boy and the man writing his story. The writer and the boy are brought into direct physical contact as the writer takes his pen and lays it in the frost-cracked gashes on the boy's feet. By using the tool with which he is communicating to his polite audience as the implement of yoking these two worlds, he also forces that audience to join him in contacting the boy. Then he brings his readers face to face with the first of many moral inversions: to survive, the slave must violate the property rights defined by society; he must steal a bag intended to help produce profit. In all this, we are forced to sense a tremendous disparity between the emotional level of the prose, running on that matter-of-fact norm, and the potential rage and violence implicit in the slave's situation. This is all part of Douglass's patient preparation for the climax of his *Narrative,* and for his final warning to his audience.

Douglass next describes how he ate: "Our food was coarse corn meal boiled. This was called *mush*. It was put into a large wooden tray or trough, and set down upon the ground. The children were then called, like so many pigs, and like so many pigs they would come and devour the mush . . ." (52). In the very next paragraph, Douglass tells of his leaving this plantation. He thus establishes the juxtaposition which will provide one underlying dialectic for the rest of the narrative, the dialectic between rural and urban existence. Here we see clearly an opposition of values between

Douglass's vision, which is representative of his Black contemporaries, and the vision dominant in most of the white literature of the period.

The movement from country to city, and the conflict between the values of these two worlds, was of course a highly conventional literary theme in ante-bellum America, with its rapid industrialization and urbanization. This is typically envisioned as a fall from rural innocence and natural happiness into the artificialities of the infernal city, as in Hawthorne's "My Kinsman, Major Molineux" and Melville's *Pierre; Or, The Ambiguities*. Outside the city is the Eden to which a conscious person may wish to return, rarely with as much success as in the visions projected by Thoreau.

For Frederick Douglass, the movement primarily means the opposite. The city to him represents consciousness and the possibility of freedom; the country represents brutalization and the certainty of slavery. So the boy, now "probably between seven and eight years old," spends almost three days "in the creek, washing off the plantation scruff," "for the people in Baltimore were very cleanly, and would laugh at me if I looked dirty" (52–53). He is going to be given a pair of trousers; "The thought of owning a pair of trousers was great indeed!" (53). To merit the trousers and the city, he must no longer be a young pig: "It was almost a sufficient motive, not only to make me take off what would be called by pig-drovers the mange, but the skin itself" (53).

In the city, Douglass becomes a house boy. His expectations about urban life are not disappointed: "A city slave," he discovers, "is almost a freeman, compared with a slave on the plantation" (60). And there he encounters simultaneously two great sources of knowledge. The first, introduced by his mistress, is the alphabet. The second, confronting him in the form of his master's reactions, is that all the values of the slave must be the opposite of those of the slaveowner. The master forbids his wife from any further instruction of the boy because "it was unlawful, as well as unsafe, to teach a slave to read":

> To use his own words, further, he said, "If you give a nigger an inch, he will take an ell. A nigger should know nothing but to obey

his master—to do as he is told to do. Learning would *spoil* the best nigger in the world. Now," said he, "if you teach that nigger (speaking of myself) how to read, there would be no keeping him. It would forever unfit him to be a slave." (58)

So the master points to consciousness as the means to freedom, to the written language as a means to increase consciousness, and to himself as the negation of consciousness, the negation that must constantly be negated in order to achieve freedom:

These words sank deep into my heart, stirred up sentiments within that lay slumbering, and called into existence an entirely new train of thought.... I now understood what had been to me a most perplexing difficulty—to wit, the white man's power to enslave the black man. It was a grand achievement, and I prized it highly. From that moment, I understood the pathway from slavery to freedom.... The very decided manner with which he spoke, and strove to impress his wife with the evil consequences of giving me instruction, served to convince me that he was deeply sensible of the truths he was uttering. It gave me the best assurance that I might rely with the utmost confidence on the results which, he said, would flow from teaching me to read. What he most dreaded, that I most desired. What he most loved, that I most hated. That which to him was a great evil, to be carefully shunned, was to me a great good, to be diligently sought; and the argument which he so warmly urged, against my learning to read, only served to inspire me with a desire and determination to learn. (58–59)

This experience, which foreshadows the climax of the *Narrative,* defines for Douglass the path to consciousness and freedom, that is, to humanity. Unlike Pinocchio, who can become human only by learning to be honest, Douglass can attain his humanity only by learning deceit and trickery. He reveals to us some of the wily and devious tricks he uses, still as a small boy, to gain from the hostile white world around him the ability to read and write. Frankness, trustfulness, passivity are all for him just so many snares that would put him back in the barnyard with the horses and pigs.

Douglass succeeds in learning how to read, and the master's worst fears come true:

The more I read, the more I was led to abhor and detest my enslavers. I could regard them in no other light than a band of successful robbers, who had left their homes, and gone to Africa, and stolen us from our homes, and in a strange land reduced us to slavery. (67)

But as his eyes are opened, as he gains intensifying consciousness of his condition, without seeing how to change it, his own transformation becomes the source of his greatest torment. He now sometimes yearns to be deprived of consciousness, to be, in fact, an unthinking animal: "I have often wished myself a beast. I preferred the condition of the meanest reptile to my own. Any thing, no matter what, to get rid of thinking!" (67).

In the following chapter his urban sanctuary is disrupted by a temporary fall back into the barnyard. The death of his legal owner forces him back to be present at the redivision of all the property. Although now only about ten or eleven years old, he understands the scene all too well. It is perhaps the most conventional scene in the slave narrative genre, undoubtedly because it was such a critical event in the actual lives of the slaves and one that displayed most dramatically the essence of chattel slavery. It is when the slaves are "divided, like so many sheep" (76). For Douglass the young city slave it is a nightmare, which Douglass the author presents as the literal embodiment of his animal imagery:

We were all ranked together at the valuation. Men and women, old and young, married and single, were ranked with horses, sheep, and swine. There were horses and men, cattle and women, pigs and children, all holding the same rank in the scale of being, and were all subjected to the same narrow examination. Silvery-headed age and sprightly youth, maids and matrons, had to undergo the same indelicate inspection. (74)

He concludes this paragraph by foreshadowing a reversal that will take place in the function of the animal imagery: "At this moment, I saw more clearly than ever the brutalizing effects of slavery upon both slave and slaveholder."

Earlier, Douglass had traced the degradation of his mistress, who "at first lacked the depravity indispensable to shutting me up in mental darkness." In order to become "equal to the task of treating me as though I were a brute," she must be transformed from being a "tender-hearted woman" to a creature of "tiger-like fierceness" (63–64). As the *Narrative* progresses, Douglass makes us increasingly aware of this other kind of animal. Just as the slaves in the early part of the book are likened to barnyard animals, the slaveowners later are compared more and more to predatory beasts. So when Douglass is lucky enough to be returned temporarily to Baltimore, the fate he thus escapes is "worse than lion's jaws" (75). But at the age of about fourteen, this is just the fate he meets, as he is returned to the plantation.

His new country master cannot tame him, even with "a number of severe whippings" (87). So he decides to rent young Douglass out to Edward Covey, a farmer notorious as a "'nigger-breaker'" (88). Douglass now finds himself, "for the first time in my life, a field hand" (89). It is now 1833, the very year in which Richard Colfax was publishing his evidence that "the Negroes, whether physically or morally considered, are so inferior as to resemble the brute creation as nearly as they do the white species."

Edward Covey is known to his slaves, significantly enough, as "the snake" (92). Vicious as he is, Covey's main weapon in breaking slaves is not the whip but work. At the very moment that Colfax is propagandizing the concept that Negroes are inherently and permanently subhuman, Douglass is learning that through unending work a person can be transformed into a beast:

> We were worked in all weathers. It was never too hot or too cold; it could never rain, blow, hail, or snow, too hard for us to work in the field. Work, work, work, was scarcely more the order of the day than of the night. The longest days were too short for him, and the shortest nights too long for him. I was somewhat unmanageable when I first went there, but a few months of this discipline tamed me. Mr. Covey succeeded in breaking me. I was broken in body, soul, and spirit. My natural elasticity was crushed, my intellect languished, the disposition to read departed, the cheerful spark that lingered about my eye died; the dark night of slavery closed in upon me; and behold a man transformed into a brute!
> Sunday was my only leisure time. I spent this in a sort of beast-

> like stupor, between sleep and wake, under some large tree. At
> times I would rise up, a flash of energetic freedom would dart
> through my soul, accompanied with a faint beam of hope, that
> flickered for a moment, and then vanished. (94–95)

This is the lowest point in Douglass's life, and its essential crisis.
Reduced to animal existence, his human consciousness seems to
serve only the function of self-torture. But even this ultimate
degradation contains the potential of human liberation.

Douglass's authorial strategy here is crucial. He is aware that
his audience may think of him as half human. He does not protest
by proclaiming that he is every bit as human as the reader. Instead, he takes the reader through his own experience of becoming, in fact, "beast-like," and not through extraordinary or exceptional torture but through unremitting, mindless labor without
end, the ordinary life of the slave. By conceding that he himself
had become like an animal *after* attaining a much higher consciousness, Douglass forces the reader to recognize that he or she,
merely by being cast down from his or her relatively comfortable
social existence, could also be reduced to the semblance of an
animal. This experience is quite different from the one in which
Douglass the child had first awakened to find himself a slave.
How could Douglass's readers possibly imagine themselves as beings who had never known any existence but that as a rural beast
of burden? The Douglass who returns to the animal farm is much
closer to the typical reader: he has lived in the city; he has
thought philosophically about freedom and slavery; he can read
and write; he has read books. Thus Douglass can serve as a surrogate for the reader, and the reader may be able to share a portion
of Douglass's slave experience. The readers can discover that all
their book knowledge and philosophical consciousness would not
serve to distinguish *them* from animals if they were suddenly
plunged into plantation slavery. The situation resembles those in
many science fiction stories, from *Gulliver's Travels* and Voltaire's *Micromegas* to *Planet of the Apes* and James McConnell's
"Learning Theory," in which human beings find themselves incapable of demonstrating to alien creatures that they belong to an
intelligent species.

Douglass, however, does find the way to demonstrate—to Covey, to himself, and thus to the readers—that he is a human being. He now speaks in the second person, addressing the reader directly: "You have seen how a man was made a slave; you shall see how a slave was made a man" (97).

Douglass discovers that it is not cranial capacity or facial angles or book knowledge or intelligence in the abstract that distinguishes the human species from brutes. It is the consciousness which allows people to alter the conditions of existence, a consciousness that develops in the struggle for freedom from brute necessity. Faced with slavery, that can mean only one thing before all: "I resolved to fight; and, suiting my action to the resolution, I seized Covey hard by the throat. . . . I told him . . . that he had used me like a brute for six months, and that I was determined to be used so no longer" (103–4). They fight for what seems hours. Douglass overcomes Covey, "the snake." Then comes the famous passage in which Douglass defines this fight as the key event in his life, the climax of the *Narrative*, and the core of his message:

> This battle with Mr. Covey was the turning-point in my career as a slave. It rekindled the few expiring embers of freedom, and revived within me a sense of my own manhood. It recalled the departed self-confidence, and inspired me again with a determination to be free. The gratification afforded by the triumph was a full compensation for whatever else might follow, even death itself. He only can understand the deep satisfaction which I experienced, who has himself repelled by force the bloody arm of slavery. I felt as I never felt before. It was a glorious resurrection, from the tomb of slavery, to the heaven of freedom. My long-crushed spirit rose, cowardice departed, bold defiance took its place; and I now resolved that, however long I might remain a slave in form, the day had passed forever when I could be a slave in fact. (104–5)

This is a troublesome passage for many academics, for it challenges their most fundamental assumptions about the relations between body and mind, and between life and art. I noted earlier that no journal except one devoted to Afro-American literature had ever found an article on the *Narrative* acceptable for publication. There may be many possible reasons for this, but one that is in hand reveals what is fundamentally at issue in the rejection of Douglass's art and vision. In recommending rejection of an article on the *Narrative* submitted to an academic journal, a referee insisted that the author made a serious error in not finding any "irony in the situation in which Douglass must reduce his conflict with the slaveholders to a question of brute strength and physical violence in order to assert his 'manhood.'" This referee went on to explain the values the author of the article *ought* to have shared to have his view of the *Narrative* acceptable:

> Does he [Douglass] learn that in matching the brute in himself against the animalism of his enslavery that he becomes the victor? If [the author of the article] is right about Douglass's genius, it would seem more convincing that Douglass recognized that his real victory over slavery and his most splendid assertion of his manhood was the *Narrative* itself: his triumph over language and his own rage.[19]

Characteristic of his social class, this academic referee equates the body and physical violence, no matter how it is exerted, with "the brute," and the mind, especially evidenced in its verbal products, with what is really human. This is based on the underlying academic dichotomy between mind and body, an expression of bourgeois ideology, which envisions workers as mindless bodies and intellectuals as pure minds whose bodily physical comforts have nothing to do with their thinking. In "On the Teaching of Literature in the Highest Academies of the Empire" (1970), I showed how this dichotomy structures the most fundamental unexamined assumptions governing the study and teaching of literature in America. The primary of these assumptions I caricatured in these terms:

> First, there is the overall relationship between art and life. Great literary art transcends life. That is, literary achievements are more significant than social or political actions.[20]

One could not ask for a better expression of this assumption than that statement by the anonymous referee about the climax of Douglass's *Narrative*.

Douglass's individual rebellion, his personal repelling "by force the bloody arm of slavery," has tremendous importance for him, for the history of nineteenth-century America, for us. As Nancy T. Clasby has shown, "Douglass's act of violent resistance and the mysterious rebirth he experienced" are "crucial thematic elements" not just in this *Narrative* but in Black literature up through the present.[21] As Clasby perceives:

> The institutions under which Douglass had lived had failed to give him a viable identity—his manhood. The fight with Covey symbolically shattered the institutions and the old identity.[22]

To be reborn as a human being, to shed the animal identity imposed upon him by the white man, this Black slave must commit the most forbidden crime of all: he must strike the white man who oppresses him.

Not to understand the meaning of this is to fail to comprehend not only Douglass's *Narrative* but the historical epoch we ourselves live in, an epoch characterized by anticolonial struggles, led by the nonwhite peoples of the world. Frantz Fanon, the Black psychiatrist and revolutionary theorist, has written several books unfolding the historical implications of the psychological truths Douglass was able to compress into a paragraph. Fanon explains that the act of violence against the oppressor, even on the individual level, is the primal event that "frees the native from his inferiority complex and from his despair and inaction; it makes him fearless and restores his self-respect."[23] For Douglass, as for the peoples studied by Fanon, the initial act of violence is the premise of a new community for the oppressed. Clasby shows that Douglass's entire subsequent life as a leader of his people flowed from this act:

> From the time of his resolution that "the day had passed forever" when he could be "a slave in fact," Douglass experienced his own

integrity, a love for his brothers, and a relationship to spiritual realities which had been denied him by the conventional societal mechanisms. For the family which had been denied him by slavery he found a new brotherhood among his fellow rebels. He traded "slaveholding Christianity" for a close-knit and loving community of suffering slaves.[24]

Douglass's creation of this *Narrative* is indeed a monumental act, but it could only happen because of what he did that day on the plantation. And the brilliant art of this narrative embodies in animal imagery his rebirth into a new identity. Unlike those who think a person becomes a "brute" when he or she fights back against oppression, Douglass has shown us that the brutes on the farm are those who remain sheepish; those who can learn how to resist and defeat slavery are truly human beings. Prior to this, as we have seen, Douglass compares himself and other slaves to those domesticated farm animals—horses, pigs, sheep—and compares the slaveowners and their accomplices to wild predators— lions, tigers, snakes. From this point on in the *Narrative,* Douglass never again likens himself or any slave to an animal. The animal imagery associated with the slaveholders, however, continues, actually building to a climax after his escape from both enslavement and the rural world. This climax takes place in the least agrarian setting—New York City. The main animal in this vision is a crocodile, not a mammal but a reptile, not American, but African. The jungle fantasies of the American ethnologists, facial angles and all, are thrown back into their own faces.

"Immediately after my arrival in New York," he tells us, "I felt like one who had escaped a den of hungry lions" (143). But this feeling "very soon subsided," as he realizes that this great metropolis of America is part of a "hunting-ground for slaveholders— whose inhabitants are legalized kidnappers" (143–44). He becomes aware that he is "every moment subjected to the terrible liability of being seized upon by his fellowmen, as the hideous crocodile seizes upon his prey!" (144). He is frighteningly alone in this urban jungle, "among fellow-men, yet feeling as if in the midst of wild beasts": "I was afraid to speak to any one for fear of speaking to the wrong one, and thereby falling into the hands of money-loving kidnappers, whose business it was to lie in wait for the panting fugitive, as the ferocious beasts of the forest lie in wait for their prey" (143–44). So Douglass turns his readers' world upside down. They may still wonder if he is really a human being like themselves or just some lower species in human clothing. He knows that *he* is human, and he warns them of what *they* will be if they collaborate with the crocodiles and other beasts whose laws govern America.

Frederick Douglass was about twenty-seven years old when he published the *Narrative,* his first book, in 1845. The following year another twenty-seven-year-old American author, Herman Melville, published, in England, his first book, *Narrative of a Four Months' Residence Among the Natives of a Valley of the Marquesas Islands; Or, a Peep at Polynesian Life.* Douglass, writing as a nonwhite slave in white America, had to veil some of his message in imagery. Melville, writing as a white American who had lived in a nonwhite society under the shadow of imperialism, spoke more bluntly when he distinguished "the white civilized man as the most ferocious animal on the face of the earth."[25] When Melville's *Narrative* was published in America as *Typee,* these words, along with many other crucial passages, were deleted. When Douglass's *Narrative* was published in America, he had to flee his native land. His owner, backed up by the laws of the United States of America, was seeking to hunt down and recapture his runaway beast of burden, the author of *Narrative of the Life of Frederick Douglass, An American Slave: Written by Himself.*

Let us go back to the year 1833. A snowy-haired gentleman in his mid-fifties sits alone in his well-furnished study. He is an educated professional man, the physician of the region, a husband, a father, and the owner of a fine residence in town and several farms. His gray eyes lift to stare menacingly at the fifteen-year-old slave who enters at his command.

> "So you want to be married, do you?" said he, "and to a free nigger."
> "Yes, sir."
> "Well, I'll soon convince you whether I am your master, or the nigger fellow you honor so highly. . . ."

"Don't you suppose, sir, that a slave can have some preference about marrying? Do you suppose that all men are alike to her?"

"Do you love this nigger?" said he, abruptly.

"Yes, sir."

"How dare you tell me so!" he exclaimed in great wrath.... "Do you know that I have a right to do as I like with you,—that I can kill you, if I please?"

"You have tried to kill me, and I wish you had; but you have no right to do as you like with me."

"Silence!" he exclaimed, in a thundering voice. "By heavens, girl, you forget yourself too far! Are you mad? If you are, I will soon bring you to your senses. Do you think any other master would bear what I have borne from you this morning? Many masters would have killed you on the spot. How would you like to be sent to jail for your insolence?"[26]

This scene appears in a mid-nineteenth-century work of American literature, a work written by one of the two participants. It was not the master who turned out to be the literary artist. Only one piece of his writing survives, the notice he had posted throughout the region when the slave ran away, and even that we must get from her book:

$300 REWARD! Ran away from the subscriber, an intelligent, bright, mulatto girl, named Linda, 21 years of age. Five feet four inches high. Dark eyes, and black hair inclined to curl; but it can be made straight. Has a decayed spot on a front tooth. She can read and write, and in all probability will try to get to the Free States. All persons are forbidden, under penalty of the law, to harbor or employ said slave.[27]

We do know that the doctor also wrote wildly obscene notes to her, but these, unfortunately, have not been preserved. He apparently did not record his own view of slavery. We may assume that it coincided with that articulated by William Gilmore Simms and Nathaniel Hawthorne.

This view is not shared by the young slave woman. She was able to evade his grasp. But to do this she had to hide for seven years in an attic crawl space less than three feet high in her grandmother's shed. This imprisonment permanently crippled her limbs. Then she managed to escape to the "free" states. In 1861, on the eve of the Civil War, she published, under the pen name Linda Brent, *Incidents in the Life of a Slave Girl,* the book in which her master goes down to posterity.

Incidents in the Life of a Slave Girl is a great work of American literature. It is also, and this is part of its greatness, an ironic statement about both the dominant ante-bellum literary form—the romance—and its readership, the relatively leisured and privileged classes.

The romance or novel was the principal literary genre before the Civil War. Most of its audience was female, leisured, and sheltered. Beginning with the earliest romances, much of the genre's excitement came from the disparity between the protected lives of the readers and the perilous adventures of the heroine or hero. One of the most popular of the earliest novelists, Susanna Haswell Rowson (c. 1762–1824), conventionalized this disparity, producing what has been called "the novel of victimization," "a novel that relies for its success on the contrast between the readers' cozy comfort and the heroine's sorrow and insecurity."[28]

Linda Brent's early life recapitulates the fictional formula. Mrs. Rowson's heroines, for example, are "deprived at a comparatively early age . . . of whatever protection they relied upon" and thereafter must "fend for themselves."[29] An orphan at seven, Linda serves until she is twelve as the slave of a kindly woman, nursed at Linda's grandmother's breast, who teaches Linda to read and who leads the slaves to expect that at her death she will free the girl. But when this kindly mistress dies, her will enslaves Linda to her five-year-old niece, effectively placing her in the clutches of that child's father, that snowy-haired professional gentleman who soon becomes obsessed with debauching the young slave. Linda is totally without protection, and she must fend for herself to the utmost of human capabilities.

The heroine of the romance often must pass through endless misfortunes, beset on all sides by perils. Through all her vicissitudes, the heroine's integrity depends on the preservation of her "virtue." Will she maintain that precious, very private property? If so, the romance may have a happy ending, and the only happy ending for most romances, needless to say, is a good marriage, blessed with future children.

The difference between the fictional life of the typical romantic heroine and the actual one of the cozy (perhaps bored) reader is no greater than that between the actual life of this slave woman and the fictional perils of the romance. Linda Brent is pursued not merely by one or two villainous seducers, but by a nightmare society based on the most naked exploitation and wallowing in the grossest forms of perversion and torture. For her, Snaky Swamp, the place where she first hides and where her body is poisoned by the bites of hundreds of mosquitoes as she fends off swarms of poisonous snakes, is literally a haven from the world of human parasites and reptiles: "even those large, venomous snakes were less dreadful to my imagination than the white men in that community called civilized" (116).

At key points in her narrative, Linda Brent addresses her audience directly, showing them that in her hideous world all the values of their lives, including their romances, are inverted. Virtue, their highest value, is the "crime" for which she must imprison herself for seven years (29). Beauty, the most desirable attribute, is to be dreaded: "If God has bestowed beauty upon her, it will prove her greatest curse. That which commands admiration in the white woman only hastens the degradation of the female slave" (27). Children, the longed-for sequel to the happy romance, are merely the property of the rapacious slaveowner, who regards even his own sons and daughters by slave women as commodities, "as marketable as the pigs on the plantation" (35).

Linda Brent states explicitly that she is writing to "the women of the North," hoping to arouse them to the suffering of "two millions of women at the South." Her narrative is an attempt to show them that: "Slavery is terrible for men; but it is far more terrible for women" (79). She opens her life to the "virtuous reader," in whom she confides that she lost her own "virtue" to a white man at the age of fifteen. But in the final chapters, she brings it all home to her readers.

By the time *Incidents in the Life of a Slave Girl* was published in 1861, the romance had reached the outer limits of its conventions. *The Scarlet Letter* (1850) had begun *after* the heroine's marriage, adultery, and the birth of her illegitimate child. *Moby-Dick* (1851) had taken the adventure story to its utmost bounds in all directions, and *Pierre* (1852) had outstripped the conventional treatment of that most shocking romantic theme, incest. Slavery itself had become a suitable subject as the War approached. *Uncle Tom's Cabin* (1851–52) had sold 300,000 copies in its first year. Harriet Beecher Stowe's sequel, *Dred: A Tale of the Great Dismal Swamp* (1856) was playing on the stage. So Linda Brent's readers were not unaccustomed to shocking revelations about the lives of slaves and the degrading effects of slavery on the white people of the South. But this was relatively far removed from their own lives. Until her final chapters, Linda Brent allows her northern readers to feel secure in their pity for the slaves and their indignation at the slaveowners and their accomplices in the South. But when she describes her adventures in the North, she, like Frederick Douglass, edges closer to the reader. One climax comes when Linda Brent achieves her freedom—only by being bought as a slave right in New York City:

> "The bill of sale!" Those words struck me like a blow. So I was *sold* at last! A human being *sold* in the free city of New York! The bill of sale is on record, and future generations will learn from it that women were articles of traffic in New York, late in the nineteenth century of the Christian religion. It may hereafter prove a useful document to antiquaries, who are seeking to measure the progress of civilization in the United States. (206)

But even at this point, her readers are relatively safe in their comfortable homes. Then Linda Brent turns directly, with all those accumulated conventions of the literary romance echoing ironically, to her "virtuous reader": "Reader, my story ends with freedom; not in the usual way with marriage" (207).

In case anybody has missed the point, she goes on: "I and my children are now free! We are as free from the power of slaveholders as are the white people of the north; and though that, according to my ideas, is not saying a great deal, it is a vast improvement in *my* condition" (207).

In the fall of 1974 I was teaching *Incidents in the Life of a Slave*

Girl in a course at Wesleyan University. There were 67 students in the class; over a third of them were Black. The discussion led to Linda Brent's use of the conventions of the romance. When we got to the statement, "Reader, my story ends with freedom; not in the usual way with marriage," two or three white students expressed doubts that she could have meant all the apparent ironies. But enough internal evidence was found to show the ironies must have been intentional. At this moment, a white student (male, and I believe an English major) began to argue heatedly that he didn't see how Linda Brent could have written the book, that it must have been written by L. Maria Child, the white abolitionist who acknowledges her role as editor. I pointed out that all authors have editors. A Black woman asked if he had any evidence to support his belief. "No," he replied, "it's just clear that an escaped slave woman *could* not have written such a consciously *literary* work." Some white students told me later they couldn't understand why the Black students, particularly some of the Black women, had gotten so "upset" by his argument.

This is not to ridicule the white students at our elite colleges. Their approach to literature (at least in the classroom) of course mostly comes directly and indirectly from the methodological assumptions governing the teaching of literature. It is not the students who are responsible for excluding the slave narrative and most other literary art by oppressed people in America from the canon of American literature. This exclusion is based upon certain assumptions about culture, and the cultural assumptions still dominant in the academy are in essence those of the class that owned Frederick Douglass and Linda Brent, or at least of the intellectuals who spoke for that class. Although everybody today says that New Criticism is dead and buried, have we in practice moved beyond the ideology which the American brand of New Criticism was originally intended to maintain? Here, presented in manifesto form as "A Mirror for Artists," is what New Critic and poet Donald Davidson meant by culture:

> In the South the eighteenth-century social inheritance flowered into a gracious civilization that, despite its defects, was actually a civilization, true and indigenous, well diffused, well established.

Its culture was sound and realistic in that it was not at war with its own economic foundations. It did not need to be paraded loudly; it was not thought about particularly. The manners of planters and countrymen did not require them to change their beliefs and temper in going from cornfield to drawing-room, from cotton rows to church or frolic.[30]

Frederick Douglass and Linda Brent show us the difference between such appearances and reality, between manners and morals, between form and content—distinctions obfuscated by all varieties of formalism, including any claim that the literary canon of a nation has been determined purely by "literary excellence."

Beyond this is another question: What were the products of this culture, in literature or in any other art? The "economic foundations" of this "gracious civilization" consisted of millions of Black slaves, and one of the main arguments in defense of slavery was that the Negroes would do the work for which they were suited, the manual work, leaving their owners free to create a fine, elegant, and lasting culture. This leisured class in fact produced virtually nothing of any artistic significance. About the best that can be said of the white literature of the slave South is this statement from a 1973 book aimed at reestablishing its glories (the quotation is from the chapter entitled "Black History or Propaganda," an attempt to expose Afro-American studies as insidious propaganda akin to that of "Bolshevik or Maoist historians"):

Anyone familiar with the *Southern Review, Russell's Magazine,* or the *Southern Literary Messenger,* or with the works of William Gilmore Simms, Edgar Allan Poe, John Pendleton Kennedy, Augustus B. Longstreet, and George Washington Harris knows that the Old South produced some outstanding writers and literature. The most versatile man of letters was Simms—novelist, short-story writer, critic, journalist, and editor. Some authorities consider his historical novels to be notable achievements in American literature. Though Poe's work transcends region, some of it is set in the South, and Poe himself aspired to be a southern gentleman.[31]

Various excuses have been offered as to why "the South" was unable to produce any more significant literature and art: There weren't enough printing facilities. " ... Northern industrialism drove the genius of the South largely into the political rather than the artistic field."[32] There were too few people to produce significant literature and art. The architecture of the southern plantation preoccupied the artistic talents of the region. The most outrageous—and revealing—excuse is that offered by Allen Tate in *Reactionary Essays on Poetry and Ideas:*

> ... in the Old South, and under the worse form of slavery that afflicts both races today, genuine social classes do not exist. The enormous "difference" of the Negro doomed him from the beginning to an economic status purely: he has had much the same thinning influence upon the class above him as the anonymous city proletariat has had upon the culture of industrial capitalism. ...
> ... the Negro, who has long been described as a responsibility, got everything from the white man. The history of French culture, I suppose, has been quite different. The high arts have been grafted upon the peasant stock. We could graft no new life upon the Negro; he was too different, too alien.[33]

All these excuses depend for any plausibility on ignoring the culture of the slaves. For the pre-Civil War South did produce great art, an art invisible only to those blinded by their own class assumptions.

It was not the slaveowner but the slave who produced the significant literature and art of the South. And although there were some splendid achievements by those slaves patient enough to write to white audiences—Frederick Douglass, James Pennington, William and Ellen Craft, William Wells Brown, Solomon Northrup, Henry "Box" Brown, Linda Brent—the transcendent artistic achievement was by the field slaves who were singing their poems to each other. As we shall see in Chapter 3, it is Afro-American music and poetry that has formed the most distinctive and influential tradition within American literature, and it is this tradition which represents the unique major contribution American poetics has made to world culture.

Even if slavery had allowed the slaveowners to develop an elegant culture, this would not in the opinion of most of us today be a weighty argument in favor of slavery. And what kind of art could be created out of the leisure wrung from such brutal and anachronistic oppression? What would be the content of such art? The art of the slaveowning class and their literary advocates, no matter how splendid in form, would have to engage in fundamental falsification of the human experience that constitutes history. The slaves, on the other hand, were in painful daily touch with the social reality at the core of American history. By revealing that reality, their art became a priceless treasure.

This is not to defend what I have named "the oyster theory," the notion that great art is like a pearl, something that can be produced only out of suffering and agony (and that therefore in a communist society where people were happy there could be no great art). In preclass societies throughout the world, not the least in North America itself, whole tribes have joined in creating magnificent art, including mythological legends, folk tales, dance, and songs. But it is true that in societies divided into social classes much of the most significant art has come from the misery of the oppressed classes, whether created by the oppressed people themselves or by socially conscious individual artists drawn from the more privileged classes. Such art remains, and will remain, important because it expresses truth, not about "the human situation" in the abstract, but about real living situations broadly representative of life during the epochs of class rule and class struggle.

CHAPTER 2

The Worker as Criminal and Artist: Herman Melville

In the 1830s and 1840s, the United States was becoming the leading maritime power in the world. Central to its growing dominance of the oceans was the industry of whaling. It was the Yankee whalemen who had, in the words of Herman Melville, "overrun and conquered the watery world like so many Alexanders; parcelling out among them the Atlantic, Pacific, and Indian oceans."[1]

The crews of the whaleships were made up of some of the most desperate men from the bottom of American society and from the dispossessed of the world, "the meanest mariners, and renegades and castaways," to whom Melville would ascribe a transcendent dignity.[2] After Linda Brent's brother escaped to the North, he shipped out on a whaler from New Bedford around 1841.[3] Several years later, Linda Brent's only son Benny, subjected to racist humiliation in the North, in desperation also shipped out on a whaling voyage.[4] Frederick Douglass was lucky enough to find employment on the whaling docks of New Bedford in 1838, and was still working there when Melville shipped out, around the same time as Linda Brent's brother, in 1841. On the Yankee whaleships, white Americans and Europeans, Black freemen and escaped slaves, American Indians and Lascars, convicts from Australia and tribesmen from New Zealand, all met as equals, worked collectively for their very survival, ate the same scurvy food, received beatings from the same whips and handspikes, and slept in the same rat- and cockroach-infested forecastle.

The large-scale agriculture developing in the South during this period was based on chattel labor. The manufacturing industry developing in the North was based on wage labor. America's vast ocean commerce was based on a condition of servitude halfway between chattel and wage labor. The differences and similarities among these three forms of labor determine much of the character and significance of the literature produced out of all three.

Of all sailors, the whalemen lived the most dangerous and physically oppressive existence. On voyages lasting for years, often out of sight of land for months at a time, they rarely tasted fresh food. The mortality rate on the average whaler was higher than that of the average warship during a declared war. Nevertheless, whalemen shared certain conditions of labor with sailors on all types of American ships during this period, including merchantmen, slavers, warships, and privateers. These conditions of labor shared the following characteristics with Black chattel slavery, characteristics different from normal wage labor:

1. Sailors stayed on the job under penalty of law. To leave the job was a specific crime (desertion).

2. To disobey orders collectively was a specific crime (mutiny).

3. Sailors were routinely flogged for negligence, shirking, insubordination, insolence, or the whim of an officer.

4. There was no appeal beyond the power of the officers.

5. Sailors were often worked or starved to death, or ordered into almost certain death, all under penalty of law. (Even coal miners, at least in theory, could refuse an especially dangerous job without losing anything more than their livelihood.) It was not at all unusual for over half the crew of a whaling ship to die in one voyage.

6. Hence many sailors, particularly on whaleships, were actually kidnapped bodily (shanghaied) into servitude to replace the dead men.

There were also certain differences from Black chattel labor and similarities to the usual conditions of wage labor:

1. Their servitude to a single master was not perpetual (if they

lived long enough). After the voyage for which they had signed on or were shanghaied, sailors had the "freedom" to try to find employment elsewhere.

2. Sailors were legally entitled to some remuneration (though, as Melville shows in several books, they were often legally cheated out of all their pay). This could be in the form of wages or the "lay" (share) system of most whalers.

3. Sailors in theory had legal rights as citizens, once they were back someplace where they could exercise them, and their service was in theory a contract between two equal parties.

These nineteenth-century sailors may thus be considered essentially peons, or temporary chattels, rather than slaves or "free" laborers. In this state of semibondage, a person experiences very directly a connection between work and what is defined as crime. Linda Brent could be whipped for "negligence" or "insolence" or imprisoned for "disobedience." Herman Melville shared this experience: he was threatened with the whip, and he was imprisoned for joining a collective refusal to work. When Frederick Douglass was planning to escape, he was committing a crime, for which he was sent to jail. Herman Melville's career as an artist began with the narrative of his first crime: desertion from work. For the whaleman, as for the Black slave, running away was a crime, resistance was a crime, and, in fact, it was a crime not to work. Melville widens this view until he reveals that for all people—except of course the rich—not to work is a dangerous crime. Hence the vision of "Bartleby the Scrivener. A Story of Wall-Street," where even an office worker who merely "prefers not to" work is sentenced to prison, and in fact his death, for the crime of "vagrancy."

Herman Melville began life as the son of a prosperous merchant. But his father died, bankrupt, when Melville was a young boy. So at the age of twelve he was forced to go to work. At nineteen he shipped out as a merchant seaman. Then in 1841, at the age of twenty-one, he left America as a common seaman on the crew of a whaleship. He returned, almost four years later, as a foretopman on a United States warship. He had been a whaler, a deserter, a mutineer, a sailor living in constant dread of his captain's whip, and a man who had lived alone among one of the nonwhite peoples being subjugated by Europe and America. He was now ready to write about what he had lived.

If Herman Melville had not fallen from a petty bourgeois family into the working class, if he had not labored in the most oppressive conditions inflicted on white workers in the mid-nineteenth century, and if he had not rebelled against these conditions with the crimes of desertion and mutiny, he might still have been an artist. But he would not be the artist we know as Herman Melville, an artist whose creative imagination was forged in the furnace of his labor and oppression, an artist who saw the world of nineteenth-century American society and its commercial empire through the eyes of its victims.

Like Frederick Douglass and Linda Brent, Melville addressed his writings primarily not to these victims but to the social class that profited from their labor. Although the battle for free public education (for whites) had been won in principle in the mid-1830s, although literacy was spreading in the working class, and although inexpensive popular novels were being published in the 1840s, the main readership for novels and romances were gentlemen and ladies of leisure and education. This social class also was the main arbiter determining what literature should be published, for the working class as well as for itself. Melville understood very well that this social class has a tendency to reduce literature to a pleasant amenity of its own comfortable existence.

So he began his career as a literary artist by defining a contradictory class relationship between himself and this audience. He ends the very first paragraph of his first romance with these words, a defiant statement from a lowly worker to the people he has served:

> Oh! ye state-room sailors, who make so much ado about a fourteen-days' passage across the Atlantic; who so pathetically relate the privations and hardships of the seas, where, after a day of breakfasting, lunching, dining off five courses, chatting, playing whist, and drinking champaign-punch, it was your hard lot to be shut up in little cabinets of mahogany and maple, and sleep for ten hours, with nothing to disturb you but "those good-for-nothing tars,

shouting and tramping over your head,"—what would ye say to our six months out of sight of land?[5]

The gentlemen critics and other literati of Melville's day, unlike many today, recognized what Melville was up to. When Melville's *Narrative* was published the following year in America as *Typee: A Peep at Polynesian Life,* his publisher forced him to delete the entire passage I have just quoted, as well as the antiimperialist guts of the book, and reissue the so-called Revised American Edition (of August 1846). During the rest of his life, this censorship was maintained on all American editions of *Typee.* It was not until 1892, the year after his death, that Melville's first book reappeared in America in an uncensored form (prepared by his literary executor following Melville's written instructions). As Mao Tse-tung puts it in "Talks at the Yenan Forum on Literature and Art," "... all classes in all class societies invariably put the political criterion first and the artistic criterion second. The bourgeoisie always shuts out proletarian literature and art, however great their artistic merit."[6]

Melville understood right away that his art would be perceived by much of his audience as just more "shouting and tramping" by one of "those good-for-nothing tars" disturbing their slumber. Some of the petty-bourgeois intellectuals were at first indulgently amused at the spectacle of this "reading sailor spinning a yarn" with "nothing to indicate the student or the scholar."[7] It was as if one of those chimpanzees we have recently taught to read were to write an account of his adventures. But they were quick to point out that this ignorant sailor should not be taken seriously, because "Mr. Melville's mind, though vigorous enough, has not been trained in those studies which enable men to observe with profit."[8]

But Melville persisted in exposing the essence of his society. The more deeply he probed, the more outraged was the response from many of the literati. His second book, *Omoo,* described the hideous conditions on a whaleship, the mutiny Melville had helped to organize, his experience as a prisoner of British imperialists, and the savage destruction of Pacific societies by European and American imperialism. His next book, *Mardi* (1849), a philosophical and political allegory, induced reviewers to demand that he go back to writing South Sea romances, stripped of such unseemly pretentiousness. In *Redburn* (1849) he described the exploitation of sailors on a merchant ship, the terrifying poverty of Liverpool, and the importation of Irish immigrants in slavelike conditions. *White-Jacket; Or, The World in a Man-of-War* (1850) tells of the brutal dictatorship that American naval seamen lived under; like *Typee, Omoo,* and *Redburn,* it is largely autobiographical. Then came *Moby-Dick* (1851). Many of the reviewers admired its "wildness," "genius," and authentic descriptions of the whaling industry, most found parts of the book "obscure" if not downright "incomprehensible," and a strident minority denounced it as "crazy," "ridiculous," "vulgar," "immoral," and "not worth the money asked for it, either as a literary work or as a mass of printed paper."[9] The judgment soon to be decisive was this one:

> "Typee" was undoubtedly a very proper book for the parlor, and we have seen it in company with "Omoo," lying upon tables from which Byron was strictly prohibited, although we were unable to fathom those niceties of logic by which one was patronized, and the other proscribed. But these were Mr. Melville's triumphs. "Redburn" was a stupid failure, "Mardi" was hopelessly dull, "White-Jacket" was worse than either; and, in fact, it was such a very bad book, that, until the appearance of "Moby-Dick," we had set it down as the very ultimatum of weakness to which its author could attain. It seems, however, that we were mistaken.[10]

When *Pierre; Or, The Ambiguities* appeared in 1852, the reviewers were shocked, although they also claimed not to understand the book. They now realized they had been too lenient and careless in their toleration of Melville's work. Even people he considered his friends among the New York literati deserted him and rallied behind those trying to silence this rude barbarian before he could do any more damage. Leading the attack was George Washington Peck, who began his article in the *American Whig Review* (November 1852) with the words, "A bad book!"

Peck explains that he is not concerned if Melville falsely depicts "South Sea savages" and sailors, but Melville's vision of polite society must no longer be allowed:

> We can afford Mr. Melville full license to do what he likes with "Omoo" and its inhabitants; it is only when he presumes to thrust his tragic *Fantoccini* upon us, as representatives of our own race, that we feel compelled to turn our critical Aegis upon him, and freeze him into silence.... he strikes with an impious, though, happily, weak hand, at the very foundations of society....
>
> We have, we think, said sufficient to show our readers that Mr. Melville is a man wholly unfitted for the task of writing wholesome fictions; that he possesses none of the faculties necessary for such work; that his fancy is diseased, his morality vitiated, his style nonsensical and ungrammatical, and his characters as far removed from our sympathies as they are from nature.
>
> Let him continue, then, if he must write, his pleasant sea and island tales. We will always be happy to hear Mr. Melville discourse about savages....

The critical aegis of polite society was partly successful. Melville was driven underground, forced to write for several years anonymously and under pseudonyms. Then, on April Fool's Day, 1857, Herman Melville published under his own name the last work of prose fiction to see print in his life, though he lived another thirty-four years. It was entitled *The Confidence-Man: His Masquerade*. It depicts capitalist society as the world of a riverboat perilously floating down the Mississippi into total darkness, a world in which every waking moment of every passenger is spent trying to fleece somebody or trying to keep from being fleeced.

Melville was rescued from deep oblivion after World War I, contemporaneously with the Harlem Renaissance, when his works were rediscovered and reprinted. The critical opinion prevailing from then until World War II summed up his main writing career in three stages: First came some fine romances of life in the South Seas and on ships. Then suddenly burst forth his masterpiece, *Moby-Dick*. After that, burned-out and more than half crazy, he lapsed into incomprehensible attempts to recapture his artistry, ending with the obscure "fragment," *The Confidence-Man*. Following World War II, the magnificent short fiction of the 1852–55 period, particularly "Bartleby, the Scrivener. A Story of Wall-Street," "Benito Cereno," and "The Encantadas," began to receive recognition, and one or two critics even began to acknowledge *The Confidence-Man* as an important book. After the Korean War, the beginning of the Indochina War, and the first Black urban rebellions of 1964–68, some people, including myself, began to perceive *The Confidence-Man* as Melville's masterpiece.

Although Melville has been released from the silence and obscurity imposed on him by the petty-bourgeois authorities of the cultural world of his own time, though his works are now taught in every college and university, and though the United States government has even issued a Moby Dick postage stamp, what is most vital and relevant about Melville is still largely suppressed and buried. For despite the deepening understanding of many teachers awakened by the historical events of the last decade, the Melville that is taught is still predominantly a denatured Melville, an academic Melville.

This is certainly ironic, for Melville was keenly aware of his alienation from the academic world. And he saw a fundamental contradiction between that world and the world in which he received his true education, his artistic training, and all that he thought worthy about himself as a human being—the world of the common seaman. As he puts it in *Moby-Dick,* speaking with the thinnest of disguises through his persona Ishmael:

> And, as for me, if, by any possibility, there be any as yet undiscovered prime thing in me; if I shall ever deserve any real repute in that small but high hushed world which I might not be unreasonably ambitious of; if hereafter I shall do anything that, upon the whole, a man might rather have done than to have left undone; if, at my death, my executors, or more properly my creditors, find any precious MSS. in my desk, then here I prospectively ascribe all the honor and glory to whaling; for a whale-ship was my Yale College and my Harvard. (Ch. 24)

Melville perceived social reality in terms of class contradictions. In *White-Jacket; Or, The World in a Man-of-War,* he presents capitalist society in microcosm as the world of a warship. His explanation of class conflict in the larger society emerges as he displays the reactions of the two main classes of men on the ship to the rumor of an impending war. All the seamen on board, "almost to a man," "abhorred the idea of going into action" (Ch. 49). Would the seaman's "wages be raised? Not a cent." "What, then, has he to expect from war? What but harder work, and harder usage than in peace; a wooden leg or arm; mortal wounds, and death?" However, the opposing class has an opposite response: "But with the officers of the quarter-deck it was just the reverse." To them it offered the possibility of "glory" and "promotion." Hence they had an objective interest in the "slaughtering of their fellow-men." Melville then generalizes from this example:

> This hostile contrast between the feelings with which the common seamen and the officers of the *Neversink* looked forward to this more than possible war, is one of many instances that might be quoted to show the antagonism of their interests, the incurable antagonism in which they dwell. But can men, whose interests are diverse, ever hope to live together in a harmony uncoerced? Can the brotherhood of the race of mankind ever hope to prevail in a man-of-war, where one man's bane is almost another's blessing? By abolishing the scourge, shall we do away tyranny; *that* tyranny which must ever prevail, where of two essentially antagonistic classes in perpetual contact, one is immeasurably the stronger?

Melville does not offer this as a picture of all human society, or as an inevitable consequence of human nature. It is capitalist society he is talking about. In fact *Typee,* his somewhat fictionalized narrative of his stay with the people of the Marquesas Islands, takes precisely the same view of the origin of classes, private property, and the state as Engels's *Origin of the Family, Private Property, and the State,* which was published almost forty years later. The society of the Typee Valley is what Marx and Engels called primitive communism. There are no social classes in this society, but rather a single extended family, living in the "harmony uncoerced," the "brotherhood of the race of mankind" that Melville cannot find in the "civilized" world:

During my whole stay on the island I never witnessed a single quarrel, nor anything that in the slightest degree approached even to a dispute. The natives appeared to form one household, whose members were bound together by the ties of strong affection. The love of kindred I did not so much perceive, for it seemed blended in the general love; and where all were treated as brothers and sisters, it was hard to tell who were actually related to each other by blood. (Ch. 27)

In a passage censored out of the American editions, Melville singles out for his special admiration the unanimity of view that flows from this communality:

There was one admirable trait in the general character of the Typees which, more than anything else, secured my admiration: it was the unanimity of feeling they displayed on every occasion. With them there hardly appeared to be any difference of opinion upon any subject whatever. They all thought and acted alike. . . . They showed this spirit of unanimity in every action of life: everything was done in concert and good-fellowship. (Ch. 27)

There is no "state" and "no established law," Melville observes in another passage censored from the revised editions, and yet every person lived without fear of crime: "in the darkest nights they slept securely" (Ch. 27). There is personal property, such as hand-carved artifacts, but no private property, such as real estate or the products of other people's labor. Melville directly contrasts this primitive communism with capitalist society:

There were no foreclosures of mortgages, no protested notes, no bills payable, no debts of honour in Typee; no unreasonable tailors and shoemakers, perversely bent on being paid; no duns of any description; no assault and battery attorneys, to foment discord, backing their clients up to a quarrel, and then knocking their heads together; no poor relations, everlastingly occupying the spare bed-chamber, and diminishing the elbow room at the family table; no destitute widows with their children starving on the cold charities of the world; no beggars; no debtors' prisons; no proud and hard-hearted nabobs in Typee; or to sum up all in one word—no Money! "That root of all evil" was not to be found in the valley. (Ch. 17)

Existence is Edenic, and "There seemed to be no cares, griefs, troubles, or vexations in all Typee" (Ch. 17).

Melville, however, does not sentimentalize life in Typee, and he is not a utopian. He realizes that a person whose consciousness has been determined by capitalist society cannot live in the society of Typee, or in some utopian community (like Brook Farm) trying to re-create such a society as an island in the midst of capitalism. In fact the very presence of the narrator begins to rend the structure of Typee society, and the final image he gives of it is a violent argument about him culminating in the symbolic end of Eden: "blows were struck, wounds were given, and blood flowed."

The actual end of this society, and of the other stable societies of the Pacific, is described at length in *Omoo* and *Typee* in passage after passage painting the hideous features of European and U.S. imperialism. Needless to say, almost every one of these passages was deleted from the revised edition of *Typee*. Melville describes the conscious destruction of the natives' culture by the Christian missionaries, the looting of their resources, the spurious claim to sovereignty over them imposed by fleets of warships and marines landing to burn down their villages, the establishment of puppet rulers, the pretexts used to impose direct colonial rule, the investment of capital, and the starvation, disease, wage and chattel slavery, and utter misery and degradation imposed by "civilization" and carried out by "the most ferocious animal on the face of the earth": "the white civilized man" (Ch. 17).

The ship which brings the narrator to the Marquesas contains the antagonistic class relationships of capitalism, the class relationships being extended throughout the Pacific by the various empires' ships of commerce and war. The purpose of the voyage is to kill whales in order to make money for the owners of the ship. The people who do the work are the superexploited sailors. The agent of capitalist authority is the captain, for whom justice resides in "the butt end of a handspike" (Ch. 4). The narrator commits the crime of desertion, a crime peculiar to this group of workers, whose condition, as we have seen, lies about midway between wage and chattel slavery. Like a slave, he has discovered that the principle of "law and equity" does not apply to his condition. He contemplates the more serious crime of organized resistance, but gives it up because "our crew was composed of a parcel of dastardly and mean-spirited wretches, divided among themselves, and only united in enduring without resistance the unmitigated tyranny of the captain. It would have been mere madness for any two or three of the number, unassisted by the rest, to attempt making a stand against his ill-usage" (Ch. 4).

The ship on which Melville left the Marquesas, the Australian whaleship *Lucy Ann,* had quite a different sort of crew, as described in *Omoo.* "They were a wild company" (Ch. 21), ready to fight back individually or collectively. Eating rotten food on a rotting ship commanded by an incompetent gentleman and swarming with cockroaches and rats, the crew eventually refuses to work, and they sign a bill of complaints drawn up by the narrator. When the British consul at Tahiti tries to force them back to work, they rise up, led by a knife-wielding sailor who proclaims "we're all a parcel of mutineers and pirates!" (Ch. 21). For this crime of refusal to work, Melville and his shipmates were incarcerated by the British.

The most serious crime Melville contemplates against lawful authority is murder. In *White-Jacket,* the captain of the ship orders the narrator to be flogged for unintentionally missing an assignment. In an apparently autobiographical passage, filled with precise physical and emotional detail, the narrator carefully calculates the force, time, distance, and moral choice necessary to rush at the captain and carry him overboard to their mutual death. I shall quote this passage at some length because it shows with burning clarity how Melville's artistic imagination was shaped by his experience of work, oppression, and resistance:

> The captain stood on the weather-side of the deck. Sideways, on an
> unobstructed line with him, was the opening of the lee-gangway,

where the side-ladders are suspended in port. Nothing but a slight
bit of sinnate-stuff served to rail in this opening, which was cut
right down to the level of the captain's feet, showing the far sea
beyond. I stood a little to windward of him, and, though he was a
large, powerful man, it was certain that a sudden rush against him,
along the slanting deck, would infallibly pitch him head-foremost
into the ocean, though he who so rushed must needs go over with
him. My blood seemed clotting in my veins; I felt icy cold at the
tips of my fingers, and a dimness was before my eyes. But through
that dimness the boatswain's mate, scourge in hand, loomed like a
giant, and Captain Claret, and the blue sea seen through the opening at the gangway, showed with an awful vividness. I cannot
analyse my heart, though it then stood still within me. But the
thing that swayed me to my purpose was not altogether the
thought that Captain Claret was about to degrade me, and that I
had taken an oath with my soul that he should not. No, I felt my
man's manhood so bottomless within me, that no word, no blow, no
scourge of Captain Claret would cut me deep enough for that....
The privilege, inborn and inalienable, that every man has, of dying
himself, and inflicting death upon another, was not given to us
without a purpose. These are the last resources of an insulted and
unendurable existence. (Ch. 67, "White-Jacket arraigned at the
Mast")

Whether or not this passage is strictly autobiographical, Melville's vision is unambiguous. Like Frederick Douglass, he discovered under the threat of the whip that a human being must sometimes be prepared to fight and die.

White-Jacket was Melville's fifth book. In each of these, except
for the experimental narrative in the latter sections of *Mardi,*
Melville writes from the point of view of a common sailor. In each
book, this common sailor is a fictionalized self-portrait. True, this
sailor is also exceptional. Although he is part of the most oppressed portion of the working class, he has fallen into that class
from above, and he figures he has a good chance of climbing back
out again. That is, like Melville, this worker is doubly declassed,
and no longer belongs simply either to the petty bourgeoisie, into
which he was born and to which he hopes to return, nor to the
working class, into which he has fallen. But to comprehend Melville's art, we must grasp the significance of his conscious choice
to present the world from the point of view of an oppressed

worker. Most other mid-nineteenth-century American authors commonly taught in the academy today saw the world from the opposite class point of view. For them workers either did not exist at all, or, if they did, they existed as objects, as exotic creatures, or, at best, poor wretches. Melville's art is a projection of the human universe through the eyes of a worker, an articulate, self-educated, passionate, philosophic, and extremely creative worker.

After these first five books with sailor-narrators comes still another, called *Moby-Dick; Or, The Whale*. Here the narrator, one of the lowest seamen on a whaler, is a philosopher and a loner who asks us to call him Ishmael. The awe-inspiring creative achievement of *Moby-Dick* flows directly from Melville's proletarian view of the most important experience of his life.

Moby-Dick is of course one of the most written-about books in literature, and it would be impossible to give a comprehensive, or even a very balanced, account of it in a few pages. Most essays and even books about *Moby-Dick* tend to distort it one way or another, for the very same reasons that Ishmael always finds himself distorting the whale: its proportions are too vast to encompass. However, I would argue that to approach *Moby-Dick* initially from any direction other than one that follows Melville's own path through the brutal but ennobling labor of the whaleman is not just to distort but fundamentally to misrepresent *Moby-Dick*. This is precisely the error I made in *The Wake of the Gods: Melville's Mythology,* and the result was to cut *Moby-Dick* from its roots and drain the life out of it.

In any and all disputes about *Moby-Dick,* there is one incontestable fact: its underlying power comes from the reality of whales and whaling, the ocean and the men who sailed it. If it were not for the precise realism and physicality of the narrative, *Moby-Dick* would be, just as Ishmael himself declares, nothing but "a monstrous fable, or still worse and more detestable, a hideous and intolerable allegory" (Ch. 45). Of course the White Whale is a symbol. But whatever he may symbolize, he is one thing for certain: a gigantic, intelligent animal actually hunted to be turned into dollars. And whatever that hunt may symbolize, it is a most dangerous, messy, physical labor going on in reality as the book is published. "For God's sake," says Melville directly to his readers in the paragraph just after his insistence that this is not mere allegory, "be economical with your lamps and candles! not a gallon you burn, but at least one drop of man's blood was spilled for it." Without the actual bones and blubber of the whales brutally slain "to light the gay bridals and other merry-makings of men" (Ch. 81), without the real-life stove boats and drowned sailors, without Melville's personal participation in all this, *Moby-Dick* would be as abstract and boring as *The Faerie Queene.* But remove all the philosophy and symbolism from *Moby-Dick,* and you still have a marvelous adventure story, and the finest account ever written of the nineteenth-century whaling industry.

The second awareness indispensable to understanding *Moby-Dick,* though here there will be much disagreement, is that it is a celebration of the transcendent dignity and nobility, in fact divinity, of the most oppressed members of the proletariat. Ishmael allows that "men may seem detestable as joint stock-companies and nations; knaves, fools, and murderers there may be," but he argues that there is in each person an essential "grand and glowing creature" representing the nobility of the race and actually made manifest in the most degraded worker, who therefore embodies the divinity of humanity:

> ... this august dignity I treat of, is not the dignity of kings and robes, but that abounding dignity which has no robed investiture. Thou shalt see it shining in the arm that wields a pick or drives a spike; that democratic dignity which, on all hands, radiates without end from God; Himself! The great God absolute! The centre and circumference of all democracy! His omnipresence, our divine equality!
>
> If, then, to meanest mariners, and renegades and castaways, I shall hereafter ascribe high qualities, though dark; weave round them tragic graces; if even the most mournful, perchance the most abased, among them all, shall at times lift himself to the exalted mounts; if I shall touch that workman's arm with some ethereal light; if I shall spread a rainbow over his disastrous set of sun; then against all mortal critics bear me out in it, thou just Spirit of Equality, which hast spread one royal mantle of humanity over all my kind! (Ch. 26)

The incarnation of the divine seaman is the heroic steersman Bulkington, holding the ship off "the treacherous, slavish shore": "Bear thee grimly, demigod! Up from the spray of thy ocean-perishing—straight up, leaps thy apotheosis!" (Ch. 23). Melville compares the whalemen with the greatest heroes and gods of antiquity and with the aristocrats who inherit their titles, always to the advantage of the workers. He warns every knight of St. George, for example, never to eye a whaleman with disdain, "since even in our woollen frocks and tarred trowsers we are much better entitled to St. George's decoration than they" (Ch. 82). The "roll of our order" includes not only "heroes, saints, demigods, and prophets" but even "the great gods themselves." The savior gods of the world's major myths are enrolled in the same clan with the illiterate seamen. The question is not whether the whalemen qualify as gods and heroes but whether the gods and heroes qualify as whalemen. So, after debating "whether to admit Hercules among us or not," Ishmael finally generously allows him into "our clan": "he may be deemed a sort of involuntary whale-man; at any rate the whale caught him, if he did not the whale" (Ch. 82).

The central ethic of *Moby-Dick* is a proletarian ethic. It is the ethic of solidarity, of unity in the face of the gravest threats to survival, and it derives from the conditions of labor. In *Moby-Dick* that ethic is symbolized in many different forms, none more graphic than "the monkey-rope." In the process of "cutting-in" to the whale, the first step is for a man, balanced on the body of the almost submerged carcass, to insert a blubber-hook and keep it secured. He "flounders about, half on the whale and half in the water, as the vast mass revolves like a tread-mill beneath him," while swarms of voracious sharks lunge for the body (Ch. 72). This man is attached by a "monkey-rope" to a man on the deck. When Queequeg, the South Seas cannibal harpooneer, is balanced on the dead whale, it is his bosom friend Ishmael to whom he is tied, for life or for death:

> . . . the monkey-rope was fast at both ends; fast to Queequeg's broad canvas belt, and fast to my narrow leather one. So that for better or for worse, we two, for the time, were wedded; and should poor

> Queequeg sink to rise no more, then both usage and honor de-
> manded, that instead of cutting the cord, it should drag me down in
> his wake. So, then, an elongated Siamese ligature united us.
> Queequeg was my own inseparable twin brother; nor could I any
> way get rid of the dangerous liabilities which the hempen bond
> entailed. (Ch. 72)

Many ties binding people to each other, like this line between
Ishmael and his "dear comrade" Queequeg, are woven throughout
Moby-Dick. Toward the end, at the moment of crucial decision,
the symbolic monkey-rope is the handhold between Captain Ahab
and the Black cabin boy Pip. This bond almost saves the crew, but
then Ahab rejects it in favor of the hempen line which fatally
lashes him to the White Whale. Severing the bond with Pip, Ahab
dooms the entire crew to death, except for Ishmael, who escapes to
tell us the tale and explain what it means.

It is no coincidence that the most important symbols of human
solidarity and unity in *Moby-Dick* are bonds between white and
nonwhite people. As Edward Grejda has shown in *The Common
Continent of Men: Racial Equality in the Writings of Herman Melville,* this is a central theme throughout Melville's entire career
as a writer, beginning with that narrative of a residence among a
nonwhite people. In *Moby-Dick,* the victimization of nonwhite
peoples by white Europeans and Americans is one of the principal
forces menacing human solidarity. The very name of the ship
hunting the White Whale, the *Pequod,* an Indian tribe extermi-
nated by the white colonists, symbolizes the historical basis of
America. Fleece, the shuffling Black cook, seems to submit to the
racist taunts of the mate Stubb, but he has the last laugh. Dag-
goo, the majestic African harpooneer, responds with violence to
the racist taunts of the Spanish sailor. Hopes of salvation are
embodied most fully by the cannibal Queequeg, who symbolically
weds Ishmael, recklessly plunges into the sea to rescue a Yankee
bumpkin who had just been insulting him, leaps into the interior
of the sinking carcass of a whale to rescue the American Indian
Tashtego, and then finally, even in his own death, saves Ishmael
as his coffin rises to the surface from the sinking *Pequod* to give
the narrator his only clutch on life.

The central philosophical exploration of *Moby-Dick* is the relation between our subjective world and the objective world in
which we live and which shapes our perception of it. Here Melville seeks an answer to the central philosophical question of the
bourgeois historical epoch, the same question Marx wrestled with
in his 1841 doctoral dissertation and *The Economic and
Philosophic Manuscripts of 1844*: In a materialist universe, is
freedom possible?

Captain Ahab, the supreme individualist, superhero, universe-
threatening aspirant to the role of the savior god, thinks he
can single-handedly achieve human freedom by imposing his
own will and ego on objective reality. To Ahab, it matters not
what things really *are*; he believes that he can fashion them into
what he wills them to be. He succeeds in subordinating the entire
crew to his personal and cosmic quest, turning their bonds of
solidarity into a tool at his command, wresting their labors away
from the purposes of the pious capitalist owners and their faithful
first mate Starbuck, who all think that the only reason to kill
whales is to make money. But in the end, objective reality incarnate in a colossal alien animal drags Ahab and his men to the
bottom of the ocean which, though vastly symbolic, is also profoundly real.

The sailors, on the other hand, are deprived of freedom because
their very essence is alienated through the alienation of their
labor. They serve the purposes of the owners, giving their lives—
almost like the whales they hunt—to generate profits. Ahab is
able to penetrate beyond this shallow motivation of capitalism
deep into the fears and desires of the crewmen, deep enough to
reach a symbol from their collective unconscious:

> How it was they so aboundingly responded to the old man's ire—by
> what evil magic their souls were possessed, that at times his hate
> seemed almost theirs; the White Whale as much their insufferable
> foe as his; how all this came to be—what the White Whale was to
> them, or how to their unconscious understandings, also, in some
> dim, unsuspected way, he might have seemed the gliding great
> demon of the seas of life,—all this to explain, would be to dive
> deeper than Ishmael can go. (Ch. 41)

The crew then shift their labor away from producing profits for the owners, luxuries for the affluent, and oil for industry. Instead they yield their labor, their unified will, and ultimately their lives to Ahab's monomaniac purpose.

Apparently in opposition to Ahab, who defies all nature and blasphemes all deities, is an undercurrent of pantheism, the worship of all nature, including its most insignificant part and summed up in the lure of the ocean. But Ahab, like Melville's pantheistic contemporaries, is also a Transcendentalist. His assault upon nature is itself a form of worship, based on a faith in a god, however malign, lurking behind the "pasteboard masks" figured forth by the world of nature. To the element of fire he shouts: "'I now know thee, thou clear spirit, and I now know that thy right worship is defiance'" (Ch. 119). Although both pantheism and Ahab's inversion of it are presented as extremely alluring, and are of course crucial in the book's dialectic, Melville displays these philosophies as treacherous. The narrative moves toward a revelation of the catastrophic and tragic flaw in Ahab's vision. And all along the way, the laboring lives of the seamen provide constant revelation of truths that cut away the delusions of all brands of philosophic Idealism.

Like Hegel, Melville sees a dialectic relationship between mind and matter, subject and object. But like Marx, he turns Hegel's dialectic upside down, standing it not on its head but on its feet. Like Marx, he shows being determining consciousness, and physical labor as the primary source of knowledge. The workers have a more authentic and profound basis for knowledge than the academic philosophers, and real freedom lies in the recognition of material and social necessity.

Melville sees truth as founded on facts apprehended most accurately through labor. If you want true knowledge of whales and their environment, if you want to understand the ocean or the industry thriving on it, you must acquire that knowledge either directly or indirectly from the people who do the labor of whaling. Like Melville, you can go whaling. Or you can read a book by someone who has gone whaling. This is in part his response to those bookish critics who claimed that "Mr. Melville's mind," the mind of a "reading sailor," "has not been trained in those studies which enable men to observe with profit." Chapter after chapter debunks the false knowledge about the oceans that comprise "two thirds of this terraqueous globe"; the illiterate whalemen are shown again and again to know more truth than all the holy scriptures and academic scientists combined. Here, for example, is what Melville has to say about the picture of the sperm whale found in Frederick Cuvier's *Natural History of Whales:*

> Before showing that picture to any Nantucketer, you had best provide for your summary retreat from Nantucket. In a word, Frederick Cuvier's Sperm Whale is not a Sperm Whale, but a squash. Of course, he never had the benefit of a whaling voyage (such men seldom have), but whence he derived that picture, who can tell?[11] (Ch. 55)

To comprehend the radical thrust of Melville's epistemology, compare it to the conventional intellectual's view, at least during that period. The following year, in *The Blithedale Romance,* Hawthorne expressed the conventional wisdom in these words:

> Intellectual activity is incompatible with any large amount of bodily exercise. The yeoman and the scholar—the yeoman and the man of finest moral culture, though not the man of sturdiest sense and integrity—are two distinct individuals, and can never be melted or welded into one substance.[12]

Melville, like Frederick Douglass and Linda Brent, takes precisely the opposite view.

One example among many, an especially brilliant one, is the chapter "The Mast-Head." Melville notes that "nowadays, the whale-fishery furnishes an asylum for many romantic, melancholy, and absent-minded young men . . . seeking sentiment in tar and blubber." These "young Platonists" dream away their time at the mast-head and therefore never spy any whales. It would be an error to equate these dreamy effete youths, hopelessly "short-sighted" because "they have left their opera-glasses at home," with either Ishmael or Melville. Ishmael is a sound seaman, entrusted with the position of bowsman to Queequeg. As for Melville himself, he was even less than Ishmael a mere bookish observer of the action. He had been a harpooneer, the position of greatest respect, physical prowess, and responsibility among the crew, the man "expected to set an example of superhuman activity" (Ch. 62). He had not only sighted whales but hurled harpoons into them. In fact, it is a harpooneer who admonishes one of these dreamy lads for never sighting a whale. When one of these young Platonists ascends the mast-head, he puts his philosophy into practice, and there he shows that the beautiful theories of Hegel and Emerson may do fine in the study but they won't do on the seas of life. Melville lets his prose drift along with the rhapsodic rhythms of the Idealist youth's reverie. Then one sudden point from the world of work punctures the illusion, proving that in the real world Platonic dreams of the Ideal can be fatal:

... lulled into such an opium-like listlessness of vacant, unconscious reverie is this absent-minded youth by the blending cadence of waves with thoughts, that at last he loses his identity; takes the mystic ocean at his feet for the visible image of that deep, blue, bottomless soul, pervading mankind and nature; and every strange, half-seen, gliding, beautiful thing that eludes him; every dimly-discovered, uprising fin of some undiscernible form, seems to him the embodiment of those elusive thoughts that only people the soul by continually flitting through it. . . .

There is no life in thee, now, except that rocking life imparted by a gently rolling ship; by her, borrowed from the sea; by the sea, from the inscrutable tides of God. But while this sleep, this dream is on ye, move your foot or hand an inch; slip your hold at all; and your identity comes back in horror. . . . And perhaps, at mid-day, in the fairest weather, with one half-throttled shriek you drop through that transparent air into the summer sea, no more to rise for ever. Heed it well, ye Pantheists!

Pierre, published the year after *Moby-Dick,* is Melville's first book which moves away from the world of ships and of work. The title character is a wealthy youth, a dreamy idealist, who seeks to redress the sins of his father and of his society. Like the "young

Platonists" who may fall from the mast-head because they confuse the rhapsodic projections from their own minds with objective reality, Pierre ends by destroying himself and all he loves after he discovers that his most self-sacrificing impulse is at bottom a disguised desire to have his sister as his lover. Pierre's tragedy concludes with his suicide in the city prison of New York.

What scandalized the critics most about *Pierre* was its uncompromising probe of the significance of sexual aberration in civilized society. As Melville was driven underground by the literary establishment, forced to write anonymously and under pseudonyms, he went much further with this exploration. Unlike Freud, he recognized that particular "aberrant" or "perverted" sexual impulses show more about the society in which they occur than they do about the particular individuals experiencing them. To some extent he foreshadows the methods and insights of Frantz Fanon, or of Eldridge Cleaver's early writings about sexual pathology. Melville shows that the most essential and grotesque sexual perversion of our society is merely an expression and product of capitalist social relations. In that vision he locates Satan more accurately than do some of our more recent sensationalist excursions into diabolism, such as the film *The Exorcist* or E. Howard Hunt's sado-masochistic novel *Coven*. To Melville, the underlying sexual perversion of our society is the enslavement of human beings, imprisoning them in factories, ships, plantations, and offices, forcing them to expend their creativity to enrich a handful of parasites who own the means of production. Master of this hell is none other than the capitalist.

On April Fool's Day, 1855, *Harper's New Monthly Magazine* published a pair of anonymous sketches entitled "The Paradise of Bachelors and The Tartarus of Maids." These are trick stories, with hidden meanings intended to expose the polite unwitting readers of *Harper's*. They display Melville's view of the two main classes in capitalist society, the working class and the owning class, in the form of a grotesque sexual allegory.

In "The Tartarus of Maids," Melville assumes the voice of a seedsman who visits the factory that produces the envelopes for his seeds. A nice germinous, procreative job. But what the seedsman represents is a perverted male sexuality entering a woman's genitals in the quest for dollars, and these woman's genitals have been captured and enslaved by the archetypal Satanic capitalist. All creativity, including procreativity, has been perverted to produce nothing but blank paper and profits.

The seedsman himself may be considered a portrait of the creative writer within capitalist society, who, like Melville himself, must sell his art as a commodity in order to live. ("Dollars damn me!" Melville said succinctly.) On another level, his business represents the expansion of industrial capitalism and wage slavery in the pre–Civil War United States: "Having embarked on a large scale in the seedsman's business (so extensive and broadcast, indeed, that at length my seeds were distributed through all the Eastern and Northern States, and even fell into the far soil of Missouri and the Carolinas)...."

The seedsman enters a valley, passing the "Mad Maid's Bellows-pipe." He passes through a "Dantean gateway": "From the steepness of the walls here, their strangely ebon hue, and the sudden contraction of the gorge, this particular point is called the Black Notch." Beyond this is a "strange-colored torrent" called "Blood River." He finally arrives at the factory, which resembles a "great whited sepulchre." It sits near the bottom of "the Devil's Dungeon."

All the workers in the factory are women, referred to consistently as "girls." The narrator asks the owner why:

> "The girls," echoed I, glancing round at their silent forms. "Why is it, sir, that in most factories, female operatives, of whatever age, are indiscriminately called girls, never women?"
>
> "Oh! as to that—why, I suppose, the fact of their being generally unmarried—that's the reason, I should think. But it never struck me before. For our factory here, we will not have married women; they are apt to be off-and-on too much. We want none but steady workers: twelve hours to the day, day after day, through the three hundred and sixty-five days, excepting Sundays, Thanksgiving, and Fast-days. That's our rule. And so, having no married women, what females we have are rightly enough called girls."

Birth, menstruation, child care—none can be permitted to interfere with the production of blank paper and profits.

The narrator is given a tour of the factory by a boy named

Cupid, who represents about all that is left of Eros in this sterile world. Cupid shows him "two great round vats . . . full of a white, wet, woolly-looking stuff, not unlike the albuminous part of an egg, soft-boiled." The boy tells him that this "white pulp" is "the first beginnings" of the paper. Cupid then takes the narrator into a room, "stifling with a strange, blood-like, abdominal heat" where "the germinous particles" were being "developed." The power for the factory comes from Blood River. A "girl" meekly tends "a vertical thing like a piston periodically rising and falling." An elderly woman, formerly a wet nurse, has come to work here because the "business" of a wet nurse "is poor in these parts." "Poisonous particles" dart from all sides through the air into the lungs. Only machinery can be heard, because "the human voice was banished." A woman looks at the narrator with "a face pale with work, and blue with cold; an eye supernatural with unrelated misery." The narrator is overwhelmed by the essential perversion and sterility of the factory:

> Machinery—that vaunted slave of humanity—here stood menially served by human beings, who served mutely and cringingly as the slave serves the Sultan. The girls did not so much seem accessory wheels to the general machinery as mere cogs to the wheels.

In the rag-room, "each girl" rubs rags across a long blade "vertically thrust up" before her like an "erected sword." The narrator apprehends these swords as fit symbols of this deadly factory in the Devil's Dungeon: "So, through consumptive pallors of this blank, raggy life, go these white girls to death." Just at this moment, two of the "girls" begin to sharpen a swordblade by rubbing it "up and down" with a whetstone. The narrator does not note the perverse sexuality all around him, but he understands clearly, in terms like those being used by Marx, that these women, alienated from their labor, alienated from the products of their labor, and alienated from their human essence, are forced to fashion the very instruments of their own destruction: "Their own executioners; themselves whetting the very swords that slay them, meditated I."

The factory is owned by a "dark-complexioned man" known as "Old Bach." The narrator doesn't notice that these are euphemisms for the Devil, but naïvely inquires whether he is a bachelor. When he finds this is so, his memory takes him back to "The Paradise of Bachelors," subject of the first sketch.

The entrance to the Paradise of Bachelors is not far from another symbolic phallus, "Temple Bar." It is an anus. To reach it, the narrator turns, "soiled with the mud of Fleet Street," site of filthy London journalism, to "glide down a dim, monastic way, flanked by dark, sedate, and solemn piles," a word signifying then, as now, a morbid dilation of the veins of the lower rectum. Inside, in the "honey-comb of offices and domiciles," like "any cheese ... quite perforated through and through with the snug cells of bachelors," he enjoys a huge feast of gluttony and good fellowship with nine bachelors, men of business and law. Beginning with "ox-tail soup," which reminds the narrator at first of "teamsters' gads and the raw-hides of ushers," they pass through a course of turbot, "just gelatinous enough, not too turtlish in its unctuousness," to cloy themselves on "a saddle of mutton, a fat turkey, a chicken-pie, and endless other savory things" washed down with round after round of wines and ale. As they give way to "unconstraint," they now bring out, "like choice brands of Moselle or Rhenish," the "choice experiences in their private lives." For instance, "one told us how mellowly he lived when a student at Oxford; with various spicy anecdotes of most frank-hearted noble lords, his liberal companions." Another tells "a strange anecdote of the private life of the Iron Duke, never printed, and never before announced in any public or private company." After dinner, they all descend to the courtyard, "two by two, and arm-in-arm." Then they divide, "some going to their neighboring chambers to turn over the *Decameron* ere retiring for the night."

For these men of wealth, pain and trouble simply do not exist:

The thing called pain, the bugbear styled trouble—those two legends seemed preposterous to their bachelor imaginations. How could men of liberal sense, ripe scholarship in the world, and capacious philosophical and convivial understandings—how could they suffer themselves to be imposed upon by such monkish fables?

> Pain! Trouble! As well talk of Catholic miracles. No such thing.—
> Pass the sherry, sir.—Pooh, pooh! Can't be!

These "easy-hearted men had no wives or children to give an anxious thought." They are as barren and sterile as the maids in the Tartarus they own and control.

In "Bartleby, the Scrivener. A Story of Wall-Street"[13] Melville probes deeper into the sterile world of capitalism. The narrator of this story is also a bachelor, a Wall Street lawyer, who, "in the cool tranquillity of a snug retreat" does "a snug business among rich men's bonds, and mortgages, and title-deeds." (His main boast is that he was formerly "not unemployed" by the late John Jacob Astor.) He is "a conveyancer and title-hunter, and drawer-up of recondite documents of all sorts." The paper mill of "The Tartarus of Maids" produces nothing but blank paper; "all sorts of writings could be writ on those now vacant things—sermons, lawyers' briefs, physicians' prescriptions, love-letters, marriage certificates, bills of divorce, registers of birth, death-warrants, and so on, without end." The narrator of "Bartleby" is the man who converts these blank pieces of paper into the documents upon which capitalism rests: bonds, titles, and mortgages which declare that all the means of production, including that very paper mill, and all the products coming from it, including the pieces of paper themselves, do not belong to the people who produced them with their entire life's creativity, but instead are the private property of a handful of rich parasites.

The narrator is not an unkind, much less a Satanic, man. But he is an employer. Hence he sees his officeworkers as objects, whose existence is to serve the function he assigns them. He considers one of his two scriveners "a most valuable person to me," and the other "a very useful man to me." His Wall Street office is made of walls surrounded by other walls. In one direction, his office "looked upon the white wall of the interior of a spacious sky-light shaft," providing a view "deficient in what landscape painters call 'life.'" In the other direction, "my windows commanded an unobstructed view of a lofty brick wall, black by age and everlasting shade."

His business becomes considerably increased when he receives the office of Master in Chancery, a kind of judgeship: "There was now great work for scriveners. Not only must I push the clerks already with me, but I must have additional help." In answer to his advertisement for "help," there arrives at his office a mysterious stranger named Bartleby.

Bartleby is informed of his duties as a scrivener, and at first "did an extraordinary quantity of writing," "copying by sunlight and by candle-light." But when the narrator off-handedly orders Bartleby to compare copy, "a request made according to common usage and common sense," Bartleby calmly responds, "I would prefer not to."

Gradually Bartleby withdraws more and more of his labor from the commands of the narrator, at each point meekly stating "I would prefer not to" go to the post office, help tie a package, examine papers, or even do any more copying. The narrator originally had considered him "a valuable acquisition." But as Bartleby's mysterious strike lengthens, the narrator finds this rebellion of "my hired clerk" shattering to all his customary assumptions, first about the relations between employers and employees, then about private property itself, and finally about the entire human condition in this society. Bartleby's "crime" is a mild, quiet version of Melville's own crimes of desertion and mutiny: it too is a refusal to work.

Bartleby's strike becomes a strange, mute sit-in, as he "prefers not to" leave the office at all, though he no longer does any work for his employer. The narrator finds himself "sort of unmanned when he tranquilly permits his hired clerk to dictate to him, and order him away from his own premises," not perceiving that his own workers might be similarly "unmanned" by the dictates and orders of their employer. But in fact what is happening is almost the opposite of what the narrator here perceives. By confronting the underlying ethic of Wall Street, which is exactly the opposite of the proletarian ethic of solidarity represented by the monkey-rope, Bartleby offers to the narrator the possibility of becoming a human being, with feelings and emotional ties to other human beings. Struck by the discovery of Bartleby's cosmic loneliness and solitude, the narrator's bachelor privacy and smugness disin-

tegrate, and he finds a revelation denied to the bachelor hedonists
of "The Paradise of Bachelors":

> For the first time in my life, a feeling of overpowering stinging
> melancholy seized me. Before, I had never experienced aught but a
> not unpleasing sadness. The bond of a common humanity now drew
> me irresistibly to gloom. A fraternal melancholy! For both I and
> Bartleby were sons of Adam. I remembered the bright silks and
> sparkling faces I had seen that day, in gala trim, swan-like sail-
> ing down the Mississippi of Broadway; and I contrasted them with
> the pallid copyist, and thought to myself, Ah, happiness courts
> the light, so we deem the world is gay; but misery hides aloof, so we
> deem that misery there is none.

But business sense gets the upper hand again, and the narrator
orders Bartleby to "quit me." When Bartleby announces that he
would prefer not to, the narrator responds as the very essence of
capitalist society, reducing all human relationships to money relationships:

> "I would prefer *not* to quit you," he replied, gently emphasizing
> the *not*.
> "What earthly right have you to stay here? Do you pay any rent?
> Do you pay my taxes? Or is this property yours?"

Gradually, however, the narrator begins to perceive something
unearthly, something perhaps even divine, radiating from
Bartleby, "this forlornest of mankind." He feels that "Bartleby was
billeted upon me for some mysterious purpose of an all-wise Prov-
idence, which it was not for a mere mortal like me to fathom." He
glimpses the message of Matthew 25, in which Christ identifies
himself with all those most miserable—strangers, the poor, the
sick, the needy, prisoners—and in which Christ promises to judge
each person on how he or she responds to these wretched of the
earth:

At last I see it, I feel it; I penetrate to the predestinated purpose of my life. I am content. Others may have loftier parts to enact; but my mission in this world, Bartleby, is to furnish you with office-room for such period as you may see fit to remain.

But the customs and usages of Wall Street overcome this resolve. The narrator buckles under "the unsolicited and uncharitable remarks obtruded upon me by professional friends." He flees from his own office, leaving Bartleby to the tender mercies of the landlord and the new tenant. Then he denies Bartleby three times, in words echoing Peter's three denials of Christ.

Next, "fearful . . . of being exposed in the papers," he returns in an attempt to help the other functionaries of capitalism to get rid of this "nuisance." He decides to offer Bartleby the choice of other things to do in this society. They range the gamut of the opportunities open to white-collar workers:

"Would you like to re-engage in copying for some one?"
"Would you like a clerkship in a dry-goods store?"
"How would a bar-tender's business suit you?"
"Well, then, would you like to travel through the country collecting bills for the merchants?"
"How, then, would going as a companion to Europe, to entertain some young gentleman with your conversation—how would that suit you?"

Bartleby prefers not to spend his life doing any of these things.

As a result, he is arrested and placed in the same New York City prison as Pierre, already known as "the Tombs, or, to speak more properly, the Halls of Justice." He is charged with being a vagrant, precisely because he refuses to become one. The walls and the physical environment of the prison, as the narrator notes, are no more unpleasant than the office world of Wall Street. There Bartleby, the mysterious stranger, curls up and dies.

At one end of pre–Civil War America stood the brick walls of the financial district of the Empire State. At the other, Black slaves produced the main cash export of the country, King Cotton, which was building the capital base for industrial capitalism. "Bartleby" shows a single white-collar worker threatening the very foundations of Wall Street with a mysterious, mild-mannered withdrawal of labor and refusal to disperse. This form of what his boss calls "passive resistance" succeeds finally in destroying only himself. "Benito Cereno,"[14] another great story of this period, describes a different form of resistance, a highly organized and bloody revolt by Black slaves. Melville locates this in the past, but his vision is obviously intended as prophetic.

The story is based on an actual slave revolt that took place on a Spanish slave ship sailing between two Spanish colonies in the New World. It is told in the third person, but from the point of view of Amasa Delano, the practical, business-minded Yankee captain of the American ship that did actually recapture the slaver and its human cargo (Melville based his story on a chapter from Delano's book).

Melville renames Delano's ship the *Bachelor's Delight,* name of a famous pirate vessel, and emblematic of its bland, utilitarian, optimistic, money-grubbing Yankee bachelor captain. On one level, the rotting old Spanish ship represents the dying Spanish empire, about to be taken over by the vigorous, rising young Yankee empire. The main focus is on the material basis of both these empires: Black slavery. Central to that is the consciousness of slaves and of masters.

The slaves are able to take over the Spanish ship easily because their owner made the fatal error of thinking—like William Gilmore Simms and Nathaniel Hawthorne—that they were content with their condition and therefore didn't need to be in chains. The Blacks are trying to return to Africa. When they see the American ship, they force the survivors of the Spanish crew to assume their original roles. So when Captain Delano comes on board, he enters the scene of an elaborate masquerade, the Blacks, now in control, pretending to be slaves again, the Spanish crew, now cringing in terror, pretending to be the masters of the Blacks and the ship.

Captain Delano cannot comprehend what is going on, because to him slaves are primarily "valuable freight," and secondarily pleasant animals who enjoy bright colors, are content with their servile lot, and are "too stupid" to organize a revolt. Delano's vision of slaves as animals is the converse of the animal imagery used by Frederick Douglass: "Captain Delano took to negroes, not philanthropically, but genially, just as other men to Newfoundland dogs." Like Linda Brent's master, Delano expects young slave women to enjoy his attention. He stares, with approval and other warm feelings, at a young nursing "negress," lying "with youthful limbs carelessly disposed . . . like a doe in the shade of a woodland rock":

> Sprawled at her lapped breasts, was her wide-awake fawn, stark naked, its black little body half lifted from the deck, crosswise with its dam's; its hands, like two paws, clambering upon her; its mouth and nose ineffectually rooting to get at the mark; and meantime giving a vexatious half-grunt, blending with the composed snore of the negress.
>
> The uncommon vigor of the child at length roused the mother. She started up, at a distance facing Captain Delano. But as if not at all concerned at the attitude in which she had been caught, delightedly she caught the child up, with maternal transports, covering it with kisses.
>
> There's naked nature, now; pure tenderness and love, thought Captain Delano, well pleased.

Delano has no inkling that this woman is a human being who is outwitting him, that her display of naked happiness is part of the masquerade contrived to escape from slavery to freedom.

But this New Englander is also a practical man of business and action. When he is told the real state of affairs, he ruthlessly organizes the recapture of the ship. His main goal is to take over the valuable slaves, killing and injuring as few as possible. This is for profits, not mercy, a fact brought out by the Americans as they murder two of the Spanish sailors incorrectly believed to have in "some way favored the cause of the negroes." But even after all is revealed to Captain Delano, he still does not comprehend that Blacks, just like whites, will fight and kill for their freedom and that Black slavery contains the seed of the devastation of his own society.

The last two full-length fictions Melville published were *Israel Potter; Or, Fifty Years of Exile: A Fourth of July Story* (1854-55)[15] and *The Confidence-Man: His Masquerade* (1857). The first is his account of the origins of the American republic; the second is his apocalyptic vision of where that American republic is heading.

Israel Potter is Melville's true history of the American Revolution, reconstructed from an autobiographical pamphlet by one of its unsung heroes. Melville's thesis is quite direct: the real heroes of the Revolution were the American yeomanry, but all they were to gain from its victories was a future of grinding labor, deepening impoverishment, a change of masters, imprisonment, and obscurity.

Born among farmers in the New England hills, Israel Potter falls into the working class—temporarily, he thinks: "he hired himself out" for a promise of land, which proves false (Ch. 2). Hunting and trading on the edges of the wilderness, he acquires "that fearless self-reliance and independence which conducted our forefathers to national freedom" (Ch. 2). He next becomes, like his nineteenth-century biographer, a harpooneer on a whaleship.

Israel Potter fights heroically in the most famous battles of the Revolution, from Bunker Hill to the conquest of the *Serapis* by the *Bon Homme Richard*. He meets Benjamin Franklin, whom Melville presents as the archetypal bourgeois mind controlling the Revolution. Manipulated by Franklin like a puppet, he ends up an exile in England, where he is "to linger out the best part of his life a prisoner or a pauper" (Ch. 1). He moves from imprisonment as a rebel to imprisonment as a worker. His job as a brickmaker recalls "The Tartarus of Maids." "Lorded over by the taskmaster," Israel "toiled in his pit," "condemned," as a worker, "to a sort of earthy dungeon." This entire proletarian environment is seen as a prison:

> The yard was encamped, with all its endless rows of tented sheds, and kilns, and mills, upon a wild waste moor, belted round by bogs and fens. The blank horizon, like a rope, coiled round the whole.

> Sometimes the air was harsh and bleak; the ridged and mottled
> sky looked scourged, or cramping fogs set in from sea, for leagues
> around, ferreting out each rheumatic human bone, and racking it;
> the sciatic limpers shivered; their aguish rags sponged up the
> mists. No shelter, though it hailed. The sheds were for the bricks.
> (Ch. 23)

Israel falls from level to level of the proletariat, eventually becoming part of the reserve army of the unemployed, who "would
work for such a pittance as to bring down the wages of all the
laboring classes" (Ch. 26).

When he finally returns to his native land, Israel finds himself
a dispossessed stranger. He fades "out of being—his name out of
memory." In and out of all kinds of prisons throughout his life,
Israel Potter is finally rewarded "for his faithful services," Melville tells us bitterly in his introduction, by being "promoted to a
still deeper privacy under the ground." Israel Potter's own autobiographical narrative appeared in 1824, before most of the
great narratives by escaped slaves. Melville describes it in his
introduction as "forlornly published on sleazy gray paper" and
"written, probably, not by himself, but taken down from his lips
by another." In Melville's vision, this narrative made Israel Potter a profound example of the victim as criminal and artist.

The Confidence-Man displays the rotten foundations of
capitalist society and prophesies its end. A meek, mysterious,
lamblike man, resembling Bartleby, opens the book by attracting
the curiosity of the more well-to-do passengers on a riverboat. His
place is then mysteriously assumed by the seemingly fawning
figure of Black Guinea, "a grotesque negro cripple" who, "opening his mouth like an elephant for tossed apples," catches the
smallest pieces of money, copper pennies.[16] Black Guinea transmutes into form after form of the Confidence Man, a mythic figure
who stalks the decks of the riverboat bringing out all the kinds of
money, and money relationships, that constitute the essence of
this society.

At the end the Confidence Man becomes a cosmic Destroyer,
appearing simultaneously as the extravagantly attired Cosmopolitan and a boy in rags with a face covered with grime. The

boy is selling locks to keep out thieves, moneybelts to wear in case they get in, and counterfeit detectors to see if the money was worth protecting in the first place.

This final scene of Melville's last fiction to be published in his lifetime recalls that scene of the first paragraph of his first book. It is a "gentlemen's cabin," in which most of the passengers are still trying to sleep. Melville, that noisy sailor, is still keeping them awake, or trying to. All the lights but one have now died out, and voices call out from the berths protesting that the verbal quest for wisdom is "keeping wiser men awake": "And if you want to know what wisdom is, go find it under your blankets."

The last passenger awake is a "clean, comely," and "well-to-do" old man. He is left with only one activity before being led away into the deepening darkness: he must sit there studying a banknote to determine whether it is counterfeit. His best clue may be a wild goose chase, a symbol, perhaps vaguely outlined on this symbolic piece of paper: "the figure of a goose, very small, indeed, all but microscopic; and, for added precaution . . . not observable, even if magnified, unless the attention is directed to it." Unknown to this affluent professional gentleman, the bank that issued the bill was part of the Mississippi Bubble, and had already gone bankrupt.

This Mississippi riverboat is steaming toward the same state. Its voyage had begun at sunrise in the slave city of St. Louis, just across the river from the "free" state of Illinois. The first half of the book takes place in daylight, as the boat glides between Illinois and the slave state of Missouri. Twilight, in this most formally perfect of Melville's books, comes in a chapter which divides the book precisely into two equal halves. It envelops the boat as it lies still at Cairo, the last point on the journey south without Black chattel slavery; from here on there is slave territory on both sides of the river and darkness continues to intensify on board.

Identities shift amidst the deepening ambiguities of action in *The Confidence-Man,* an unsurpassed display of the art of the fictionist, but Melville's values burn brilliantly. His quest for truth and the possibility of freedom strips mask after hypocritical mask from the smiling faces of polite society. For Melville here is dealing only with the passengers and their world: the sailors who work this boat remain as invisible to the readers as they are to the passengers.

One of the most revealing exchanges takes place between a gruff, eccentric, rifle-toting Missourian on the one hand and the Confidence Man in the guise of an affable herb doctor on the other. The Missourian, named Pitch, is a farm owner who here seems to oppose slavery, but who will later agree to purchase a boy to work on his land (from the Confidence Man, this time representing an employment agency known as the Philosophical Intelligence Office). Here Pitch, before revealing his own opinions, demands to know where the herb doctor stands on the question of slavery:

> "You are an abolitionist, ain't you?" he added, squaring himself with both hands on his rifle, used for a staff, and gazing in the herb-doctor's face with no more reverence than if it were a target. "You are an abolitionist, ain't you?" (Ch. 21)

The herb doctor's answer tells us what he represents, for we have heard his voice in response to every movement for human liberation:

> "As to that, I cannot so readily answer. If by abolitionist you mean a zealot, I am none; but if you mean a man, who, being a man, feels for all men, slaves included, and by any lawful act, opposed to nobody's interest, and therefore, rousing nobody's enmity, would willingly abolish suffering (supposing it, in its degree, to exist) from among mankind, irrespective of color, then am I what you say."

Pitch, still wielding his rifle, the instrument that was shortly to be used both to defend and to abolish Black slavery, then accurately labels this liberal gentleman:

"Picked and prudent sentiments. You are the moderate man, the invaluable understrapper of the wicked man. You, the moderate man, may be used for wrong, but are useless for right."

Pitch comes from Missouri, where the voyage of the riverboat had begun. In 1820–21, the liberal northern capitalists had reached that convenient arrangement with the southern plantation owners known as the Missouri Compromise, which provided that Missouri would be the only slave state in the Louisiana Purchase north of 36° 30′. But in 1854, three years before the publication of *The Confidence-Man*, Congress had reached a new compromise, the Kansas-Nebraska Bill, which explicitly repealed the Missouri Compromise and opened up the possibility of slavery in Kansas. In 1856 the proslavery militia sacked the town of Lawrence, Kansas. In response there emerged a figure less ambiguous than Melville's rifle-toting Missourian, a man named John Brown, who began armed counterattacks against the slavery men in May 1856.

Two years after *The Confidence-Man*, John Brown led the attack on Harper's Ferry. Brown was convicted of treason against the United States of America, and of urging and inciting slaves to treason and murder. He was hanged in December 1859, by the government of the United States. In 1861 the Civil War began, with the government of the United States still firmly committed to the support of slavery.

In 1866, the year after the war ended, the slaves now officially freed, Melville published a volume of Civil War poems entitled *Battle Pieces and Aspects of the War*. The first poem, "The Portent," is a memorial to John Brown. It begins by describing Brown "Hanging from the beam, Slowly swaying (such the law). . . ." *Battle Pieces* concludes with a "Supplement" in which Melville affirms that the white people of the South had been "cajoled" into supporting an armed attempt to establish "an Anglo-American empire based upon the systematic degradation of man." He insists that we "remember that emancipation was accomplished not by deliberate legislation; only through agonized violence could so mighty a result be achieved."

Pierre had ended with the would-be hero committing suicide in prison. "Bartleby" concludes with the mysterious stranger who had disrupted the routine of Wall Street dying in prison. Israel Potter, the revolutionary hero, is imprisoned, in one form or another, for most of his life. The rebel leader of the slave revolt in "Benito Cereno" is imprisoned and then executed by hanging. So is John Brown, who initiated the war that freed the slaves. When Melville died in 1891, he left one last work of fiction, published first in 1924. It too deals with a heroic man hanged by the forces of law and order.

Billy Budd, Sailor opens with another metamorphosis of Black and white. First we see a Black African as the Handsome Sailor, a godlike man, combining "strength and beauty," the "champion" and "spokesman" of his shipmates, workers of "such an assortment of tribes and complexions" they could serve as "Representatives of the Human Race."[17] His figure merges into that of Billy Budd, an Anglo-Saxon version of the same heroic sailor.

Billy Budd is Adam before the Fall, a man of natural goodness and innocence. He is beloved by all his shipmates on the merchant ship *The Rights of Man*. Symbolically kidnapped from *The Rights of Man*, he is impressed into service on the aptly named warship of the British empire, H.M.S. *Bellipotent*. The time is shortly after the American and French Revolutions, and the British crown, representing the main reactionary force in the Western world, is faced with rebellions by the sailors of its own fleet.

Claggart, the head of the secret police on board the *Bellipotent*, a human version of a "snake" or "torpedo-fish," falsely accuses Budd of fomenting mutiny. Budd, whose only defect is that he stutters in highly emotional situations, becomes too choked to speak in his own defense. He involuntarily strikes out with his fist, accidentally killing Claggart with that one blow.

This confrontation has been arranged by the captain, with himself as the sole witness, to test the truth of the accusation. He is an intellectual, somewhat bookish, staunchly tory officer aptly named "Vere" (the original spelling for the nautical term for shifting before the wind). Captain Vere knows that Budd is both morally and legally innocent of murder and mutiny, but decides immediately that he must be hanged as an example to the rest of the crew. So he calls together a drumhead court, handpicked by himself from among the officers of the ship. When these three officers hear the evidence, even they—culled from the class *White-Jacket* shows to be "essentially antagonistic" to the seamen—do not want to convict Budd. So Vere takes over the "trial," essentially dictating the verdict he had already reached. He argues that they must convict, though it is obviously against nature, because they serve the King, as opposed to nature. He further argues that they should disregard both their "heart" and their "private conscience," because their only loyalty as the King's officers is to the "imperial . . . code" (110–11). Accordingly, the best man and the truest sailor on the ship is hanged.

Much of the criticism of *Billy Budd* has consisted of a debate about Captain Vere, as if the key issue of the story were to decide whether Melville was condemning or approving his action. I am not going to restate the correct side of this argument, which many students of Melville have set forth, for there is overwhelming evidence in the story, and throughout Melville's other works, that Vere stands for all Melville found most detestable, inhuman, and menacing: arbitrary authority; oppression; military tyranny; legalism; the officer class and its support of war; hypocrisy; loyalty to kings and empire; legalized murder; disregard of nature, the human heart, and the dictates of conscience.

The real issue about Vere is not whether he is right or wrong, but whether he is sane or mad. I do not believe that Melville wrote *Billy Budd* to convince readers not to hang innocent people, or to argue that they should rebel against eighteenth-century British monarchy and imperialism. *Billy Budd* assumes these values, and insofar as it focuses on Vere, who is, after all, quite secondary to Billy Budd himself, it is a psychological study, the tale of a diseased mind that can argue with learning, calmness, and plausibility that the best thing to do is to murder the best person in your world.

The question of Vere's sanity is raised privately by the ship's surgeon, and Melville then asks each reader to answer "by such light as this narrative may afford" (102). He provides the answer in a philosophical disquisition on "Natural Depravity." Talking in particular about the obvious example of Claggart, he frames a general definition which fits Captain Vere even more precisely. The best examples of this depravity "invariably are dominated by intellectuality" (75). "Civilization, especially if of the austerer sort, is auspicious to it. It folds itself in the mantle of respectability" (75).

> But the thing which in eminent instances signalizes so exceptional a nature is this: Though the man's even temper and discreet bearing would seem to intimate a mind peculiarly subject to the law of reason, not the less in heart he would seem to riot in complete exemption from that law, having apparently little to do with reason further than to employ it as an ambidexter implement for effecting the irrational. That is to say: Toward the accomplishment of an aim which in wantonness of atrocity would seem to partake of the insane, he will direct a cool judgment sagacious and sound. These men are madmen, and of the most dangerous sort, for their lunacy is not continuous, but occasional, evoked by some special object; it is protectively secretive, which is as much as to say it is self-contained, so that when, moreover, most active it is to the average mind not distinguishable from sanity, and for the reason above suggested: that whatever its aims may be—and the aim is never declared—the method and the outward proceeding are always perfectly rational. (76)

Essential to these men is a secret passion, a force driving their *will,* which dominates their conscience. Using as metaphor the profession Melville finds most contemptible, the very one Vere assumes at the critical moment, he tells us that "Claggart's conscience" was "but the lawyer to his will." And what was Vere's secret passion, that degrades his conscience to the role of lawyer? Vere's "spirit . . . 'spite its philosophic austerity may yet have indulged in the most secret of all passions, ambition" (129). Vere is Claggart in the most subtle form.

What are we to make of the fact that to some academics Captain Vere seems a good man, an admirable man? It has actually been written that Vere is Melville's one true "hero," and the one character in all his fiction with whom Melville can best be identified. Such admiration is appalling, but it should be no great surprise. For the image of Vere is a reflection of an actual social type: the bookish man of authority, the figure of minor power who adroitly veers in the service of his country's global empire, the intellectual who can make the most atrocious act of murder seem rational and just while arguing that a spontaneous act of self-defense is violence demanding the most severe punishment, the bland advocate and moral philosopher whose own hands remain spotlessly white while he sanctions the killing of the most innocent among the oppressed.

On the other side are the oppressed people, the victims of the Captain Veres and the powers they serve. When Billy Budd is hanged, in his death he becomes a kind of god to the sailors of the entire fleet. Any chip from the spar from which Billy was hanged is for them "as a piece of the Cross." The last words of the story—and the last words of Melville's life as an artist—are in the form of a "rude" ballad, made by the "tarry hand" of "another foretop-man . . . gifted, as some sailors are, with an artless *poetic* temperament." The poem, "Billy in the Darbies," narrated by Billy as he lies in chains awaiting his execution, is of course really Melville's. For Melville himself was a foretopman.

Part II

History

CHAPTER 3

Plantation to Penitentiary: Songs of Slavery, Peonage, and Prison

A. Songs of Slavery

In 1845 the following passage appeared in an article entitled "Who Are Our National Poets?":

> Who are our true rulers? The negro poets, to be sure! Do they not set the fashion, and give laws to the public taste? Let one of them, in the swamps of Carolina, compose a new song, and it no sooner reaches the ear of a white *amateur,* than it is written down, amended, (that is, almost spoilt,) printed, and then put upon a course of rapid dissemination, to cease only with the utmost bounds of Anglo-Saxondom, perhaps of the world. Meanwhile, the poor author digs away with his hoe, utterly ignorant of his greatness![1]

In 1971, a century and a quarter later, Eileen Southern approvingly quoted this passage in *The Music of Black Americans.*[2] Then Eugene Genovese quoted the same passage in *Roll, Jordan, Roll,* again with approval.[3] The man who first wrote these words, James Kennard, Jr., must have writhed in his grave. For he meant this statement to be satire, an example of the utmost conceivable absurdity to which poetic taste and judgment could fall! There is a world of knowledge about poetry, the criticism of poetry, and the social functions of poetry to be comprehended from meditating upon this.

Like any competent satirist, Kennard was relying on the fact that he and his readers shared certain assumptions and values. If we examine the poetry being written by most of his contemporaries in America, we discover that his belief was well founded. Open the pages of any literary or general magazine of antebellum America, and you will find endless examples of poetry written by aspiring literati who shared James Kennard's assumptions. Most of it is unreadable, except as quaint specimens of curiosa. This poetry of the genteel tradition is characterized by ideality, stilted "poetic" diction, abstractions, grandiose phrases, passionate exclamations, evocations of the eternal verities, a parade of the various poetic figures of speech, glimpses of romantic European scenery (especially from Greece, Italy, and the Rhineland) displaying the author's foreign travel, and ornamental references (especially to Greek and Roman mythology) displaying the author's liberal education. It strives for elegance, universality, and timelessness.

Kennard was not arguing that Negro poets were beneath contempt. He assumed this. His main target was the rising belief in the values of national cultures, particularly manifest in those calls, during the second half-century of the Republic, for an American literature and poetic. He accurately perceived the long-range dangers posed by the desire for an American literature. The exaltation of any poetry as national threatened his central criterion of universality, and in the particular case of the American nation there was a potentially devastating challenge to the cultural hegemony of his social class. This threat was incarnate in the Black slave.

"What is necessary to make the poet national?" Kennard asks. He answers, with heavy-handed sarcasm:

> Certainly, liberal education and foreign travel cannot assist him in attaining this desirable end; these denationalize a man; they ren-

der any but the narrowest soul cosmopolitan. By these means the
poet acquires a higher standard than the national. By a kind of
eclecticism, he appropriates forms and thoughts, images and modes
of expression, from all countries and languages; by comparing the
specific, the transient, and the idiosyncratic, he arrives at the general and the permanent. . . .[4]

This is of course the classical theory of the Ideal in artistic creation, articulated most systematically by Joshua Reynolds, dominant in eighteenth-century British cultural criticism, and under
attack by some of the English Romantics and other progressives
seeking to extend in culture the advances of the American and
French Revolutions. Unlike many modern purveyors of this critical system, Kennard was well aware of its class content. Hence, as
he satirically assumed the pose of an advocate of the opposition to
elegance, universality, and timelessness, he pointed to a particular social class as the living embodiment of the negation of his
ideals:

... in what class of our population must we look for our truly
original and American poets? What class is most secluded from
foreign influences, receives the narrowest education, travels the
shortest distance from home, has the least amount of spare cash,
and mixes least with any class above itself? Our negro slaves, to be
sure! *That* is the class in which we must expect to find our original
poets, and there we *do* find them. From that class come the Jim
Crows, the Zip Coons, and the Dandy Jims, who have electrified the
world. From them proceed our ONLY TRULY NATIONAL
POETS. (332)

Kennard was attempting to alarm his readers, who already had
started to succumb to the values emanating from the slave songs.
If you abandon our standards of poetic excellence, he warns, the
poorest, least cultured, most ignorant and stupid Negro will be in
fact the national poet. Furthermore, the process of debasement
had already commenced. Kennard was especially repulsed by the
spectacle of "a hundred thousand of the sweetest voices in christ-

endom," the voices of refined young white maidens, singing songs originating among subhuman Black men. He turns directly to his "most beautiful, accomplished, delicate and refined lady-reader":

> You cannot hold yourself above him, for you imitate him; you spend days and weeks in learning his tunes; you trill his melodies with your rich voice; you are delighted with his humor, his pathos, his irresistible fun. Say truly, incomparable damsel! is not Sambo the realization of your poetic ideal? (335)

Kennard was especially sensitive to the menace because the tunes sweeping the civilized world were not even the original Black songs but the pale imitations of them from the enormously popular minstrel shows. Even these laundered and denatured songs, set in shows consciously intended to support the institution of Black slavery,[5] had somehow set the white world dancing and singing to Black art. What if Afro-American music, song, and poetry itself were unleashed among polite white society?

Kennard's fears are an early form of a recurrent, almost obsessive, theme in American culture. Seventy-five years after Kennard's satire, Henry Edward Krehbiel, ostensibly writing as a learned white champion of Afro-American music, voiced the same kind of alarm as a wave of Black music swept through Europe and white America in the wake of Dvořák's symphony "From the New World," with its heavy use of Afro-American song. Authentic Black dance music, in the form of the "debased offspring" of the pure slave songs, Krehbiel wrote, now "tickles the ears and stimulates the feet of the pleasure-seekers of London, Paris, Berlin and Vienna even more than it does those of New York."[6] Krehbiel's strategy is to try to build a wholesome but patronizing appreciation of the folk songs of the plantation, which had been purified, by the slaveowners' regulations, of the orgiastic "African savagery":

> ... in this year of pretended refinement, which is the year of our Lord 1913, the dance which is threatening to force grace, decorum

and decency out of the ballrooms of America and England is a
survival of African savagery, which was already banished from the
plantation in the days of slavery. It was in the dance that the
bestiality of the African blacks found its frankest expression.[7]

He quotes one of his authorities:

All the more undisguised is the crude sensuality among the lower
classes of the Haytian population. Here every motion is obscene;
and I am not at all considering the popular merrymakings or dance
festivals secretly held partly in the open, partly in the forests,
which are more like orgies, in which the African savagery, which
has outlived centuries, has unbridled expression.[8]

So Krehbiel, like Kennard, admonishes: "It can scarcely be set
down to the credit of American and English women that in adopt-
ing the tango they are imitating the example, not of the ladies of
Argentina, but of the women of the Black Republic."[9]

Within just a few years, American society would be entering an
era which white writers and cultural critics would define in terms
of Black music: the Jazz Age. Then came the reaction, including
New Criticism, that cultural formalism aimed at restoring the
elegance, universality, and timelessness of poetry by separating
it totally from both history and popular culture. The class content
of this formalism was clear to its practitioners, who saw in the
dominance of jazz and the movies two of the most appalling forms
of cultural degradation. In 1930, at the close of the Jazz Age,
appeared *I'll Take My Stand,* the cultural manifesto of the New
Critics (a book whose title, ironically enough, was taken from
"Dixie," a song used as a "walk-around" in an 1859 New York
minstrel show). *I'll Take My Stand* issued this jeremiad:

The shop-girl does not recite Shakespeare before breakfast. Henry
Ford's hired hands do not hum themes from Beethoven as they go
to work. Instead, the shop-girl reads the comic strip with her bowl
of patent cereal and puts on a jazz record while she rouges her lips.
She reads the confession magazines and goes to the movies. . . . Nor

have we much reason to hope that the ravages will eventually be
limited to the vulgar enterprises I have named, of which the movies
offers perhaps the most convincing example. . . .
    At this point somebody might argue that the lower classes never
produced or enjoyed good art, anyway.[10]

So the guardians of culture were now concerned about the degradation not only of refined, leisured white women but also of
working-class white women.

Although formalism did achieve hegemony in the academy, its
victories were all hollow. Afro-American music continued to
overwhelm all the levees and undermine all the dikes built to
confine it to its proper channels. By the time rock-and-roll broke
through the pallid "cool" jazz of the Eisenhower years, the de-
fenders of cultural elegance, confronted by a sea of gyrating hips,
might have wished young white women were still merely playing
1929 jazz records, doing the 1913 version of the tango, or trilling
the melodies of that 1845 "Sambo." Despite all the satire and
invective, lamentations and sermons, lectures and anthologies
put together by those who would present poetry as the precious
private property of a coterie of great geniuses, Afro-American
culture had restored poetry to some of its primary social
functions, intimately related to music, dance, work, and sex.

Two poles provide opposing views of poetry, its functions, and
its values. We may call one the view of James Kennard, Jr., and
the other the view of the slaves he is ridiculing. From Kennard's
view, poetry is an amenity of refined life, the accomplishment of
individual men of genius whose minds have been enriched by
books, leisure, travel, and the philosophical pursuit of ideal truth
and beauty. From the slaves' view, poetry is first of all a necessity
of physical survival, something to be created collectively out of
shared experience. Kennard's view of poetry, which is at the core
of the bourgeois theory of poetry, may be essentially an aberration in the cultural history of the human species. The slaves' view
has at least a deeper tradition.

Poetry is a universal human activity: all peoples, nations, and
tribes all over the world engage in poetic creation. Furthermore,
in all societies, including modern capitalist industrial society, the

majority of people love poetry, feel a need for it, listen to it daily, and often voice it and discuss it. If this statement is surprising, that is only because all classes in capitalist society tend to accept the bourgeois separation between music and what they have come to think of as "poetry." Most people in America have had some exposure to poetry in a classroom; the typical response is boredom and a feeling that "poetry is not for me." This same student will then turn on the radio or the record player and listen to—poetry. But now that student has been conditioned to think of "poetry" as academic and to regard the poetry on radio, records, or tapes as something altogether different. Why? Because it is sung, because it is about common life, and because it is entertaining.

Whether the poetry being sung on these records and tapes, at discotheques and parties, and in the shower is as "good" as the poetry in literary anthologies and English classes is a subject of debate; that question tests all kinds of aesthetic theories and their consequences. But it is beyond any debate that these songs are a form of poetry. Curiously and ironically enough, poetry, one of the most oral of all art forms, becomes the special object of expropriation as the bourgeoisie attempts to control language and art through its domination of writing. To understand what poetry is, we have to grapple briefly with another very large question— the relation between oral and written literature.

Despite the apparent contradiction in terms, most of the world's literature is now, or has been, oral. This includes many of the epics and holy "scriptures" of East and West—from the *Iliad* and the *Odyssey* to the *Ramayana* and *Mahabharata*—as well as ritual chants and hymns, ballads and songs, legends and tales. We can strip away many layers of mystification about written literature simply by reminding ourselves that writing itself is primarily a social convenience, a method of recording, preserving, and transmitting oral communication. Of course the written preservation of some early oral literature, though this was un- doubtedly a minute portion, was a monumental human accom- plishment; it has bequeathed to us some great treasures whose very existence we otherwise might not even have suspected. Writ- ten literature can also be stored and transmitted conveniently. And it does have certain important aesthetic advantages. It can be reworked and improved upon systematically. It appears as stable, constant, consistent works of art. On the other hand, it also has some great aesthetic disadvantages. Its stability represents a terrific price paid in spontaneity and improvisation. Written down and stored, it is thus separated from the living emotional and intellectual contexts that are its matrix. Poetry in particular tends to lose important qualities of rhythm and timbre, of the indefinable nuances of the most exquisite known instrument—the human voice.

Now I am not suggesting that written poetry is less legitimate, less "good," or less worthy to be studied than oral poetry. Written poetry is in no danger of banishment from the academy. What I am arguing is that oral poetry is also legitimate, also good, also worthy of study, and that it should not be segregated from written poetry. Those who question the holiness of the canon are often called reductionists; but the true reductionists are those who reduce literature to the dimensions of that canon. To teach written poetry as the only authentic poetry—which is basically what we do in the classroom and its adjuncts (literary criticism and scholarship, anthologies, doctoral examinations, degree requirements, academic hiring and firing, etc.)—is to gut the life from a precious and vital human activity. This is not to imply that written poetry is irrelevant to most people's experience. It is we teachers of literature who make written poetry irrelevant by presenting it as separate and distinct from the people's living tradition of oral poetry.

Worst of all, we not only denigrate oral literature through unfounded exaltation of written literature, but actually use the written language to demean the spoken language. We push this so far that the main lesson taught about writing in our schools, from first grade through the doctorate, is that the majority of people are incapable of doing it. After mystifying and traumatizing most of our students for twelve or more years about writing, we then write articles speculating about why they can't write. We teach writing as though grammar were the true path to eloquence, and grammar as though it were a set of laws engraved on a tablet on Mount Sinai, having nothing to do with the way people actually speak the language (except to regulate it). We forget that the grammar of a language is defined primarily by living usage, not by the rationalist theories of late seventeenth- and early eighteenth-century grammarians, and we also forget that the English language reached one of its most eloquent moments in Renaissance drama and poetry, almost a century before any formal grammar was codified (and while the academic authorities of that day were still maintaining that the "vulgar" language, the language of "the rude multitude, in contrast to the learned few," could not produce significant literature).[11] Thus it is no wonder that those of us who teach English find ourselves in the role of the verbal police force, the punitive arm that reaches out from the printed page to throttle natural speech and to guard the hallowed precincts of literature from the hordes of unwashed students. Every teacher of English has more than once had this conversation:

"What do you do for a living?" asks a new acquaintance.

"Oh, I teach."

"What do you teach?"

"English."

"Uh, oh," says our new acquaintance, with an exaggerated air of mock—or real—fright, "I better watch how I talk."

The radical split between oral and written literature, between "low" and "high" culture, between Black and white, leaves us with strange contradictions and paradoxes. Song and dance have been largely exiled from daily life in polite society, first to the plantation, and then to the ghetto. Precisely because the poetry and the music of Afro-Americans are thus placed somewhat beyond the reach of the sterilizing and homogenizing powers of the bourgeois cultural superstructure, they are able to exert a profound and intensifying cultural influence on American society as a whole. For almost a century and a half the idea has spread, among both Blacks and whites, that Black people have more innate sense of rhythm than white people. Meanwhile white arbiters of culture can find no Black poetry "good" enough in form to be included in courses and anthologies.

It is only since the triumph of the most prosaic class in history, the modern bourgeoisie, with its virtually conscious attempts to remove rhythm from human intercourse, that poetry has to any serious extent been divorced from music, dance, drama, labor, and sex. But people in general still love poetry and song, music and dance, because we need rhythm in our daily lives, just as we need food, air, water, sunshine, exercise, love, and comradeship. We are all social creatures, as Melville shows in the collectivity of Marquesan Islanders, African slaves, and polyglot sailors, and, by negative example, in the lonely, self-consuming egoism of Ahab, Bartleby's boss, and Captain Vere. And we are all rhythmic creatures, pulsing to an internal beat, owing our very conception to an act of rhythm, as Black culture, like most of the cultures in the history of the world, affirms without hesitation. So James Kennard, Jr., despite his own satirical intentions, was articulating more truth than he meant when he asserted that the "negro slaves" are "our ONLY TRULY NATIONAL POETS." Those Afro-American slaves, and their descendants, have also been our most international poets, uniting American poetics with the main body of living poetry among the peoples of the world, forming the essential link between the songs of the most primitive hunting and gathering tribes and the songs of the most advanced modern industrial nations.

The primal origin of poetry is hidden in inconceivable depths of time. Some students of language believe that poetry is intimately tied to the origin of language itself, and even that the first human speech was a form of poetry. In any event, "primitive man," as Otto Jespersen puts it, "was constantly reduced to using words and phrases figuratively: he was forced to express his thoughts in the language of poetry."[12] Certainly poetry in all societies arises epochs before there is a written language, and, when writing does appear, written poetry develops as an art form long before written prose does: ". . . any literature which has been historically studied shows that accomplished prose does not arise until after a long practice of accomplished verse";[13] "Just as in the literature transmitted to us poetry is found in every country to precede prose, so poetic language is on the whole older than prosaic language."[14] Evidence from anthropology, classical studies, and physiology indicates that some poetry may have originated in the processes of labor.[15] Whether or not poetry did originate this way in the prehistoric past, a question that will always remain somewhat speculative, the actual creation of poetry in the labor process has been a widely observed phenomenon. In order to survive, people have always had to work together. In order to work together, it is often necessary for people to join together in rhythm and word. This is particularly true in some of the earliest forms of human labor, such as lifting large weights, paddling or rowing a canoe or boat, reaping and mashing grain, digging, herding animals, marching long distances, tramping grapes, pounding, chopping, etc. Thus a very early form of poetry, if not the earliest, comes from human beings engaged in collective labor, their bodies sharing rhythmical movements, their wills sharing common words and thoughts. Our individual sense of rhythm as human beings springs from that which is most private, the beat of our own heart and pulses, our breathing, the movement of our own hips and limbs and head. Singing or chanting together, people link their individual private rhythms into a collective rhythmic time and verbal meaning. Music, dance, and poetry thus are often intimately connected, and all three arts come to enrich sex, the primal rhythmic activity that antedates labor.

The universality of poetry as a human activity is astonishing. There has yet to be discovered a people or a tribe, no matter how small, that does not have a developed body of poetic tradition. (The Netsilik Eskimos had a population of about 300 in 1922 when many songs were collected from them and the population of Ifaluk Atoll was 260 when an entire volume of impressive songs was collected from them in 1953.)[16] In nonliterate societies, poetry is always a part of daily life, playing a vital role in courtship, child care, religious ritual, combat, labor, mourning, and many other human relationships. In these societies, there are often men or women who specialize in creating poetry as their primary social role. However, in many, apparently most, primitive societies virtually every man and every woman is a poet. This has been verified by anthropological research among Polynesians, Melanesians, Eskimos, Australian aborigines, and tribes in Southeast Asia, South America, and all sections of the African continent. Typical observations are the following, the first made about the stone-age people of the Andaman Islands in the Bay of Bengal, the second about the Copper Eskimos, the third about the

Dobu Islanders of the Western Pacific:

> Every one composes songs. A man or woman would be thought little of who could not do so. Even the small children compose their own songs. Each person composes his own.[17]

> Every man, and most of the women, have their own songs with which they have been inspired and then composed themselves.[18]

> Every Dobuan is a song-maker.[19]

The ability of each individual to create poetry survived even in some literate societies, such as the Tuareg of northern Africa: "The art of poetical composition is in the nature of a polite accomplishment, common to all, and enjoyed by all, and the love of poetry and song is one of the most characteristic and striking features of Tuareg social life."[20] Poetry in nonliterate societies is almost always sung, rarely recited. For example, Ojibway "poetry is not only inseparable but indistinguishable from music."[21] "Words fitted to music are the songs and poetry of the people. . . . There is no conception of poetry without a tune."[22] This bond between poetry and music is not restricted to primitive societies. This was equally true of the advanced feudal societies of Europe and western and northern Africa. Just as the troubadours and trouvères of medieval France composed both their melodies and what we may still call "lyrics," the poetic peoples of the eighteenth- and nineteenth-century Ashanti kingdoms improvised music and words together as a common art.

So the slaves kidnapped from Africa brought with them a rich and varied heritage of poetry wedded to music and social life. Some of these people came from primitive hunting and gathering tribes, but far more came from agricultural societies in either the slave stage (not unlike early Athens) or the more advanced political economy of feudalism. These Africans transported into American slavery all came from cultures in which song was a daily activity, part of labor, love, ritual, and entertainment. Even those scholars most hostile to the theory of the central role of the work song in the creation of poetry have had to concede its tremendous importance in Africa, and therefore in Afro-American culture and its later influences. John Greenway, one of the most extreme debunkers of the importance of the work song, reveals a great deal when he offers the following as an argument: "The fact that the African social and economic organization produced communal work songs which transferred so well to the Negro folk group forming on American soil has greatly exaggerated the importance of this category of literature in our minds."[23] Suddenly, on the slave ships, their native African songs were transformed into the immediate means of physical survival. In order to keep them from dying "slaves were encouraged, sometimes forced, to dance and sing during the daylight hours allowed them on deck. There are old prints which show cargoes of slaves being whipped into song."[24]

The Africans spoke different languages and dialects, all of which were soon made illegal by the slaveowners. In America, their own musical instruments, their own religions, their own songs, and their own dances were also made illegal; all became acts of crime. The slaves were forced to adopt the English language, together with English music and religious symbolism. In one of the most dramatic creative acts in human history, the slaves then adapted this alien music, religion, and language to the survival needs of their slave labor situation. Hence arose the original slave work songs, with their veiled content, alluding to escape and rebellion. These included spirituals, which expressed their own oppression and yearnings for liberation in the mythology of their masters.

The first widespread white attention to the slave songs came in the early 1830s, coinciding with the transformation of slavery into large-scale agribusiness, with its attendant phenomena: the redefinition of Africans as a subhuman species, the rebellions of Nat Turner and others, laws making it a crime for Negroes (slave or free) to learn to read. This first white recognition took the form of the wildly popular "Jim Crow" song and dance routine, started by Thomas Rice around 1830, and soon developed into the minstrel craze of the early 1840s. By 1845, James Kennard could assume an audience that would intellectually regard Black poetry as the creation of subhuman primitives but an audience that had also somehow been deeply influenced even by the grotesque white parodies of this Black poetry.

During the ensuing decade, some serious white interest in the slave songs began to appear in the form of scattered comments by European and British residents and travelers in the South. And some of Kennard's worst fears began to come true, for the songs of the Black slaves were becoming a main symbol of America. When Franklin Pierce won the presidency in 1852, he rewarded his faithful campaign biographer and fellow antiabolitionist, Nathaniel Hawthorne, with the United States Consulship to Liverpool. Four years later, Hawthorne in his British travels ran head-on into the ironies of this cultural situation, as he dined with the officers of the North Cork Rifles on April 1, 1856:

> The regimental band played during dinner, and the Lieutenant-Colonel apologized to me for its not playing Hail Columbia, the tune not coming within their musical accomplishments. It was no great matter, however; for I should not have distinguished it from any other tune; but, to do me what honor was possible, in the way of national airs, the band was ordered to play a series of negro melodies, and I was entirely satisfied. It is really funny that the "wood-notes wild" of those poor black slaves should have been played in a foreign land as an honorable compliment to one of their white countrymen.[25]

In America, one of the first signs of serious white interest in the slave songs was the article "Negro Minstrelsy—Ancient and Modern" by J.J. Trux in *Putnam's* in 1855. Although Trux still treats the subject with banter and whimsy, though he believes that Negroes are incapable of remembering the words of a song while they are not singing it because "their intellects could only retain the words when assisted by the music," though he sees in their poetry "looseness and negligence in respect to rhyme," "carelessness and license in the metre," and "incoherence" in "the constantly recurring refrain," Trux expresses a romantic and not entirely patronizing admiration for the slave songs and their imitations in the minstrel shows. He is reminded of "the old, plain songs which Shakespeare loved" and the "ancient English and Scottish ballads" collected by Percy. With real enthusiasm he exclaims, "The song which is sung in the parlor, hummed in the kitchen, and whistled in the stable, may defy oblivion."[26]

The Civil War brought a different kind of recognition to the slave songs. As northern abolitionists were finally able to wage their part of the struggle in the slave states themselves, some of these northerners now heard the slave songs directly from the slaves. They listened with seriousness and respect, and they were overwhelmed by the tremendous power and beauty of what they heard. The first major collection was published in 1867 by Thomas Wentworth Higginson, the great abolitionist, prolific author, confidant of Emily Dickinson, who had been the commander of the first Black regiment organized during the war.[27] This was followed within a few months by *Slave Songs of the United States,* edited by William Francis Allen, Charles Pickard Ware, and Lucy McKim Garrison.

Most of the songs contained in these two collections were religious, at least on the surface. Colonel Higginson glimpses the yearnings for earthly freedom under that surface, and he records the militant "Many Thousand Go," with its ringing celebration of rebellion and escape from slavery. Higginson actually hears a song in the process of development as one of his men, while pulling an oar, begins to sing his own composition about "de ole nigger-driver" and the other oarsmen pick it up "as if it were an old acquaintance, though they evidently had never heard it before." Many of the songs transcribed by Higginson express the fundamental ethic of oppressed working people, the same ethic Melville had imaged forth in the monkey-rope in *Moby-Dick,* the ethic of solidarity and brotherhood. For example, in "Wrestling Jacob":

> O, I hold my brudder wid a tremblin' hand;
>   I would not let him go!
> I hold my sister wid a tremblin' hand;
>   I would not let her go!

Higginson states, "I never overheard in camp a profane or vulgar song," but he also suggests that there were apparently songs he was never meant to hear. One day when a squad of men are returning from picket duty, they boisterously begin a stanza about the typical white ("buckra") soldier, "De buckra 'list for money," but quickly break it off when they see Higginson. Allen, Ware, and Garrison are disappointed in finding so few secular songs: "We had hoped to obtain enough secular songs to make a division by themselves; there are, however, so few of these that it has been decided to intersperse them with the spirituals. . . ."[28]

Apparently the slaves, even in the company of the most sympathetic and antislavery whites, still kept much of their oral poetry to themselves. In *Clotel; Or, The President's Daughter: A Narrative of Slave Life in the United States* (1853), that powerful novel by the runaway slave William Wells Brown, there is a most revealing scene. It is the night of the slaveowner's death, and his daughter and her husband-to-be from the North hear the slaves singing. The couple decide to eavesdrop. "'We must not let them see us,'" she warns, "'or they will stop singing'":

"Who makes their songs for them?" inquired the young man. "Oh, they make them up as they sing them; they are all impromptu songs." By this time they were near enough to hear distinctly every word; and, true enough, Sam's voice was heard above all others. At the conclusion of each song they all joined in a hearty laugh, with an expression of "Dats de song for me;" "Dems dems."

"Stop," said Carlton, as Georgiana was rising from the log upon which she was seated; "stop, and let's hear this one." The piece was sung by Sam, the others joining in the chorus, and was as follows:

Sam.

"Come, all my brethren, let us take a rest,
    While the moon shines so brightly and clear;
Old master is dead, and left us at last,
    And has gone at the Bar to appear.
Old Master has died, and lying in his grave,
    And our blood will awhile cease to flow;
He will no more trample on the neck of the slave;
    For he's gone where the slaveholders go.

Chorus.

"Hang up the shovel and the hoe—
Take down the fiddle and the bow—
Old master has gone to the slaveholder's rest;
He has gone where they all ought to go."[29]

The remaining three stanzas of this song were also not meant for any white ears. Nor was this "jubilee" song recorded by another runaway slave, Frederick Douglass, in *My Bondage and My Freedom* (1855), the first expanded version of the 1845 *Narrative:*

We raise de wheat,
Dey gib us de corn;
We bake de bread,
Dey gib us de cruss;
We sif de meal,
Dey gib us de huss;
We peal de meat,
Dey gib us de skin,
And dat's de way
Dey takes us in.
We skim de pot,
Dey gib us the liquor,
And say dat's good enough for nigger.
  Walk over! walk over!
  Tom butter and de fat;
  Poor nigger you can't get over dat;
    Walk over![30]

So from the very beginning, the songs the slaves sang among themselves expressed a vision of them as the working class producing everything of value for a parasitic owning class. In *Clotel,* William Wells Brown records a spoken poem articulating this vision concisely:

The big bee flies high,
The little bee make the honey;
The black folks makes the cotton,
And the white folks gets the money.[31]

We can only surmise how widespread these lines were during the days of chattel slavery by their omnipresence in the early twentieth century when Black people were laboring under somewhat different forms of slavery. Variants of these lines appear as song stanzas heard in all parts of the South from Mississippi through North Carolina. Here, for example, is a version collected in Natchez, Mississippi, in the early 1920s:

> Old Bee make de honeycomb,
> Young Bee makes all de honey.
> Nigger makes de cotton and corn,
> White man gits all de money.[32]

The secular slave poetry we do know about almost all recurs in one form or another as living folk songs throughout much of the twentieth century. The themes and even the words of the secular slave songs continue to develop as poetry, especially in the blues and convict work songs, until, as we shall see, they become the core of a highly developed poetic art in the prisons of the 1960s and 1970s.

Meanwhile, the slave spiritual has won admiration—and singers—throughout the world. The triumphs of the spiritual have also given rise to two major controversies.

From the beginning, it was obvious that the words of the spirituals were not merely religious. Even the most sympathetic of white auditors, however, failed to comprehend how pervasively the spirituals conveyed hidden yearnings for escape and rebellion. For example, even after he was told that slaves had actually been imprisoned in Charlestown, South Carolina, for singing "We'll Soon Be Free," Higginson was unable to accept its double meanings, although some of them are slyly explained to him:

> "De Lord will call us home," was evidently thought to be a symbolical verse; for, as a little drummer-boy explained to me, showing all his white teeth as he sat in the moonlight by the door of my tent, "Dey tink *de Lord* mean for say *de Yankees*."[33]

Nevertheless, Higginson declares that all "suspicion" that the words of this song refer to fighting against slavery is "unfounded":

> We'll soon be free, *(three times)*
> When de Lord will call us home.
> My brudder, how long, *(three times)*
> 'Fore we don sufferin' here?
> It won't be long *(three times)*
> 'Fore de Lord will call us home.
> We'll walk de miry road *(three times)*
> Where pleasure never dies.
> We'll walk de golden street *(three times)*
> Where pleasure never dies.
> My brudder, how long *(three times)*
> 'Fore we done sufferin' here?
> We'll soon be free *(three times)*
> When Jesus sets me free.
> We'll fight for liberty *(three times)*
> When de Lord will call us home.

This song seems explicitly enough a message of rebellion. And as early as 1855, Frederick Douglass had explained in *My Bondage and My Freedom* that many of the spirituals had double meanings:

We were, at times, remarkably buoyant, singing hymns and making joyous exclamations, almost as triumphant in their tone as if we had reached a land of freedom and safety. A keen observer might have detected in our repeated singing of

> "O Canaan, sweet Canaan,
> I am bound for the land of Canaan,"

something more than a hope of reaching heaven. We meant to reach the *north*—and the north was our Canaan.

> "I thought I heard them say,
> There were lions in the way,

> I don't expect to stay
>   Much longer here."
> Run to Jesus—shun the danger—
> I don't expect to stay
>   Much longer here,"

was a favorite air, and had a double meaning. In the lips of some, it meant the expectation of a speedy summons to a world of spirits; but, in the lips of *our* company, it simply meant, a speedy pilgrimage toward a free state, and deliverance from all the evils and dangers of slavery.[34]

Then there were other songs, never sung in the presence of a white person, in which an occasional call to "dear Lord" was merely a call for divine assistance in the earthly struggle to destroy slavery. William Wells Brown, whose main job as a slave was to supervise groups of slaves being transported on riverboats down the Mississippi to be sold in the New Orleans market, recorded in *Narrative of William W. Brown, A Fugitive Slave. Written by Himself* (1847) an example of one of these songs:

The following song I have often heard the slaves sing, when about to be carried to the far south. It is said to have been composed by a slave.

> See these poor souls from Africa
> Transported to America;
> We are stolen, and sold to Georgia,
> Come sound the jubilee!
>
> See wives and husbands sold apart,
> Their children's screams will break my heart;—
> There's a better day a coming,
> Will you go along with me?
> There's a better day a coming,
> Go sound the jubilee!
>
> O, gracious Lord! when shall it be,
> That we poor souls shall all be free;
> Lord, break them slavery powers—
> Will you go along with me?

> Lord break them slavery powers,
> Go sound the jubilee![35]

Although this was evidently quite a common slave song, there is, as far as I am aware, no record of any white person ever having heard it. (If this song sounds less "authentic" than those recorded by most white transcribers, it is partly because Brown refuses to adhere to the practice of transcribing Black pronunciation as dialect, as though they alone of all Americans pronounced words differently from how they are spelled; to restore any lost sense of "authenticity," change the spelling to "dese po' souls," "Dar's a betta' day," etc.)

Certainly many of the spirituals, at least when sung by some slaves, contained double meanings about the horrors of slavery and hopes for deliverance through the Underground Railroad, a return to Africa, rebellion, or a war of liberation. Whether these double meanings permeate the spirituals to such an extent that the religious terms become primarily camouflage, as argued by Miles Mark Fisher in *Negro Slave Songs in the United States*, may be debatable. As Eugene Genovese puts it in *Roll, Jordan, Roll:*

No choice need be made between this-worldly and otherworldly interpretations of the song sung by slaves in Mississippi:

> But some ob dese days my time will come,
> I'll year dat bugle, I'll year dat drum,
> I'll see dem armies, marchin' along,
> I'll lif' my head an' jine der song.

Or of "Didn't My Lord Deliver Daniel," or of "Joshua Fit de Battle ob Jericho," or of "Oh, Mary, Don't You Weep," or of "Go Down, Moses." They do not necessarily refer to deliverance in this world or in the other, for they might easily mean either or both.[36]

As a number of recent books have shown at length, the main achievement of the spirituals and the other slave songs was the creation of a people's culture, the most essential part of the creation of a people.[37]

This leads to the second major controversy about the spirituals. As these songs won admiration, some critics began to argue that they were not much of an achievement, after all, because they were really just derivations from white spirituals. This in turn led to a reaction which emphasized the African influences in both the music and the poetic content, as well as the materials which dealt specifically with the lives of the Black slaves. It is not my intention here to attempt to resolve these debates. Some points, however, seem to me to have been established beyond argument: the spirituals, and even more the secular work songs of the slave, do show important survivals of African musical and poetic traditions, and do contain abundant materials from the experience peculiar to the Afro-American people; on the other hand, many of the spirituals, hymns, and ballads do derive directly from white songs and poems, especially English, Irish, and Scottish. It seems unlikely that any clear distinction between the African and the European proportions could ever be established, because of the enormously complex interweavings of musical, as well as poetic, traditions in Afro-American songs. The spirituals of the white "shouting" sects, made up of cast-out elements of the European and American peasantry, pauperized workers, and even outlaw-vagabonds pushed onto the frontier, did indeed influence Black spirituals, but that influence soon was flowing in both directions. In fact, as Eileen Southern points out, "The camp meeting was an interracial institution; indeed, sometimes there were more black worshipers present than white."[38] Not only in the spirituals, but in the work songs as well, an intricate interchange went on over a considerable period of time. In the labor songs, white workers assimilated the polyrhythmic interpretations of the Blacks, including such supposedly distinctive features as neutral or alternating thirds, while the Blacks were acquiring the ballad repertoire of the whites.[39] This process took on special importance in the polyglot work world of nineteenth-century sailing ships.

Song played as vital a role on the ocean as it did on the plantation. In order for a small crew of men to hoist the heavy, cumbersome canvas sails, it was necessary for them to coordinate their efforts with rhythmic chants and songs. This was particularly true on the Yankee whaleships, with their very small crews and huge sails. These crews, as Melville shows, were international in their composition; he, for example, sailed with Englishmen, Spaniards, Irishmen, Maori tribesmen, West Indians, Scots, Frenchmen, Welshmen, Polynesians, Germans, Danes, Australian convicts, American Indians, native Africans, and Afro-American ex-slaves. All contributed portions of their musical and poetic heritages to the sea shanties, and, when they returned to land, they brought the music and poetry of the sea shanty into the labor processes of the docks, railroads, mines, mills, and farms. In *Music and the Bourgeois; Music and the Proletarian,* a monumental work of scholarship recently published in an English edition in Hungary, János Maróthy accurately sums up the contribution of the sea shanty:

> The significance of the *sea-shanty* is not merely that it was the bearer of communal continuity right up to the modern proletariat, but also that it was the first to undergo proletarian transformation of music on an *international scale,* effecting a means of exchange between various peoples and various sea- and land-work processes—from the English railway worker, through the Irish sailor, to the Negro dock worker. The process of synthetisation was rendered easier by the *variative structure* (leader-chorus, slogan variation, stable refrains and improvised solo insertions) which can be found in the variative layer of all folk musics in some form or other....[40]

Maróthy discusses as one of several examples a shanty displaying a startling synthesis of Irish and Afro-American traditions, with an intermingling of labor processes from the ship, the loading dock, and the plantation:

> Oh! away down south where I wuz born, Roll the cotton down!
> Oh! away down south around Cape Horn, We'll roll the cotton down!
> Roll the cotton, Roll the cotton, Moses!
> Roll the cotton, Oh! roll the cotton down![41]

The sea shanty, as Maróthy demonstrates, does penetrate deeply into American folk song, Black and white, creating a mingling effect in this one area of culture. But Maróthy goes much further, accepting the concept, on both an economic and cultural level, of some "melting-pot" which boils down all national cultures within America into some transcendent unity:

> America is ... an immense melting-pot where, on a broad international scale, a levelling tendency emerged which destroyed all earlier tribal provincial guildlike and national communities, all non-capitalist strata, and impelled them into the common destiny of the wage-earning worker. In America, English outlaw, Irish miner, French craftsman, Hungarian peasant, Chinese coolie— unless they made their fortunes—ended in a similar way as the "Nigger."[42]

But this is not the history of America, in fact, and to apply such a notion to Afro-American song is to misunderstand its most profound characteristics.

Black people in America have never shared the same historical destiny as any section of the white population, no matter how impoverished, and this awareness is at the center of the Black musical and poetic tradition. No matter how multinational their source materials, the songs of the Black slaves had as their primary historic achievement the creation of a national culture, the culture of the Afro-American *people*. Unlike any of the white nationalities with whom they came in contact, Afro-Americans had the common collective experience of being imprisoned as a people within the boundaries of another nation, and it is this experience of national imprisonment that defines and distinguishes Afro-American culture in all its aspects. Certainly Afro-American song has attained an international outlook, but that is on the basis of its national identity. There is nothing paradoxical about this dialectic, for to be truly *inter*national a people must have a national identity; otherwise they would be merely *non*national. The innermost secret content of the slaves' songs is that they were turning the conditions of their own oppression into the materials of their own cultural unity. Their songs and music—which constituted the slaves' only property—created a culture that belonged to their whole people.

The collective historical experience of the Afro-American people manifests itself throughout the vast body of their songs. These songs expropriate materials from many different sources, transmuting all of them into part of their own cultural framework. Harold Courlander has shown that "it would be possible to put a large body of Negro religious songs together in a certain sequence to produce an oral counterpart of the Bible; if printed, they would make a volume fully as thick as the Bible itself."[43] Yet each portion of this oral Bible is distinctively Afro-American in both form and content. That is the innermost "double meaning" of the spirituals, as, for example, in one of the most famous, "Go Down Moses":

> When Israel was in Egypt's land,
>   Let my people go.
> Oppressed so hard they could not stand,
>   Let my people go.
> Go down, Moses, way down in Egypt's land,
>   Tell old Pharaoh, let my people go.

Or take the many modern prison versions of the work song "Hammer Ring," in which the convicts shift back and forth between their own hammer or axe and the tools wielded by Noah (Norah):

Oh Black a Betty's got a baby, let your HAMMER RING.
A-well he crazy like his daddy, let your HAMMER RING.
A Jack O Diamonds was his daddy, let your HAMMER RING.
A-well it's God told Norah, let your HAMMER RING.
"I want you to build me a ark-a," let your HAMMER RING.
"Oh, how high do you want it," let your HAMMER RING.
"I want it one hundred cubies," let your HAMMER RING.
"Oh and go and warn the people," let your HAMMER RING.[44]

Within this enormous range of poetry and music, there is
virtually no line between the creation of the people as a whole and
the creations of the individuals who constitute that people.

B. Songs of An Imprisoned People

In *Poetic Origins and the Ballad,* an extended polemic, Louise
Pound attempted to demonstrate that the oral folk poetry of both
whites and Blacks in America is little more than a debasement of
the received literary tradition. She argued that "the process in
literature" is "a downward process, from the higher to the lower,
rather than one of ascent from lower to higher," that the only
apparent accomplishments of Afro-American oral poetry actually
derived from white ballads which in turn had merely preserved
old written poems, that "it is obvious that negro songs do not tend
to assume a narrative type but retrograde to a simple repetition of
phrases," and that "the real songs emerging from the unlettered
are too crude, ungrammatical, fragmentary, uninteresting to at-
tract any one but the student of folk-song."[45]
It is especially important to this line of argument to belittle the
role of collective or communal creation of poetry. Much of Pound's
polemic is in fact an effort to show that poems are almost always
made by single individuals, and that any "real communalistic or
popular poetry . . . is crude, structureless, incoherent, and lacking
in striking and memorable qualities."[46] When such a line of argument, with its categorical distinctions between individual and
collective composition, is applied to Afro-American culture, the
results are especially destructive. For whether or not it is a single
individual who makes up the words of a work song or a spiritual
or a "toast" (an urban ghetto or prison narrative in rimed coup-
lets) or a sermon or a political speech, the entire group almost
always has a hand in the process of creation.
The Black preacher, for example, does not usually speak *to* or *at*
a silent congregation that sits there staring back or fidgeting; he
speaks *with* and *for* a collective group actively participating in
both the content and the rhythms of the sermon. Although I am a
white person, used to speaking to predominantly white audiences

and with fairly fixed patterns of speech, I have found when speaking to a large group of Black people that they soon are guiding both my thoughts and my rhythms with precisely timed interjections. Most teachers of literature, whose experience in speaking is limited largely to the classroom, probably have little conception of the effects upon an individual speaker's words when other individuals in the group call out, at just the right moment, "Isn't it the truth?," "Run it down," and "Teach, brother." In *Caste and Class in a Southern Town*, John Dollard describes the act of collective creation that takes place in a Black church:

> The intensive participation of the audience is seemingly required by the minister and is obviously of greatest aid. I had never truly understood the meaning of the term "collective experience" until participating in a well-planned Negro revival service.... In the Negro churches it is a case of every man with the preacher and the boundaries of the self are weakened. There is an obvious eagerness for sympathetic contact, a willingness to be stirred and caught up in a powerful story and to abandon in song, speech and spastic gesture the strictures of the controlling self of everyday life.[47]

When Dollard is asked to speak before the church, he directly experiences collective verbal creation:

> Helped by appreciative murmurs which began slowly and softly and became louder and fuller as I went on, I felt a great sense of elation, an increased fluency, and a vastly expanded confidence in speaking. There was no doubt that the audience was with me, was determined to aid me in every way.... the audience was actually ahead of me, it had a preformed affirmation ready for the person with the courage to say the significant word.... it was exactly the intensive collective participation that I had imagined it might be. No less with the speaker than with the audience there is a sense of losing the limitations of self and of unconscious powers rising to meet the unbound, unconscious forces of the group.[48]

The most intense collective experience in Afro-American history was that of slavery. This experience did not stop with Emancipation, however, as we shall see in some detail. Certainly the prisoners throughout the South who were literally chained together while they worked and while they ate and while they slept had an experience no less oppressive and no less collective than their ancestors in chattel slavery, and work songs have been every bit as important to their survival. Hence the twentieth-century convict work song is the most available and most dramatic test of collectively created oral poetry. Louise Pound agrees that the chain gang and the American prison in general should be the ideal ground for a confrontation between the two main contending approaches to poetry. She, however, argues that common prisoners do not produce any significant songs and ballads, and therefore the supremacy of the written literary tradition, and its special claim to serious attention, remain beyond dispute:

> And do prisoners in stripes and lock step ever invent songs? Granting the "communal conditions" theory, our penitentiaries should be veritable fountains of song and balladry. As a matter of fact, the most famous of prison ballads is the masterpiece of an accomplished poet,—Wilde's "Ballad of Reading Gaol."[49]

The songs and ballads of the chain gang cannot be isolated from either Afro-American history or Afro-American poetic culture, for the central fact in chain gang poetry is that Black convicts are part of an imprisoned people. Neither their experience, nor their songs and ballads, are fundamentally separate or distinct from the rest of the Afro-American nation.

In fact, Black prisoners embody in both their lives and their culture the most thorough historical continuity within Black experience in America. An immensely revealing fact is that authentic versions of old slave work songs survive as convict work songs well into the 1960s. Here, for example, is a song a good deal more famous than "Ballad of Reading Gaol," in a version recorded in a Texas prison, as a living work song, in 1964:

> Well old marster told old mistress I could pick a bale a cotton.
> Old marster told old mistress I could pick a bale a day.

You big enough and black enough to pick a bale a cotton,
You big enough and black enough to pick a bale a day.

Chorus

But never will I pick a bale a cotton,
How in the world can I pick a bale a day?

You jumps around, you turns around to pick a bale a cotton,
I went to Loosiana just to pick a bale a day.

Yet most of the stanzas of this widely diffused twentieth-century convict work song were evidently composed in prison.[50]

Black slavery in the United States did not end with Emancipation; it merely changed its forms somewhat. When the slaves were "freed," they were not given the promised forty acres and a mule. Without land, they had no means of livelihood except to sell their labor to the landowners, their former masters. But the old slaveowning class had no intention of allowing the Black population to become an agricultural proletariat, a class of "free" laborers able to move about at will and compete on the labor market. So they devised a pervasive, intricate apparatus of law, custom, and brute force to keep the Blacks in perpetual bondage. Central to this historical redefinition of the role of Black people was an ideological redefinition of them. No longer were they just a subhuman race; now they were to be thought of as a race of criminals. This definition was to become increasingly important throughout American culture, right on up through the white code words of the 1960s and 1970s, such as "black militants," "welfare cadillacs," "violent-prone," "crime in the streets" (as opposed to "safe streets"), and "racial disorders" (as opposed to "law and order").

No pretext had been necessary to kidnap Africans and bring them to America as slaves. But pretexts would be necessary to kidnap Black Americans and reenslave them to work first the plantations, and then the canals, the coal mines, the turpentine and lumber camps, the track-laying and tunneling crews for the railroads, the prison factories, the state prison farms, and the roads needed for automobiles. The victims would have to be perceived as criminals, and they would thus be forced, for their very survival, to become artists of song and ballad and, later, of political autobiography, poetry, drama, and fiction.

The necessary transformation in the structure of law was effected in 1865, in the very Amendment to the Constitution which abolished the old form of slavery, Article 13:

> Neither slavery nor involuntary servitude, except as a punishment for crime whereof the party shall have been duly convicted, shall exist within the United States, or any place subject to their jurisdiction.

From the ratification of that Amendment in December 1865, through the present, a person can legally become a slave in the United States only after being defined by one of the states, or the federal government, as a criminal.

Even before the end of the Civil War, a new system had been emerging to take the place of the older form of slavery: the convict lease system (*Gone with the Wind* actually uses this new form to glorify the older slavery by comparison). This system appeared to have a great advantage for the landowners: they did not own the convicts, and hence could afford to work them to death. The President of the Board of Inspectors of Convicts for the State of Alabama, R. W. Dawson, discovered that in 1869 the death rate among leased Alabama Black convicts was 41 percent.[51] Some restraints were obviously necessary; Mississippi managed to reduce its annual death rate for leased Black convicts between 1882 and 1887 to a mere 15 percent.[52] Southern states now also began to rely on strict laws defining "vagrancy" and "loitering" and "having no visible means of support" as crimes. Under these laws, virtually every recent victim of slavery would almost certainly have to be considered a criminal.

Alongside the relatively small but rapidly growing convict lease system, there began, also before the end of the Civil War, the much more far-reaching contract system for farm workers. Illiterate Black ex-slaves were forced to sign contracts with their previous owners. These contracts bound them to servitude, often even stipulating that they required the landowner's permission to set foot off the plantation.[53] From now on, any person leaving this servitude would be, under the law, a criminal.

Under the convict lease system, prisoners were rented out to landowners, railroad and mining companies, or contractors who then sublet them to employers. The private lessee guarded, disciplined, fed, housed, and worked the convicts as he saw fit. This system was indistinguishable from slavery except for the element of "crime" and the much higher mortality rate. By the beginning of the twentieth century it was under much attack and was gradually being replaced by more sophisticated systems, most of which have persisted through the present. There is the "state account" method, in which the state actually goes into business, selling the products of convict labor on the market. The enormously profitable prison farms of Arkansas, Texas, and Mississippi are a form of state account. There is "state use," in which the state does not sell but uses the products of convict labor. Using convicts for public works, such as the chain gangs who built and maintained most of the roads in the South, is actually a form of state use. Under the "contract" system, a private employer contracts with the state for the use of a certain number of convicts, but, unlike the convict lease system, the state still maintains custody of the prisoners (this system, once in disfavor, is now being reinstituted as a "liberal" reform). Throughout the Black Belt in the South, all these methods were until very recently fed by the fee system. In this system, many local deputy sheriffs and police received no regular salary, but were paid a fee for each person arrested. The judge who tried the accused then drew his pay from the court costs he levied against those he found guilty. As Pete Daniel demonstrates at length in *The Shadow of Slavery: Peonage in the South, 1901–1969,* this system also abundantly fed the omnipresent institution of debt peonage, which itself "practically reinstituted slavery."[54]

Before the Civil War, Black people were enslaved just for being Black. But after Emancipation, Black people had to do one of three things to be bound by law into servitude: (1) "voluntarily" sign a contract they could not read; (2) become indebted to the people who owned all the land and commodities; or (3) commit a crime as defined by an all-white criminal justice system. The most typical crimes were vagrancy, loitering, no visible means of support, drunkenness, prostitution, possession of drugs or illegal alcohol, lewd and obscene conduct, assault, robbery, rape, burglary, abusive language, and disturbing the peace. (Meanwhile, between 1877 and 1966, which included the period of rampant lynching, only one southern white man was formally indicted for the first-degree murder of a Black.)[55]

Whenever landowners, railway and construction companies, labor contractors, or the state itself needed a supply of cheap labor, these local sheriffs, police, and judges operating on the fee system obliged with alacrity. Black men or women just standing around talking to each other would be rounded up, thrown in jail, convicted, and given fines they were of course unable to pay. Then they were either leased out, contracted out, put to work on state chain gangs, or bound over to their creditors. In these last cases, private contractors or farm owners would arrive in the nick of time to pay their fines, and the Black people thus became legally their debtors. Most of the southern states had laws making it a crime for persons in debt to leave the employ of their creditor; hence they became debt peons, virtual slaves or prisoners on farms or railroad construction crews, in turpentine camps or mines, surrounded by armed guards and bloodhounds.

One of the most common songs to grow out of this widespread and long-standing practice was "Standin' On De Corner." Variants of this song were collected all over the South prior to World War II. Here is a 1930s' version:

> Standin' on de corner, weren't doin' no hahm,
> Up come a 'liceman an' he grab me by de ahm.
> Blow a little whistle an' ring a little bell;
> Heah come 'rol wagon a-runnin' like hell.
>
> Judge he call me up an' ast mah name.
> Ah told him fo' sho' Ah weren't to blame.
> He wink at 'liceman, 'liceman wink too;
> Judge he say, "Nigger, you get some work to do."
>
> Workin' on ol' road bank, shackle boun'.
> Long, long time 'fo' six months roll aroun'.

> Miserin' fo' my honey, she miserin' fo' me,
> But, Lawd, white folks won't let go holdin' me.[56]

Among the many transcribed versions of this song is one where the first stanza is transposed, appropriately enough, into the middle of what is apparently an original old slave song, "Ole Marse John."[57]

Just as there is a continuity back into the slave past, other songs take the experience forward into the chain gang itself. Instead of "Standin' on de corner ... doin' no hahm," the singer is now "standin' on the road side, Waitin' for the ball and chain," as in this version of one of the many songs entitled "Chain Gang Blues":

> Standin' on the road side,
> Waitin' for the ball an' chain.
> Say, if I was not all shackled down
> I'd ketch that wes' boun' train.
>
> Standin' on the rock pile
> Wid a hammer in my hand,
> Lawd, standin' on rock pile,
> Got to serve my cap'n down in no-man's land.
>
> The judge he give me sentence
> 'Cause I wouldn' go to work.
>   .   .   .   .
>
> My gal she cried las' night,
> She cried the whole night long;
> She cried because judge sentence me,
> 'Cause I had to go so long.
>
> My gal she cried all night,
> I told her not to worry at all.
> I'm goin' on the chain gang,
> I 'spec' I'll be back in the fall.[58]

The forcible separation of men and women is much more extreme under the prison system than it was under slavery. For in the pre–Civil War South, when individuals were removed from their wives or husbands or lovers they at least were allowed to live with other people of both sexes. In the modern prison system, people are removed from all members of the opposite sex, often for decades or even the rest of their lives. One way to deal with unemployed young Blacks was—and is—to keep them from either competing on the labor market or reproducing by sending them up for long terms, no matter what the crime. As *The New York Times* reported in the midst of the Depression, on October 1, 1936:

> Alabama's new Burglary Law was applied here for the first time today when a jury found James Thomas, Negro, guilty of burglary in which $1.50 was the loot and fixed his punishment at life imprisonment. The jurors had heard a strong plea from the prosecutor for the death penalty.

Bukka White, a great convict blues artist, compressed the essence of this experience into "Parchman Farm Blues," a song about the 16,000-acre Mississippi prison farm which was that state's single main source of revenue, where White was sent to toil on a life sentence. All that he can now give his wife is his "lonesome song":

> Judge give me life this mornin' down on Parchman Farm, *(twice)*
> I wouldn't hate it so bad, but I left my wife and home.
>
> Oh, good-bye wife, all you have done done, *(twice)*
> But I hope some day, you will hear my lonesome song.[59]

Most commonly it is the man who is taken away from the woman. But often it is the woman who is kidnapped for "crimes" just as arbitrarily defined:

> . . . on Nov. 15, 1909, Mary Jackson, for using abusive language, was fined $10 plus $25.10 costs and hired out as a farm hand for eight months and eleven days at $4 per month.[60]

Milly Lee was a Negro woman convicted of using "abusive language" and fined one dollar and costs. She worked out the fine in two days, but it required nearly a year of labor to satisfy the "costs" consisting of fees to judge, sheriff, clerks and witnesses, totaling $132.[61]

Women prisoners performed many of the jobs required by the developing state apparatus, sometimes even on chain gangs:

The campus of Georgia State College was dug by aged Negro women working under the supervision of armed guards whilst young girls carried their picks to the road camps. Small wonder that a Negro's "heart struck sorrow" when he saw his girl join the long chain for a sentence of "11.29"—a year, which under these conditions would seem an eternity.[62]

Leroy Carr, another great ex-convict blues artist, puts this into the song "Eleven Twenty-Nine Blues":

Now I'm gonna see that judge and talk to him myself, *(twice)*
Tell him that he sent my gal to the county road and left me by myself.

Now never felt so sorry till the keeper walked down the lane, *(twice)*
And my heart struck sorrow when he called my good gal's name.

Then I heard the jailer say, "Hello! Prisoners all fall in line, *(twice)*
I'm also talkin' about that long-chain woman that got 11.29."

I've got the blues so bad that I just can't rest, *(twice)*
I'm gonna ask that jailer, "Can I do my good gal's time myself?"[63]

The blues form itself developed with the prison experience at its core, explicitly in songs such as "Penal Farm Blues," "Prison Bound," "'Lectric Chair Blues," "Back in Jail Again," "Mississippi Jail House Groan," "Shelby County Workhouse Blues," "The

Escaped Convict," "My Home Is a Prison," "Jailhouse Fire Blues,"
"High Sheriff Blues," "Heah I Am In Dis Low-Down Jail," and the
many different songs entitled "Prison Blues," "Jailhouse Blues,"
and "Chain Gang Blues." Many of the finest artists were prisoners and ex-prisoners: Bukka White, Leroy Carr, Charley Pat-
ton, Cow Cow Davenport, Robert Pete Williams, Texas Alexander, Son House, Willie Newbern, and of course Lightnin' Hopkins,
whose ankles bore the scars of chain gang shackles, Leadbelly,
and Billie Holiday.

Billie Holiday was first jailed at the age of ten for resisting
a sexual assault. The great-grandchild of a slave, she describes
this experience in words that recall those of Linda Brent: "So they
hauled me off to jail, not for anything I did, but for something
I wouldn't do."[64] As she continues, however, it is clear that she
grew up in the age after slavery:

> Those were rotten days. Women like Mom who worked as maids,
> cleaned office buildings, were picked up on the street on their way
> home from work and charged with prostitution. If they could pay,
> they got off. If they couldn't, they went to court, where it was the
> word of some dirty grafting cop against theirs.[65]

Whether or not the individual blues artist had ever been in
prison, he or she sang of a condition common to a whole people.
Actual imprisonment, the threat of imprisonment, and day-to-day
imprisonment on the tenant farms or in the ghettoes were central
to the life of Black people. The blues artist who sang about prisons
in the rural "juke" joints, Chicago and Kansas City clubs, or on
the radio or phonograph records was not separate from his or her
Black audience, and certainly was not on exhibit to them as a
specimen criminal or ex-prisoner. (That is, as we shall see in later
chapters, a role in which white ex-prisoner artists were and are
often cast.) Any poor or working-class Black could sing:

> I 'hind de bars, he 'hind de bars,
> All us niggers 'hind de bars.[66]

If the only Black people counted as prisoners were those actually convicted of a crime, prisoners would probably constitute only a minority of the Black population in any period from slavery days to the present. But from the Civil War until World War II, a majority of Black Americans were imprisoned as peons or semipeons, whether or not they had ever been convicted of a crime.

The fundamental labor system of the South during this period was a mixture of sharecropping and tenant farming, and both were based directly on debt peonage.[67] In many cases, sharecroppers and tenants were hypothetically free to leave—once they paid off their accumulated debts to the landowners. But many were legally bound into servitude. Well into the 1930s, vast numbers of Black people were still being forced to sign contracts in which they agreed to work under armed guards, to be locked up at night for "safe keeping," and to pay for any expenses incurred in recapturing them should they run away.[68] Peonage often, like slavery or prison, involved the forcible separation of husbands and wives, or parents and children.[69] Peons were often worked to death or even murdered because "unlike slaves, these peons had no monetary value; they could be replaced at the nearest jail."[70] Near one camp of debt peons doing construction work for the railroads, local people had stopped fishing in the river because it "was full of dead negroes."[71] Enough statistics and individual cases could be adduced to fill volumes. One published autobiographical narrative, however, alone gives a clear picture. This remarkable document, published in 1904 under the title, "The New Slavery in the South—An Autobiography, By a Georgia Negro Peon," is discussed in detail in the following chapter.

Before 1927 few people, even those participating in one way or another in debt peonage, had any conception of the extent of this system throughout the Black Belt. Then came the great flood of the Mississippi River in 1927. As the waters rose, first thousands of Blacks were rounded up and forced to work at gunpoint on the levees. When the levees broke, hundreds of these forced laborers were killed. Then the flood waters revealed that in the entire Mississippi valley south of Memphis, "by far the majority of the Negroes were share-croppers, held in perpetual peonage by the planter."[72] Hundreds of thousands of peons were flooded off the land on which they were held. Immediately the National Guard of the three states, Arkansas, Louisiana, and Mississippi, were mobilized to round up these refugees, herd them into camps fenced with barbed wire, and keep them under armed guard. The state governments regarded these people as the chattels of the landowners to whom they were in debt. The troops patrolling these camps shot down and killed anybody trying to escape. Several hundred thousand peons, overwhelmingly Black, were kept in these "concentration camps," the term used to describe them by the man who ran them, Herbert Hoover, acting as agent of the Red Cross.[73] The Red Cross commissaries, where small quantities of food were doled out, were actually conscription points for anyone escaping the dragnet, as Alabama Sam sang in "Red Cross Blues":

> ... She talked last night, talked for an hour,
> "Go and get a sack of that Red Cross flour."
>
> I tol' her, "Nooo ... I don't wanna go,"
> I said, "Y'know I cannot go down to the Red Cross sto'."
> ... "But you know the Government takin' a change,
> Say they gonna treat everybody right,
> They got them two cans of beans and one little can of tripe."
>
> I tol' her, "Noo ... I don't wanna go,
> I'll wait till I get a job."
>
> I said, "You know I can't go down to the Red Cross sto'."
>
> You go early in the morning, "Boy, how you feel?"
> You ask 'em for a li'l rice and they give you a bowl of meal.
>
> I tol' em "Noo ...
> An' I ain't goin' down to that Red Cross Sto'."[74]

For Black people during this period, the situation was in some respects more hopeless than during pre–Civil War slavery. The nineteenth-century slaves could look forward to the possibility of "freedom" through individual escape to the North, Canada, or Mexico, or even to revolt and the emancipation of the whole people. But there was no Underground Railroad to help the twentieth-century bondspeople escape, for there was no place to which they could escape. And relatively few white people even comprehended that Black people were still enslaved.

In this historical situation, the work songs of Black convicts assumed much the same function as the work songs of their slave ancestors. Indeed, many of the old slave songs persisted, to be modified and added to as events wore on. No verbal description of convict work songs can do more than hint of their beauty and enormous power. Fortunately, many of them have now been preserved on records; among others, any of the following gives a good small sample: *Negro Prison Camp Work Songs* (Folkways FE-4475), *Negro Prison Songs from the Mississippi State Penitentiary* (Tradition TLP-1020), *Prison Worksongs* (Folk-Lyric LFS A-5), *Negro Work Songs and Calls* (Library of Congress Archive of American Folk Song L-8). To get an inkling of the range and scope of the convict work songs, I recommend Bruce Jackson's marvelous book, *Wake Up Dead Man: Afro-American Worksongs from Texas Prisons*. Recording in only three prisons in the huge Texas system, Jackson was able to amass a rich and deep book-length collection of songs and ballads.

He also gathered from the prisoners themselves descriptions of the functions served by this poetry and music. In addition to timing the work so they can endure from sunup to sundown, the prisoners also use the songs to prevent any individual from being singled out for punishment for working too slowly, since they are all working to the same beat. One long-time man told him:

> You get worked to death or beat to death. That's why we sang so many of these songs. We would work together and help ourselves as well as help out our fellow man. Try to keep the officials we was workin' under pacified and we'd make it possible to make a day.[75]

In addition to the more obvious functions, Jackson believes that:

> The songs change the nature of the work by putting the work into
> the worker's framework rather than the guards'. By incorporating
> the work with their song, by, in effect, co-opting something they
> are forced to do anyway, they make it *theirs* in a way it otherwise is
> not.[76]

This is a reincarnation of the historic role of the slaves' songs: the
development of an oppressed people's culture, fashioned from the
very experience of their own oppression. Like the slaves, the prisoners' only property of any importance, in their eyes or anybody
else's, is the collective property embodied in their poetry and
music.

The work songs of the convicts do create a body of thematic
materials which were apparently not in the slave songs, or at
least did not play such an important role. Since Afro-Americans
had been redefined as a criminal people, it became only appropriate and fitting to fashion images of the criminal as hero. Hence
the rise of the Black Bad Man in song and ballad. And in a situation of historical impotence, it was possible to project onto the
legendary Black Bad Man all the desire for rebellion against the
white man's law and order.

One of the classic Bad Man ballads widely used as a prison
work song, and probably composed in prison, is "Po' Laz'rus." A
thrilling version has been recorded by Alan Lomax as a gang of
men were working at Camp B, Mississippi State Penitentiary at
Lambert (available on Prestige/International 25009). Here it is
used as a logging song. The men singing it are performing a kind
of labor that requires them all to move their bodies to the same
beat over a very extended period of time. The gang must swing
their axes high in the air, and then bring them down all at once.
The only instrument, like one of the most primitive percussion
instruments, is the axes as they strike the wood, and thus strike
the beat. The men sing about the legendary Lazarus, a Black Bad
Man, who single-handedly defies the law, like those other Black
Bad Men of myth and perhaps history, Railroad Bill and Stagolee.
Clearly the men are projecting onto Lazarus their own feelings of
defiance of the criminal justice system that has enslaved them.
The monotonous chop of their axes is transmuted into punctua-

tion and emphasis for the words of their tragic song. (I have indicated each heavy chopping sound with this symbol: ˆ .)

> Óh well the high sheriff, he told his deputý, "Won't you go ouf and
>   bring me Laz'ruś." (*twice*)
> "Bring him dead or alivé, Lord oh Lord, Bring him dead or alíve."
> Óh well the deputý, he told the high sheriff, says, "I ain't gonna méss
>   with Laz'ruś." (*twice*)
> "Well, he's a dangerous mán, Lord oh Lord, he's a dangerous mán."
> Óh well the high sheriff, he found Laz'ruś, he was hiding in the fiéld
>   of a mountaiń. (*twice*)
> With his head hung dówn, Lord oh Lórd, with his head hung down.
> Óh well the high sheriff, he told Laz'ruś, says "Laz'rus I cóme to
>   arrest yoú." (*twice*)
> "Bring 'n dead or alíve, Lord oh Lórd, bring 'n dead or alíve."
> Óh then Laz'ruś, told the high sheriff, says, "I never béen arrestęd,"
>   (*twice*)
> "By no one mán, Lord oh Lórd, by no one mán."
> Óh well the high sheriff, shot Laz'ruś, yes, he shot him with a gréat
>   big numbeŕ.
> Óh well the high sheriff, shot Laz'ruś, yes, he shot him with a
>   mighty big number,
> With a forty-fíve, Lord oh Lórd, with a forty-fíve.
> Óh then they take 'n po' Laz'rus, and they laid him on the cóm-
>   missary carriagé. (*twice*)
> He said, "My wound is hígh, Lord oh Lord, yes my wound is hígh."

We must be wary of sentimentalizing either the form or the
content of these enslaved work songs. They are marvelous
achievements, both formally and as an expression of human consciousness and strength, given the situation, but that enslaved
situation places severe limits on them. The rhythms are bound to
an almost inflexible meter, becoming at length almost as
monotonous as the work itself, because the demands of the labor
prevent rhythmic development. The singers are literally chained
to the very rhythms of work which make the song essential. In
fact we can hear in songs of cotton picking, where individuals can
work more or less at their own speed, a much more elaborate
rhythmic structure. And as for content, how far can people go
under the eyes and ears of overseers or prison guards? Here too

we should not sentimentalize the spontaneous level of consciousness. Endurance is admirable, but ultimately it represents a form
of acceptance or at least nonresistance. This is not the fault of the
prisoners. The options of active resistance or rebellion, even in
poetry and song, are not always open.

One of the most beautiful, and certainly one of the most an-
guished, of convict work songs is "Go Down Old Hannah," which
is usually sung while picking cotton, cutting cane, or weeding
with hoes. It has been widespread and well known among Black
prisoners. John A. Lomax collected ten versions among Texas
convicts, one of which, by "Iron Head" Baker and his group, can
be heard on *Negro Work Songs and Calls* (Library of Congress
AAFS L-8). The most famous recording is Leadbelly's on *Last
Sessions* (Folkways FA 2941). Lightnin' Hopkins manages to sing
it with a wry comic twist (now distributed in *An Anthology of Folk
Music,* Sine Qua Non—102).

"Go Down Old Hannah" is definitely the creation of Black prisoners. Leadbelly had never even heard the expression "Old Hannah" before he was in prison; as he says in *The Leadbelly
Songbook*:

> They called the sun Old Hannah because it was hot and they just
> give it a name. That's what the boys called it when I was down in
> prison. I didn't hear it before I went down there. The boys were
> talking about Old Hannah—I kept looking and I didn't see no Han-
> nah, but they looked up and said, "That's the sun."[77]

Like all widely diffused work songs, "Go Down Old Hannah"
picks up stanzas as people create and transmit it. Known stanzas
refer to historical events from 1910 to 1944. The most common
stanzas are these, which form a frame for the rest:

> Oh go down Old Hannah, well well well,
> Don't you rise no more, don't you rise no more,
> Why don't you go down Old Hannah, don't you rise no more.

Well I looked at Old Hannah, well well well,
She was turning red, she was turning red,
Well I looked at Old Hannah, it was turning red.

Well I looked at my partner, well well well
He was almost dead, he was almost dead,
Well I looked at my partner, he was almost dead.[78]

Go down old Hannah, don't you rise no more
And if you rise in the morning, set this world on fire.

If you had been on the river somewhere in 1910,
They was driving the women just as hard as they do the men.

You go down old Hannah and don't rise no more,
So if you rises in the morning bring judgement day.

So why don't you go down old Hannah, don't you rise no more,
And if you do rise in the morning, change this world around.[79]

Well you ought to been down on this old river, well, well, well,
Nineteen forty-four, nineteen forty-four,
Oughta been down on this old river, nineteen forty-four.
Well you could find a dead man, well, well, well,
On every turn row, on every turn row,
You could find a dead man, on every turn row.

I say get up dead man, well, well, well,
Help me carry my row, help me carry my row,
I say get up dead man, help me carry my row.
Well my row so grassy, well, well, well,
I can't hardly go, can't hardly go.
Well my row so grassy, I can't hardly go.[80]

All these words lose a great deal taken out of context. Like any art form, the prison work song must be understood in its own human situation. The best explication I know is one provided to Bruce Jackson by a convict who was telling him about prison slang and then "lapsed into an annotated version" of "Go Down Old Hannah." His brief comments put the life back into not only this song, but all those work songs stretching back into the days of slavery:

Go down old Hannah, ("Hannah means the sun")
Don't you rise no more. ("It means it's real hot")
If you rise in the mornin', Lord, Lord, Lord,
You bring judgment sure, you bring judgment sure.

Well I look at old Hannah,
She was turnin' red, ("Means it's late in the evenin'")
Well I look at my partner, ("That's the one on the row with you")
He was almost dead.

I say, "Oh, wake up, old dead man,
Help me carry my row. ("This is what his partner say when he
     couldn't hardly make it")
Well my row is so grassy,
I can't hardly go, I can't hardly go." ("And this is what he told
     him":)

"You ought been back on the river,
Back in nineteen ten.
They was drivin' women,
Like they was drivin' men, like they was drivin' men."

I look back at my partner,
I said, "A-partner, let's go."
Well my partner looked up at the sun,
Said, "I can't go no mo', I can't go no mo'."[81]

In the period between the Civil War and World War II, the
forms of convict labor spilled over and intermingled with "free"
labor:

Thus we find Virginia convicts being worked by a canal company.
Tennessee worked a part of its convicts within the prison walls, a
part on farms, and the rest were leased to railway companies and
coal mines. North and South Carolina employed a portion of their
convicts within walls. The rest were scattered over the state under
various lessees. Much of the tunnelling of the Western Carolina
Railroad through the Blue Ridge was accomplished by convict
labor. Georgia's convicts were leased to lumber camps and brick
yards. Alabama employed hers in railroad building, in mines and
saw mills. Mississippi's convicts were leased to railway contractors
and planters. Until 1883 the lessees of Texas convicts employed a
portion of them in a cotton mill and at other trades within the walls

of the penitentiary and placed the remainder in railway construction camps. Arkansas convicts were let to plantation owners and coal mines. In Florida the majority of the convicts were leased to turpentine farms; a smaller number were employed in phosphate mines.[82]

So the work songs of the convict camps, of the chain gangs, and of the mines and railways mostly developed as the common creation of prisoners and "free" laborers.

Gangs of "free" workers labored to collective rhythms and words explicitly about being arrested and sent away into convict labor. Here, for example, "free" Black men sing about a notorious Georgia judge whose usual sentence for vagrancy was forty-five dollars or ninety days on the chain gang (the *"huh!"* is the heavy expiration of breath from their exertion):

> Thought I heard—*huh!*
> Judge Pequette say—*huh!*
> Forty-five dollars—*huh!*
> Take him away—*huh!*[83]

In another work song, a group of "free" Black coal miners apply the language of the prisons directly to their own work situation:

> 'Way up in the mountain
> Diggin' coal,
> All I hates about diggin' coal,
> I can't find my parole.[84]

The term "captain" becomes interchangeably used for the supervisors at prison or on "free" jobs. Here a gang of "free" railroad workers sings a variant of one of the oldest hammer songs:

> I ask de captain—*wham*!
> Won't he hab mercy—*wham*!
> Naw boy!—*wham*!—naw boy!—*wham*!

Dat dere hammer—rung like mine.
Dis dat hammer, killed my partner,
Killed 'em dead—*wham!*
Killed 'em dead—*wham!*[85]

Perhaps an even older hammer song is the famous "Take My Hammer," which probably goes back to slavery days. Here is a version sung by a "free" worker in Alabama who thinks of his job in the same terms as all the other slaves and prisoners singing this song and contemplating escape:

Take my hammer,
Carry it to the captain,
Tell him I'm gone,
Tell him I'm gone.
If he ask you was I running,
Tell him no,
Tell him no.
Tell him I was going across the Blue Ridge Mountains
Walking slow, yes, walking slow.[86]

Legend has it that this very same song was sung by John Henry as he worked himself to death driving steel in the Big Bend tunnel of West Virginia in the year 1870.[87]

"John Henry" has been called "the best-known (and best) Negro ballad, the best-known Negro work song, the best song of protest against imminent technological unemployment."[88] It has from the time of its creation always been sung interchangeably by convict and "free" laborers:

If there is a single secular song in American Negro tradition that can be safely said to be known on every railroad gang, in every prison camp, in every "jookin' joint," and, probably, in every Negro cabin in the South, it is "John Henry." The song appears in many lengths and forms, and can be heard as a worksong, a field blues, an urban blues, a washboard band tune, a harmonica or guitar theme, a dance melody, and even in prose narrations.[89]

Well over a hundred versions of "John Henry" have been made on phonograph records. John Greenway lists sixty-five in *American Folksongs of Protest;* of these, fourteen are recordings of individual convicts or groups of convicts singing this song in prisons in Arkansas, Alabama, Mississippi, Tennessee, Virginia, Florida, and Georgia. Two older books on "John Henry" still remain excellent introductions: Guy B. Johnson, *John Henry: Tracking Down a Negro Legend* (Chapel Hill, 1929) and Louis B. Chappell, *John Henry: A Folk-Lore Study* (Jena, 1933).

Writing on the very eve of the Crash and the Depression, Guy Johnson could say with accuracy:

> John Henry is, I suppose, the Negro's greatest folk character. His fame is sung in every nook and corner of the United States where Negroes live. . . .
> Ask almost any Negro working man who John Henry was, and he will reply with, "He's man beat the steam drill," or "He's best steel driver the world ever afforded," or some such statement. Some will tell a detailed story of how John Henry competed with a steam drill, won the contest, but dropped dead. . . . John Henry has become a byword with them, a synonym for superstrength and superendurance. He is their standard of comparison. They talk him and they sing him as they work and as they loaf.
>
> These stories, narrative ballads, and work songs constitute the John Henry tradition. Beginning some sixty years ago, it is now known in one form or another to about nine-tenths of the Negro population.
>
> Wherever Negroes drive steel or dig or do any sort of work that requires regular muscular movements, the chances are that they sing as they work. The chances are, further, that they don't sing very long without mentioning John Henry in one way or another.[90]

Johnson's statements were made during the age of the triumph of industrial capitalism, in its closing days. The legend of John Henry was also created during that age, in its opening days. Just as surely as the legend of John Henry measures the historical distance between ante-bellum America and the sweeping triumph of industrial capitalism that followed the Civil War, Johnson's statements measure the historical distance between his age and ours, the era that began with the first worldwide crisis of capitalism.

Whether or not a real man named John Henry did drive steel faster than a steam drill in West Virginia (or Alabama), only to die from the effort, we probably never will know for certain. But what John Henry symbolizes is a historical certainty: both the passing of the age of hand labor, with its songs, into an age dominated by machinery, and the heroism of the workers who were forced to build, largely with hand tools, the very machinery that would make their labor unwanted—the railroads, the mines, the mills, the roads, the factories, the engines.

The actual setting in which "John Henry" was created, the rock tunnels dug with hand-held steel drills to set the blasting charges, echoing with work songs, was described by the Reverend William E. Barton in 1899, less than thirty years after John Henry's legendary feat:

> To hear these songs, not all of which are religious, at their best, one needs to hear them in a rock tunnel. The men are hurried in after an explosion to drill with speed for another double row of blasts. They work two and two, one holding and turning the drill, the other striking it with a sledge. The sledges descend in unison as the long low chant gives the time. I wonder if the reader can imagine the effect of it all, the powder smoke filling the place, the darkness made barely visible by the little lights on the hats of the men, the echoing sounds of men and mules toward the outlet loading and carting away the rock thrown out by the last blast, and the men at the heading droning their low chant to the *chink! chink!* of the steel. A single musical phrase or a succession of a half dozen notes caught on a visit to such a place sticks in one's mind forever. Even as I write I seem to be in a tunnel of this description and to hear the sharp metallic stroke and the syncopated chant.[91]

The ballad versions of "John Henry" are of course more elaborate than the versions used as hammer songs. Printed, oral, and recorded poems telling of John Henry include almost countless stanzas. Taken together, they comprise an epic of the Black worker who died transcending the machine that took away his livelihood. A version that includes the most common stanzas was sent to Guy Johnson by a prisoner in Ohio State Penitentiary who found that "it was necessary to interview a number of Old-Timers of this Penitentiary to get some of the missing words and to verify my recolections."[92] Some of these stanzas are:

When John Henry was a little boy,
Sitting upon his father's knee,
His father said, "Look here, my boy,
You must be a steel driving man like me,
You must be a steel driving man like me."

John Henry started on the right-hand side,
And the steam drill started on the left.
He said, "Before I'd let that steam drill beat me down,
I'd hammer my fool self to death,
Oh, I'd hammer my fool self to death."

The steam drill started at half past six,
John Henry started the same time.
John Henry struck bottom at half past eight,
And the steam drill didn't bottom till nine,
Oh, the steam drill didn't bottom till nine.

John Henry said to his shaker,*
"Shaker, why don't you sing just a few more rounds?
And before the setting sun goes down,
You're gonna hear this hammer of mine sound,
You're gonna hear this hammer of mine sound."

John Henry hammered on the mountain,
He hammered till half past three,
He said, "This big Bend Tunnel on the C. & O. road
Is going to be the death of me,
Lord! is going to be the death of me."

John Henry hammering on the mountain
As the whistle blew for half past two,

shaker: the steel driver's partner, who holds and turns the drill for him.

The last word I heard him say,
"Captain, I've hammered my insides in two,
Lord, I've hammered my insides in two."

This convict version also includes the most famous stanza of all, a stanza that appears in 64 percent of the versions collected by Johnson. (Only one other stanza appears in over half the versions known to Johnson; that is the first one given above.) It is the stanza that expresses the essence of the epic of John Henry:

John Henry said to his captain,
"A man, he ain't nothing but a man,
Before I'd let that steam drill beat me down,
I'd die with the hammer in my hand,
Oh, I'd die with the hammer in my hand."

"John Henry" is still one of the great monuments of American literature. But it no longer has the same meaning as it did for the Afro-American people when Guy Johnson was writing in 1929. "Nine-tenths of the Negro population" no longer know John Henry; "John Henry" is no longer widely sung at work; John Henry is no longer the "standard of comparison" for the Black worker, in prison or outside. "John Henry," a song and perhaps a man who came to fame in 1870, represents the age when new ways were being sought, and found, to superexploit Black labor. Within months of the publication of Johnson's book about "John Henry," the worldwide crisis of capitalism suddenly struck the United States. From that date on, in addition to the characteristic feature of industrial capitalism, a vast reserve army of the unemployed ready to be pressed into labor, there arose a new feature, characteristic of monopoly capitalism, an equally vast *permanent* army of the unemployed, who would never find work, even in the periods of boom between "recessions." (The only exception has been World War II and a brief period following.) From now on, there would be a shift, first gradual and then more abrupt, in the function of prison for Black people. Slavery had bound the entire

Black population in forced servitude. Peonage and convict labor had provided a virtually unpaid work force to help build industrial capitalism. In the final stage of capitalism, the stage of decay, it would be necessary to imprison a significant section of the young Black population to keep them permanently out of the labor market.

In the Black song ' Scottsboro," written and sung to protest the legal frameup of nine young Black men in Alabama in 1931, there are lines that, like "John Henry," also date an age while expressing a historical truth spanning several ages:

> Worse ol' crime in white folks lan',
> Black skin coverin' po' workin' man,
> Black skin coverin' po' workin' man.[93]

Soon the word "workin'" would become superfluous.

CHAPTER 4

A History of Literature by Convicts in America

The sheer quantity of literature by American convicts in the nineteenth and first half of the twentieth centuries is far beyond what I had supposed when I began this study. Most of this writing has great historical interest; much of it is deeply moving; some of it is great literature by almost any modern criteria. Yet there have been virtually no critical, scholarly, or even bibliographical publications on this literature.[1] In this chapter, I shall attempt to trace the historical development of literature by convicts up to the early 1960s, provide a theoretical structure for approaches to it, relate it to the literature by slaves, peons, and prisoners discussed in the earlier and following chapters, and give some sense of its range, diversity, and quality. If nothing else, I hope that I succeed in opening this literature for wider reading and serious study.

Personal narratives of the lives of criminals—both fictional and actual—made their appearance along with colonialism and large-scale mercantile capitalism in the sixteenth century. Ever since, they have been developing as an integral part of the culture of capitalist society. In fact, the principal literary form of the capitalist epoch, the novel, originated as extended prose narratives of the lives of criminals.

The modern novel first appeared in the form of picaresque fiction, in sixteenth-century Spain. Whereas *Don Quixote* (1605–15) was to mark the transition from feudalism to capitalism by parodying the aristocratic hero of feudal romance, the picaresque novel was already embodying this same transition by presenting the life story of what was to become the bourgeois hero, the self-made man who begins as an outlaw and, living by his own wits and energy, tries to make it for himself on a grand scale. At the very pinnacle of Spanish imperial power came *Lazarillo de Tormes* (1554), which broke away entirely from the maidens fair and knights errant of medieval romance; it is the tale of the archetypal Lázaro, who, cast out as a boy, lives among beggars, thieves, and swindlers, becoming cynical, self-seeking, and independent. In the next half-century, some of the outlaws and bandits, usurers and confidence men springing up amidst the collapse of feudalism were beginning to transform themselves into powerful and respectable merchants. The first full-length realistic novel in European literature, Mateo Alemán's *Guzmán de Alfarache,* presents this rise of the bourgeoisie in microcosm. In Part 1 (1599), the picaresque hero Guzmán details his adventures as a street urchin, a beggar, a gambler, a thief. In Part 2 (1604), he steals his way to a fortune and becomes a wealthy merchant. He is then found out, loses his fortune, and is imprisoned. Then he repents, gets a new wife, and starts on the way up again, this time by being her pimp. Down he falls again, now becoming a galley slave. Tortured by the captain of the ship, he is approached by his fellow galley slaves, including Moors, to be part of a planned rebellion. He manages to get a private word with the captain, betrays the would-be rebels, and is rewarded with his freedom. *Guzmán de Alfarache* thus epitomizes the underlying quest of the bourgeois epoch—to escape from rags to riches. And its archetypal man who makes himself by living by his wits is the living embodiment of the underlying epistemological, and even ontological, vision of bourgeois culture—"*I* think, therefore *I* am." Descartes was just eight years old when this criminal hero has the wit to achieve his own freedom by betraying his fellow slaves.

From that moment until the present, real criminals and imagined criminals have been narrating their lives at length in European literature and in the literature of the European colonies, including such places of exile for transported convicts as America and Australia. Throughout this literature, certain features have been consistently present and for a long time were predominant. One is a special relationship between the narrator, whether fictional or actual, and the presumed audience. The criminal narrator characteristically is confessing his or her crimes, and this confession, especially its moral lesson, is ostensibly the purpose of the whole narrative. In Daniel Defoe's *The Fortunes and Misfortunes of the Famous Moll Flanders, &c. Who was Born in Newgate, and during a Life of continu'd Variety for Threescore Years, besides her Childhood, was Twelve Year a Whore, five times a Wife (whereof once to her own Brother) Twelve Year a Thief, Eight Year a Transported Felon in Virginia, at last grew Rich, liv'd Honest, and died a Penitent* (1722), Moll Flanders tells us in all earnestness that her "publishing this Account of my Life, is for the sake of the just Moral of every part of it, and for Instruction, Caution, Warning and Improvement to every Reader."[2] Obviously, however, most readers are not perusing the intimate details of Moll's criminal life, or those of any of the countless other rogues, for the purpose of moral betterment. Whatever "Instruction, Caution, Warning and Improvement" the readers may hope to find is largely about the details of how professional criminals operate, the better to avoid their wiles (or, perhaps, to learn their craft). The main interest lies in vicarious participation in their thrilling, sordid adventures.

The criminal narrator is sharply marked off from the readers. He or she speaks as a lone "I"—an outlaw, a desperado, a deviant, or a member of an alien underworld—to society in general, or, more usually, a respectable reading public, incarnate in the reader. This relationship has much in common with that between the authors of the slave narratives and their audience, or between Melville and his audience, as he explicitly defines it in the first paragraph of *Typee*. The most extreme alternative to such a relationship lies in the songs of Black slaves and convicts, because there the audience is none other than the artists themselves.

America in its very origin was a society abounding in criminals and ex-prisoners, including those Puritans who came from the prisons of old England to New England. Throughout the eighteenth century, the shortage of labor in America and the heavy crime rate in England combined to make the transportation of felons to the American colonies a major component of British penology.[3] All the colonies, especially Virginia and Maryland, received continual mass shipments of convicts to serve as cheap labor, usually for a seven-year indenture. The conditions and the death rate on these sea passages approached those for African slaves.[4] This practice ended only with the American Revolution, after which Australia became Britain's main convict colony. And lawlessness was the essence of colonial life, for the colonies prospered through the mass murder of the native peoples and the theft of their lands. Whatever domestic tranquility reigned on the farms and in the villages that sprang up on the conquered land, there was always the frontier to provide more bloody conquest, an area beyond all laws except those which grew directly out of the barrel of a gun. So it is no surprise that by the early nineteenth century the lives of criminals were becoming an especially popular American literary form. In eighteenth-century England, novels about criminals flourished among their more-or-less authentic biographies and autobiographies. In America there was very little picaresque fiction, but there were many narratives about actual criminals. Perhaps people felt little need to create fictional criminals to supplement the ones all around them.

The earliest literature by convicted American criminals of which I am aware is purely confessional. The author offers himself as an example for all other members of society to shun, and he seeks forgiveness not in this world but the next. An example is a broadside by Philip Kennison, published in Boston in 1738, "The Dying Lamentation and Advice of Philip Kennison, Who Was Executed at *Cambridge* in *New-England* (for burglary) on Friday the 15th day of *September, 1738....* All written with his own hand, a few days before his death." For forty stanzas, Kennison elaborates on his exemplary predicament:

> Good People all both great & small,
>   to whom these Lines shall come,
> A warning take by my sad Fall,
>   and unto God return.

> You see me here in Iron Chains,
>   in Prison now confin'd,
> Within twelve Days my Life must end,
>   My Breath I must resign.[5]

This purely confessional mode continued throughout the nineteenth century and on into the twentieth. For instance, James A. Clay's *A Voice from the Prison; Or, Truths for the Multitude and Pearls for the Truthful* (Boston, 1856), written during his incarceration in Augusta, Maine, consists of 362 pages of moralizing based on his reformation; and *Echoes from the Living Grave. By a Convict in Sing-Sing Prison* (New York, 1869) is merely a conversion tract dedicated "to all prisoners" as "a beacon to guide them out of the midnight darkness of Sin and Unbelief into The Glorious Light of the Gospel." Toward the end of the nineteenth century, Hiram Peck McKnight, a prisoner in the Ohio Penitentiary, compiled an anthology of pious poems by himself and other inmates, *Prison Poetry* (Columbus, Oh., 1896). We even have an occasional throwback to this archaic tradition today, such as convicted Watergate conspirator Charles Colson's book about his religious conversion, *Born Again* (1976). But whatever wider significance this confessional mode may once have had, it had become of little consequence even by the middle of the nineteenth century.

By then the dominant mode of autobiographical convict narrative was confessional only in the conventional manner of the picaresque novel. In fact, the earliest known extended narrative by a convicted American criminal reads just like a tale told by a fictional picaro. This book, which compares favorably in quality with all but a very few picaresque novels, is *A Narrative of the Life, Adventures, Travels and Sufferings of Henry Tufts* (1807). It is yet one more discovery by Thomas Wentworth Higginson, who described it in a penetrating essay, "A New England Vagabond," in *Harper's Monthly Magazine,* March 1888 (later included in his *Travellers and Outlaws,* Boston, 1880). Tufts sprinkles occasional pious sentiments of confession throughout the narrative, and concludes by offering himself as a "negative example" to steer his readers from "the monster sin" to a life of "virtue": "Should any of the rising generation, by a perusal of my story, learn to avoid those quicksands of vice, on which I have been so often wrecked, I shall feel myself amply compensated for the trouble I have taken in its compilation."[6] But the real purpose of his long tale is obviously not to reform but to entertain his readers. As Tufts narrates his roguish escapades in crime and love, he also gives a vivid, priceless picture of life in the American colonies of the northeast in the latter half of the eighteenth century. After some minor thievery in his native New Hampshire, making love "with ardor" to a "damsel" who unfortunately becomes pregnant, marriage to another of his lovers, more thievery, and his first of many stays in jail, Tufts runs off in 1772 to live among the Indians in Sudbury, Canada, where "I successfully prosecuted my amour" with a "beautiful savage." Later he enlists as a private in the revolutionary army, passes counterfeit money, practices Indian medicine as a herb doctor, commits countless burglaries, makes love with many women while keeping several as wives, passes himself off in a church as a "saint" although publicly denounced by a young female parishioner who declares that Tufts had "first surveyed my face, then my feet, then my whole person, in such a carnal way and manner, that I perceived he had the devil in his heart." Tufts then discovers his true calling, that of a horse thief, which he describes in such meticulous detail that his narrative sometimes sounds like an instruction manual, and pursues his criminal and amatory adventures until he barely escapes hanging and achieves reformation.

In the next few decades personal narratives by American criminals were to become commonplace. Just as Tufts gives us an irreplaceable view of late eighteenth-century American life from its seamy side, these narratives do the same for early nineteenth-century American life. Most of them are also told in the picaresque mode. They are often far more realistic than most early American fiction, and the wide-ranging activities of their rascally heroes give authentic scenes of early American experience filled with frankness, vitality, and intimate detail. A good example is *Sketches of the Life of William Stuart, The First and Most Celebrated Counterfeiter of Connecticut, Comprising Startling Details of Daring Feats Performed by Himself—Perils by Sea*

*and Land—Frequent Arrests and Imprisonments. . . . As Given by
Himself*, "Printed and Published by the Author" in Bridgeport,
Connecticut, 1854. Though he acknowledges "I am the hero of my
own story," Stuart professes that "my heroism was displayed in
direct opposition to the laws of the land" (p. 3), and he then mouths
the conventional confession expected of all rogues who narrate the
thrilling stories of their lives: ". . . if I stand now as a beacon to
warn the young and ambitious against vice and crime, my history
will be a gain to the world." After some more pious professions,
Stuart launches his fine narrative of counterfeiting and other
wild adventures covering even more territory than Tufts. Around
1807 he works a con game in the South as partner with a free
Negro who runs away to rejoin Stuart each time Stuart sells him,
until one day when he fails to reappear. Later our hero ships out
on a privateer aiding South American states in revolt against
Spanish rule. Stuart, as expected, tacks on the usual self-
condemning moral at the very end.

By the time Melville published *The Confidence-Man* in 1857,
the lives of famous "bad men" were a staple in the literary diet of
America. As the passengers board his Mississippi River steam-
boat, they are given a wide choice of narratives about bloodthirsty
outlaws and bandits. But Melville, who sets this scene in a book
displaying all the tricks of riverboat confidence men and counterfeiters as a synecdoche for the criminality of capitalism itself,
suggests that these passengers are being warned about the wrong
kind of criminal:

> . . . still another versatile chevalier, hawked, in the thick of the
> throng, the lives of Measan, the bandit of Ohio, Murrel, the pirate
> of the Mississippi, and the brothers Harpe, the Thugs of the Green
> River country, in Kentucky—creatures, with others of the sort, one
> and all exterminated at the time, and for the most part, like the
> hunted generations of wolves in the same regions, leaving com-
> paratively few successors; which would seem cause for unalloyed
> gratulation, and is such to all except those who think that in new
> countries, where the wolves are killed off, the foxes increase.[7]

The adventures of horse thieves, highwaymen, rustlers, bank
robbers, counterfeiters, riverboat gamblers, and assorted confi-

dence men were narrated both as sensationalist tales by professional writers and as picaresque confessions by themselves.
Meanwhile, another kind of "criminal" was also publishing autobiographical narratives, often involving revelations of life in
prison. These were what we would now call political prisoners.

Some of the earliest political prisoners were rebels who had
risen up in open class warfare against semifeudal land tenure in
the New York State Anti-Rent Wars of 1839–46. One of the imprisoned leaders of the Anti-Renters, Mortimer Belden ("Little
Thunder"), improvised songs, accompanied by his fiddle, for his
fellow inmates. His "The Prisoners in Jail (Lines Composed in the
Columbia County Jail, July 9, 1845)," reprinted in the Anti-
Renters' journal, *The Albany Freeholder,* protested against both
prison and the oppression that led to their incarceration. Among
the fourteen stanzas are these:

> The sheriffs will out with their array of men,
> The County will find them what money they spend;
> They will seize upon prisoners, and into the cell—
> If there's anything worse, it must be in Hell,
>   In these hard times.
>
> And there they will keep them confined in the jail,
> Without any liberty for to get bail;
> They will do as they please in spite of your friends,
> And God only knows where this matter will end,
>   In these hard times.
>
> The judges and jurors are a very fine crew,
> They take the poor prisoners and drive them right thru;
> The sheriffs will falter, all hell they don't fear,
> They will bring them in guilty if they prove themselves clear,
>   In these hard times.[8]

Most political prisoners prior to the Civil War were jailed for
antislavery acts. Some of these people were conscious
abolitionists, such as George Thompson, who was incarcerated for
over four years, during which he wrote *Prison Life and Reflections*
(Oberlin, Oh., 1847) and *The Prison Bard; Or, Poems on Various
Subjects. Written in Prison* (Hartford, Conn., 1848). Others were

just individuals like Lewis W. Paine, a white machinist from the North working in Georgia, who decided to help a slave escape; Paine describes his decision and resulting imprisonment in *Six Years in a Georgia Prison* (New York, 1851).

These autobiographies by antislavery political prisoners have much the same intention as the narratives by escaped slaves: both attempt to use the authors' personal experience as a means of awakening the audience to the real nature of slavery and activating them to join the struggle against it. They attack the existing legal structure of society, which defines the slaveowners as respectable citizens and those who subvert slavery as "criminals." Thus both these autobiographical forms are diametrically opposed to the narratives of the lives of professional criminals, which are presented ostensibly as warnings about outlaws and confirmations of the conventional definition of crime.

Viewed in the light of these contrasting forms, *The Confessions of Nat Turner* appears fundamentally different from the kind of document it is usually taken to be. Here a slave who has led a major revolt against slavery does not manage to escape and to write or tell his own narrative. Instead he falls into the clutches of the slaveowners, who not only try him, convict him, and execute him as a criminal, but actually force him to present the story of his life in the form of a conventional criminal confession. Rather than the voice of a rebel against slavery, *The Confessions of Nat Turner* is a narrative constructed by Thomas R. Gray, its white recorder and publisher, to fit into a widely read popular genre, the lives of bloodthirsty outlaws and bandits. A political prisoner is thus transmuted into a conventional criminal.

Gray's introduction sarcastically introduces "this 'great Bandit,'" and claims that the purpose of publishing this narrative is "the gratification of public curiosity."[9] Gray describes "Nat Turner, and his band of ferocious miscreants" as "remorseless murderers." This was a "fiendish band," Gray tells us, and "no cry for mercy penetrated their flinty bosoms" (129–30). As usual in this confessional mode, this criminal now "frankly acknowledges his full participation in all the guilt" (129). Nat Turner's "own account" is offered as "an awful, and it is hoped, a useful lesson"

(130). The underlying moral purpose of publishing this document is explicitly the preservation of slavery and the social status quo, exactly opposite from the narratives of imprisoned abolitionists and escaped slaves:

> It is calculated also to demonstrate the policy of our laws in restraint of this class of our population, and to induce all those entrusted with their execution, as well as our citizens generally, to see that they are strictly and rigidly enforced. Each particular community should look to its own safety, whilst the general guardians of the laws, keep a watchful eye over all. (131)

Prior to the Civil War, two types of narratives by criminals were well established: one by the amateur or professional criminal writing in a confessional, often picaresque, mode, the other by the political reformer imprisoned as a criminal for an act many readers would commend. *The Confessions of Nat Turner* represents perhaps the earliest example of one form of overlap between these two types. Since Nat Turner was not a reformer but a revolutionary, his captors define him as just another criminal, an especially vicious and dangerous criminal. Until the rise of anarchism in the early twentieth century, autobiographical narratives by convicted revolutionaries were rare. But by the early 1860s another kind of overlap between the two forms was beginning to emerge, as some common criminals began to write the narratives of their lives, particularly their lives in prison, with a political perspective. Rather than wallowing in guilt, or professing to wallow in guilt, about their own crimes, these convict authors began to turn a critical gaze upon society. In these early works by prisoners the key question of much later prison literature was already beginning to emerge: Who is the real criminal, the prisoner or the society that imprisons people?

The modern prison system, based on the religious concept of the "penitentiary," developed first in the United States, in the late eighteenth and early nineteenth centuries, and then rapidly spread to Europe. Its first implementation, under the leadership of Pennsylvania Quakers, was in the solitary cells established in 1790 in the Walnut Street jail in Philadelphia for the purpose of meditation and reformation; this is often referred to as the birth-place of the modern prison system. The first prison physically designed to achieve total isolation of each inmate was the Eastern State Penitentiary, better known as Cherry Hill, in Philadelphia, constructed in 1829 with cells laid out so that no prisoner ever saw another person but his guards.

Initially, this system was administered by idealists who en-couraged what they believed to be moral growth among their captives. There were even a few successful examples of reforma-tion, such as George Reno, who in 1844 published in Philadelphia, under a literary pseudonym, *Buds and Flowers of Leisure Hours, by Harry Hawser, Sailor, &c.,* a collection of rather well-executed poems, including a very moving antislavery piece entitled "On the Dying Slave." In his preface, Reno asserts that the author "regards his confinement at Cherry Hill the happiest event of his life."

The "separate system" represented by Cherry Hill was being rivaled by an alternative, designed specifically for exploiting mass convict labor, the "silent system," under which prisoners were housed in solitary cells but worked together all day as an ideal source of cheap reliable labor, under rigorous enforcement of the rule that all convicts must maintain total silence. The model for this system was set up at Auburn, New York, in 1825, where they initiated the "lockstep" so that guards could maintain strict control as the prisoners marched back and forth between their cells and their industrial workshops.

Neither of these two competing systems apparently produced many successors to George Reno; extremely few subsequent pris-oners have much good to say about any of the variants of modern prisons. (The last published work I have been able to find by someone confined under the "solitary system" is *Selections from the Writings of Jesse Harding Pomeroy, Life Prisoner Since 1874,* published in Boston in 1920; Pomeroy began his forty-three years of solitary confinement at the age of fourteen and was not re-leased into the general prison population until 1917; his pathetic writings include a Rip Van Winkle experience, "My First Movie Show.") In fact, as industrial capitalism rapidly developed in the middle of the nineteenth century, the prisons rapidly shed much of their early pretense of being places of reformation and became frankly acknowledged as places of cheap mass production. With this shift, literature by convicts became increasingly a form of protest literature against the brutality of prisons and sometimes against the prison system itself.

A remarkable early work in this genre appeared in the first years of the Civil War, shortly before the mass use of convict labor to replace slavery. This book, *An Autobiography of Gerald Toole, the State's Prison Convict, who murdered Daniel Webster, Warden of the Connecticut State Prison, on the 27th of March, 1862 (Written by Himself) Being a Full Confession of Crimes for which he was sent to the State Prison. . . ,* was published in 1862 in Hartford, Connecticut. The title would seem to indicate that this is a confession in the same vein as *The Confessions of Nat Turner,* and, as in that earlier work, the criminal's "confession" is framed by the legal documents which preceded his execution. The main difference between the two works comes from the fact that Toole is actually speaking for himself, not having someone else narrate his alleged "confession." Hence Gerald Toole, unlike Nat Turner, has the opportunity to articulate a political defense of the "murder" he committed. His position is precisely the same as the one Frederick Douglass presents in describing his physical attack on the "nigger-breaker" Edward Covey and the one that Melville presents in White Jacket's preparations to murder his captain; it is the uprising, as a basic act of self-defense, of the slave against his oppressor. In fact Toole was defending himself against exactly the same punishment as the one that menaced Douglass and Melville—a flogging.

Despite the misleading title, Toole confesses nothing, including the "Crimes for which he was sent to the State Prison," an alleged arson of part of the building which housed his small shop. In the main body of his story, he tells not of his own guilt but of the viciousness of the guards and prison officials, and of their slave-driving management of the convict labor. Along with Melville's "The Tartarus of Maids" (1855) and Rebecca Harding Davis's *Life in the Iron Mills* (1861), this stands as one of the first American literary narratives set inside an industrial workshop. And Toole describes the actual scene of production in words that recall Melville's picture of the life-robbing paper factory in "The Tartarus of Maids":

> In the shop were about thirty men whose pale, emaciated looks showed that the very life blood was being worked out of them. They were all working at boot making. The coffers of unblushing contractors are filled from the labors of these poor convicts who work from dawn to dark. (17)

Toole is set to work and then severely flogged for failing to produce twelve pairs of boots in a day. The next day, his back and shoulders still oozing blood, he is again being driven off to the flogging dungeon for punishment. As Captain Webster starts pushing him with a heavy mounted stick to the place of his torture, Toole stabs him with a shoe knife. "At that time had Webster twenty lives, I should have taken them," Toole tells us with defiance and dignity. Toole is stomped, beaten, and whipped "until my whole body became one mass of torn flesh" (31), then tortured for a week, convicted of murder, and executed at the age of twenty-four. Toole's autobiography is not a confession at all, but a justification of his act of rebellion against what he perceived as a criminal system.

Just as the flogging of slaves is often central to personal narratives and fiction about slave life, and the flogging of seamen is often central to nineteenth-century literature about sailor life, the flogging of prisoners is a common theme in many works of convict literature for the next hundred years. Many readers of this book may not comprehend the severity of this punishment; a flogging is not what is usually thought of as a spanking or a paddling or a switching. It is administered with a long, heavy strap often weighted at the tip with metal; many prisoners describe guards and "captains" practicing by breaking bricks with a single blow of this whip. Prison literature contains innumerable scenes of convicts being flogged to death. I do not wish to inflict on the readers many of the detailed descriptions of floggings found in prison literature from the 1860s through the 1970s. These descriptions become increasingly appalling, and increasingly excellent as narrative prose, as our literary standards move toward approval of concrete, realistic detail and away from emotional adjectives. Whenever flogging is mentioned, the reader might envision the experience as described, with the purity and precision of a simple modern style, by Dale Woodcock in *Ruled by the Whip; Hell behind Bars in America's Devil's Island—the Arkansas State Penitentiary* (New York: Exposition Press, 1958):

> I was given twenty-seven lashes as I lay on the concrete floor. The warden threw his weight behind each lash and pulled on the whip as it struck my buttocks, thus twisting and tearing the skin. Soon blood and skin together were flipped away at every blow.... Blood was pouring from my rectum. (126)

In the period immediately following Toole's autobiography, prison literature began to present prisoners as a definite category of being in society, rather than merely individual criminals being punished. Less than a decade after Emancipation, there appeared a personal narrative by an anonymous convict who saw prisoners as the most oppressed people in society, *An Illustrated History and Description of State Prison Life,* published in Toledo, Ohio, in 1871. The author describes himself as writing in a cell in Southern Indiana State Prison "not for compensation or fame, but in defense of the most unfortunate being on earth, the convict" (14). He tells a grisly tale of torture, convict labor, and the routine rape of female inmates by prison officials, concluding with an ardent plea to the reader to do something about reforming or abolishing prisons.

Up through the first half of the nineteenth century, literature by convicts, except those convicted of political crimes, had appeared as the words of *criminals,* whether they were sincerely confessing to help their readers avoid their life of sin or merely conventionally confessing to entertain their readers with their life of rascality. But with the development of prison as a systematic means to achieve its professed goals of punishment and reformation, and its practical purpose of cheap convict labor, literature by convicts more and more appeared as the words of a new sub-

class in society, *prisoners.* By the turn of the century, this shift is
quite striking.

Even in works primarily intended to use an individual convict's
own life as a means of exploring the sociology and psychology of
the *criminal,* the main interest often shifts to the sociology and
psychology of the *prisoner.* For example, *The Autobiography of a
Thief,* recorded by Hutchins Hapgood (New York, 1903), starts off
as a narrative of criminal life but soon becomes an investigation
into prison life. The anonymous author tells us that he was born
of "poor but honest parents" in 1868, but "I have been a professional thief for more than twenty years. Half of that time I have
spent in state's prison . . ." (15). He tells of his crimes and his
various imprisonments, including stretches in Sing Sing and the
Dannemora asylum for the criminal insane. He documents the
viciousness of the prison system and describes the new class of
being it is creating. For example, here he shows the responses of
prisoners to an environment designed to deprive them of love and
human affection:

> Convicts, particularly if they are broken in health, often become
> like little children. It is not unusual for them to grow dependent on
> dumb pets, which they smuggle into prison. . . . The man in stir who
> has a white mouse or robin is envied by other convicts, for he has
> something to love. (326)

The very same year these words were being published, 1903,
another ex-convict writer was explaining that his own personal
descent, at the age of eighteen, into this subclass below the industrial proletariat had been the turning point in his life. Rather
than making him a crippled and pathetic victim, this experience
had converted him from "rampant individualism" to revolutionary socialism. Jack London describes this change in his life
in "How I Became a Socialist," first published in *The Comrade*
(March 1903). According to London, "no economic argument, no
lucid demonstration of the logic and inevitableness of Socialism
affects me as profoundly and convincingly as I was affected on the
day when I first saw the walls of the Social Pit rise around me and

felt myself slipping down, down, into the shambles at the bottom."[10] The decisive event had come in 1894, when, as a tramp "I strayed into Niagara Falls, was nabbed by a fee-hunting constable, denied the right to plead guilty or not guilty, sentenced out of hand to thirty days' imprisonment for having no fixed abode and no visible means of support, handcuffed and chained to a bunch of men similarly circumstanced, carted down country to Buffalo, registered at the Erie County Penitentiary, had my head clipped and by budding mustache shaved, was dressed in convict stripes, compulsorily vaccinated by a medical student who practised on such as we, made to march the lock-step, and put to work under the eyes of guards armed with Winchester rifles."[11]

London's crime was the same as that of Melville's Bartleby. But by this point, forty years later, imprisonment for vagrancy was not intended merely to get nuisances out of sight; prisoners were now used as part of a slave labor force, even if they preferred not to work. London's experiences as a tramp and as a prisoner led him to his understanding of how both groups form a critical part of the surplus army of labor essential to the survival and growth of capitalism, as he explains at length in "The Class Struggle" (*The Independent,* November 5, 1903) and "The Tramp" *(Wilshire's Magazine,* February 1904). In the latter article he shows how thin a line separates the employed worker from either the tramp or the criminal:

> The tramp is one of two kinds of men: he is either a discouraged worker or a discouraged criminal. Now a discouraged criminal, on investigation, proves to be a discouraged worker, or the descendant of discouraged workers; so that, in the last analysis, the tramp is a discouraged worker. Since there is not work for all, discouragement for some is unavoidable.[12]

In 1907–08, London published *My Life in the Underworld* as a series of articles in *Cosmopolitan Magazine,* narrating his life as a tramp and his month as a convict in the Erie County Penitentiary. In "Pinched: A Prison Experience" (July 1907) and "The 'Pen': Long Days in a County Penitentiary" (August 1907), he explains in vivid detail how his arrest, his so-called trial, and what he lived through in prison shattered all his earlier concepts of the police, the laws, the criminal justice system, and his own relation to them all. He shows how this experience led directly to his political and social analysis. But here he is less concerned with his analytical procedure than his emotional response, for his adolescent, naïve, heroic, superman view of himself had collapsed beneath the iron heel of the American state, and he had come to *feel* what it is like to be part of the class routinely crushed at the bottom of this society:

> I saw with my own eyes, there in that prison, things unbelievable and monstrous. And the more convinced I became, the profounder grew the respect in me for the sleuth-hounds of the law and for the whole institution of criminal justice. My indignation ebbed away, and into my being rushed the tides of fear. I saw at last, clear-eyed, what I was up against.[13]

The same year as this autobiographical narrative, London put all these ideas and feelings into the novel I regard as his master-piece, *The Iron Heel,* perhaps the first vision of the fascist night-mare which was to haunt the rest of the twentieth century, at least through the present. Jack London imagined capitalism, faced with socialist revolution, turning its whole society into one gigantic penitentiary.

As long-term prisoners began to write of themselves as a sub-class, as that category of slave laborers provided for in 1865 by Article 13 of the Constitution, they began to express a sense of being branded as outcasts, of being treated as less than human, caged up and walled off in the midst of society. This dehumaniza-tion is summed up for them in the practice of assigning numbers to convicts to substitute for their names. Thus American convicts become the first people actually to experience the exact form of what was to become that recurrent nightmare of the twentieth century—living as a nameless number in a society of numbers.

Their situation, however, was even worse than this nightmare, for their numbers also separated and distinguished them from a surrounding society, stigmatizing both them and their families. "Mourn Not for Me (To His Wife)," a poem published by two prisoners, James Stell and John Null, in *Convict Verse* (Fort Madison, Ia., 1908), expresses this double branding and alienation:

> Mourn not for me because my shame
> Is hedged by towered walls,
> And black across my humbled name
> A hated number falls.
>
> Weep for yourself, and not for me;
> Dear, all your flood of tears
> Can never set the captive free
> Nor cleanse his sullied years.
> . . . . .
>
> Weep not for me; for always, wife,
> The angry coals of shame
> Burn deepest in the guileless life
> That bears the branded name. (41)

In the same year, a novel entitled *9009* (New York, 1908), written as an indictment of the prison system by James Hopper and Fred R. Bechdolt (neither of them convicts as far as I know), achieves a bone-chilling effect by consistently using "9009" as the name of the protagonist. (Eugene Zamiatin's enormously influential Soviet antiutopian novel *We,* with its city-state in which all citizens have numbers for names, was not to appear until 1924.) This was rapidly becoming a convention used, and somewhat overused, by prison writers in books with purposes as varied as these: *Life in Sing-Sing* (Indianapolis, 1904) by "Number 1500," who still resents being incarcerated with "cheap criminals"; *Thru the Mill, by "4342"; A Prison Story That's Different* (Saint Paul, Minn., 1915), a rather dry but quite informative circumstantial account of Minnesota State Prison at Stillwater;*A Tale of a Walled Town, and Other Verses by B. 8266,——Penitentiary* (Philadelphia, 1921), a collection of the author's archaic religious poetry.

The significance of having a number for a name, and the estranged relationship between the prisoner-author and his audience, form part of the design in *An Open Letter to Society from Convict 1776* (New York, 1911). This thoughtful, well-constructed disquisition of the prison system by a seven-time loser carries the form of the prison narrative to a logical, if rather bizarre, extreme: a 160-page letter addressed from this author with a patriotic, revolutionary pseudonym to "My Dear Madam Society." Convict 1776 asserts that he does "not in the least justify crime, whether it is committed by us against you, or by you against us" (17). His analysis, however, proceeds from the fact that "the greater part of our offences is against your accepted suitor, Mr. Dollar" (15).

In order to understand what all this *is,* it may be helpful here to see, through contrast, what it is *not.* Except for London, these white prisoners see themselves first as isolated individuals, then as members of some social subclass defined by their alienation from the rest of their society. As I discussed at length in the preceding chapter, this is not at all the situation of Black prisoners, whose situation is qualitatively little different from the rest of their people. A personal narrative published during this same period, the opening years of the twentieth century, displays how this Black situation contrasts starkly with the white.

This remarkable document, "The New Slavery in the South— An Autobiography, By a Georgia Negro Peon" (1904), transcribed by a reporter "who took the liberty to correct the narrator's errors of grammar and put it in form suitable for publication,"[14] chronicles the development of a plantation from chattel slavery to convict slavery. The twentieth-century illiterate Black narrator opens his story just like the narrative of a nineteenth-century fugitive slave: he confesses that he knows neither the date of his birth nor the identity of his father. He figures he must have been born during the Civil War: "I reckon by this time I must be a little over forty years old"; "I never knew who my father was or anything about him." When he is about ten years old, he is "bound out" to a plantation owner. Around the age of seventeen or eighteen, he goes to a neighboring plantation and hires himself out. His former contractor immediately reclaims him, and gives him

"thirty lashes with a buggy whip across my bare back" for running off. At the age of twenty-one, he is allowed to contract himself for annual terms. When the owner dies, his son takes over:

> . . . this son had been serving at Atlanta in some big office to which
> he had been elected. I think it was in the Legislature or something
> of that sort—anyhow, all the people called him Senator. At the end
> of the fifth year the Senator suggested that I sign up a contract for
> ten years; then, he said, we wouldn't have to fix up papers every
> year. I asked my wife about it; she consented; and so I made a
> ten-year contract. (410)

Shortly thereafter, the Senator has constructed a "long, low
shanty" with "a double row of stalls or pens" which "looked for all
the world like stalls for horses":

> Nobody seemed to know what the Senator was fixing for. All doubts
> were put aside one bright day in April when about forty able-
> bodied negroes bound in iron chains, and some of them handcuffed,
> were brought out to the Senator's farm in three big wagons. They
> were quartered in the long, low shanty, and it was afterward called
> the stockade. This was the beginning of the Senator's convict camp.
> (410)

The narrator tells us that "when I saw these men in shackles, and
the guards with their guns, I was scared nearly to death. I felt like
running away, but I didn't know where to go." He and the other
peons under contract had considered themselves "free laborers";
they meet, and send a representative with a threat to quit. Then
they learn just how much difference there is between Black convicts and free Black people:

> Word came back that we were all under contract for ten years and
> that the Senator would hold us to the letter of the contract, or put
> us in chains and lock us up—the same as the other prisoners. It was
> made plain to us by some white people we talked to that in the

contracts we had signed we had all agreed to be locked up in a
stockade at night or at any other time that our employer saw fit;
further, we learned that we could not lawfully break our contract
for any reason and go and hire ourselves to somebody else without
the consent of our employer; and, more than that, if we got mad and
ran away, we could be run down by bloodhounds, arrested without
process of law, and be returned to our employer, who, according to
the contract, might beat us brutally or administer any other kind of
punishment that he thought proper. In other words, we had sold
ourselves into slavery—and what could we do about it? The white
folks had all the courts, all the guns, all the hounds, all the railroads, all the telegraph wires, all the newspapers, all the money,
and nearly all the land—and we had only our ignorance, our poverty and our empty hands. (410–11)

The Senator begins to add additional stockades, bring in more
convicts, and buy more land:

Within two years the Senator had in all nearly 200 negroes working on his plantation—about half of them free laborers, so-called,
and about half of them convicts. The only difference between the
free laborers and the others was that the free laborers could come
and go as they pleased, at night—that is, they were not locked up at
night, and were not, as a general thing, whipped for slight offenses.
(411)

But all this is in the relatively happy days of "contract" labor,
when there was still some faint distinction between the "free
laborers" and "the other prisoners." The real "troubles of the free
laborers began at the close of the ten-year period." Then they
discover that, since they all had been compelled to buy all their
food, clothing, and other supplies on credit from the Senator's
commissary, they were now debt peons. Henceforward, "we were
treated just like convicts." He is locked up in one of the filthy
stockades, which "were but little more than cow lots, horse
stables or hog pens." When he is put in the stockade, his nine-
year-old son is given away to someone in South Carolina and his
wife is taken into the "Big House" to serve as one of the white

men's mistresses. The ante-bellum split between house slaves and field slaves is reproduced:

> ... the poor negro women who were not in the class with my wife fared about as bad as the helpless negro men. Most of the time the women who were peons or convicts were compelled to wear men's clothes. Sometimes, when I have seen them dressed like men, and plowing or hoeing or hauling logs or working at the blacksmith's trade, just the same as men, my heart would bleed and my blood would boil, but I was powerless to raise a hand. It would have meant death on the spot to have said a word. (412)

What kind of crime had these convicts committed? The narrator learns that the great majority were convicted of the usual minor offenses established to provide a constant flow of cheap convict labor. The most common crime of convicts on the Senator's farm, and several other convict farms in the area, was adultery, committed in a certain county in south Georgia "'way down in the turpentine district":

> ... I learned that down in that county a number of negro lewd women were employed by certain white men to entice negro men into their houses; and then, on certain nights, at a given signal, when all was in readiness, raids would be made by the officers upon these houses, and the men would be arrested and charged with living in adultery. (413)

To the Black convict or peon, imprisonment did not mean becoming an alien being isolated from the rest of his people but rather becoming the typical representative of his people. Even during the early years of the twentieth century, some white prisoner-authors began to perceive their own situation as not entirely different. Convict 1776 shows a class perception of social reality when he argues to Madam Society that "the vagrancy laws should be strictly enforced against the tramp and the millionaire alike" (153). John Carter, whose poems were published in *Century*

Magazine, Harper's Weekly, The Bellman, The Smart Set, Cos-mopolitan, and *Lippincotts' Magazine,* divided his collection of prison poems, *Hard Labor, and Other Poems of Prison Life* (New York, 1911), into two sections indicating a perception of society to be expressed by the Black Panther Party half a century later. The poems about life in prison he places in the section entitled "Under the Lash"; the poems about "free" life he places in the section entitled "In the Greater Prison." Then in 1912 appeared a very influential work by a convict who claims that he is not a criminal, though he is a burglar, because he belongs to an entire social class driven to "crime" in order to survive—Donald Lowrie's first book, *My Life in Prison.*

Lowrie writes as a poor person to "the taxpayers and the conscientious citizens of the community," hoping to move them toward the reformation of prison and society.[15] His first words establish the relationship between himself and his reader, and between the two social classes embodied by them:

> I was broke. I had not eaten for three days.
> I had walked the streets for three nights. Every fibre of my being, every precept of my home training protested against and would not permit my begging.
> I saw persons all about me spending money for trifles, or luxuries. I envied the ragged street urchin as he took a nickel in exchange for a newspaper and ran expectantly to the next pedestrian. But I was broke and utterly miserable.
> Have you ever been broke?
> Have you ever been hungry and miserable, not knowing when or where you were going to get your next meal, nor where you were going to spend your next night? . . .
> If you have not felt each and all of these things, it will, perhaps, be futile for you to read what they brought to one who has felt them. . . . (1–2)

Lowrie's books did have some effect on the movement toward prison reform and were also studied by later prison authors, as attested to in the confessional, picaresque autobiography of the professional thief Jack Black, *You Can't Win* (New York, 1926), when he praises "Donald Lowrie, whose writings did for American prisons what John Howard's did for those of England" (368).

And already another kind of convict was writing not from a reformist but a revolutionary perspective. These were prisoners serving time for revolutionary political crimes, and they brought into the prisons a theoretical class perspective, even though some of them lacked the proletarian class experience of most "common" criminals.

An important early book by a committed revolutionary was Alexander Berkman's *Prison Memoirs of an Anarchist* (New York, 1912). In 1892 the Carnegie Steel Corporation locked out the Iron and Steel Workers union from its Homestead, Pennsylvania, plant. Henry Frick, the company's superintendent, brought in a boatload of three hundred Pinkerton gunmen to put down the protesting strikers. A pitched battle was fought, in which ten men were killed, and the three hundred Pinkertons surrendered as "prisoners of war" to the armed workers. The workers, however, were then crushed by thousands of Pennsylvania state militiamen. Berkman, hearing of the outrages committed against the defeated workers, went to Homestead, where he shot and stabbed Frick in an unsuccessful assassination attempt. Imprisoned, Berkman narrates the story of his own actions in the Homestead strike, then carefully interrelates the class oppression of the workers and his fellow prisoners. He dedicates his book "To all those who in and out of prison fight against their bondage."

My main concern throughout this chapter is with people who became creators of literature because of their incarceration as victims of American society. Although there are many twentieth-century prisoner-authors convicted for outright political crimes whose perception of society has been deeply intensified, if not fundamentally altered, by their prison experience, I am essentially limiting my analysis to "common criminals" whose understanding of their own situation developed directly as a consequence of their crime and punishment. The reader should, however, be aware of the rich and ever-increasing body of twentieth-century writing by political prisoners, dating at least from Berkman. These include such notable early works as Carlo de

Fornaro's *A Modern Purgatory* (New York, 1917) a narrative of life in the New York City Tombs by "an artist, writer, editor, revolutionary"; *A Fragment of the Prison Experiences of Emma Goldman and Alexander Berkman in the State Prison at Jefferson City, Missouri, and the U.S. Penitentiary at Atlanta, Georgia* (New York, 1919); *Bars and Shadows: The Prison Poems of Ralph Chaplin* (New York, 1922), including some fine sonnets by this leading I.W.W. organizer; *In Prison* (New York, 1923) by Kate Richards O'Hare, who spent fourteen months in the Missouri State Penitentiary and became committed to prison reform; *Wall Shadows: A Study in American Prisons* (New York, 1927) by Frank Tannenbaum, whose many years of work on prison reformation began while he was serving a year for unlawful assembly in 1913–14; and Eugene Debs's *Walls and Bars* (Chicago, 1927). (Debs's cellmate in the Atlanta Penitentiary, the forger Roger Benton, devoted a chapter of his own book, *Where Do I Go From Here?* [New York, 1936] to "A Man Named Gene Debs," "the most Christ-like man I have ever met in my life.")

Another group of convict writers beyond the main scope of this chapter are those who were professional writers before they became convicts. One of the most popular and prolific American authors, Julian Hawthorne, who published close to forty books of fiction, essays, and biography, far more than his father Nathaniel, was sent to the Atlanta Federal Penitentiary (for mail fraud) at the age of sixty-seven and the height of his career. He served almost a year. When he got out, he immediately began work on *The Subterranean Brotherhood* (New York, 1914) a narrative of prison life, written with more passion and commitment than any of his other works I have read. In his preface, Hawthorne declares that "these chapters were begun the day after I got back to New York from the Atlanta Penitentiary" and that he worked on the book without interruption until it was complete. "Though I had read as much in 'prison literature' as most people," he discovered that he had very little conception of what life in prison really meant. His experience leads him to the "radical and astounding" conclusion that there is only one solution: "nothing less than that *Penal Imprisonment for Crime be Abolished*" (xiii). Julian Hawthorne penetrates, through his experience, to part of the historical significance of the prison system:

> Before the Civil War there were some millions of negro slaves in the South, whom to set free we spent some billions of dollars and several hundred thousand lives. It was held that the result was worth the cost. But to-day we are creating some five hundred thousand slaves, white and black, each year. . . . (149)

Hawthorne repeats the deeply held belief of "every convict and ex-convict": "Let every judge, attorney general, district attorney, and juryman at a trial spend a bona fide term in jail, and there would be no more convictions—prisons would end" (320).

This last statement is borne out by still another group of prisoner-authors I pass over without much attention, the prominent and respectable citizens who suddenly awake to find themselves convicts. For example, Charles Stuart Wharton, former Illinois congressman, for many years an assistant district attorney in Cook County, and then a prominent businessman, was convicted of being an accomplice in a spectacular armed mail robbery in 1928. After serving his two-year sentence at Leavenworth, he describes that institution and prison in general, to which he had sent many a criminal, in *The House of Whispering Hate* (Chicago, 1932):

> Leavenworth is a great mill through which men pass in an endless chain to be turned out as ex-convicts. It is as useful as a sausage machine which grinds up meat with poison. Most of the men it sends forth will be a burden on their communities, and the few who can ever benefit themselves or the world at large after their release are made fearful by the brand upon them. (305)

The literature about prison experience written by highly educated, formerly respectable convicts, even that by a leading professional author such as Julian Hawthorne, rarely matches the quality of writing, at least by late twentieth-century standards, of much proletarian and lumpenproletarian prison literature (just as the slave songs of the nineteenth century now seem to us finer literary creations than most of the elegant poetry of the literary periodicals). These respectable citizens tended to follow the archaic literary models then in fashion, and their prose is therefore generally lifeless, vague, effusive, humorless, verbose, and now rather difficult to read. Many of the "common" criminals, however, wrote with direct, economical, colloquial, often raw prose, filled with frank realism and spiced with humor; their books still bubble with life.

There was, however, one formerly respectable citizen who, by learning the lingo of his fellow criminals and convicts, was to achieve a wide popularity and deep, though perhaps transitory, influence on the writing of fiction. This was William Porter, whose strange career was to anticipate much literature by twentieth-century criminals just as the equally strange career of his sidekick Al Jennings, also once a respectable citizen, was to echo much literature by nineteenth-century criminals.

Al Jennings was one of the last of the famous outlaws of the Wild West, leader of the daring Jennings Gang of train robbers. Fleeing to Honduras with $30,000, he there met Bill Porter, on the lam from a bank embezzlement charge. The two traveled around Mexico and Central America together, Porter living off the loot of Jennings, who at one point shot a man about to stab Porter. Both eventually ended up in the State Penitentiary at Columbus, Ohio, where each began serious writing. Jennings's life story, *Beating Back* (New York, 1914), was one of the final tales of the nineteenth-century picaros, with its thrilling adventures and detailed how-to-do-it accounts of robbing trains. Much earlier, while still in prison, Porter was smuggling out his characteristic short stories to be published under the name O. Henry. Some of his best-known stories were published in this manner, including "A Blackjack Bargainer," "A Fog in Santone," "An Afternoon Miracle," "Money Maze," "No Story," "The Enchanted Kiss," "Hygeia at the Solito," "Rouge et Noir," "The Marionettes," and "The Duplicity of Hargraves."

O. Henry did not publish as an acknowledged prison author. In fact, it was not until after his death in 1910 that it became widely known that he had been a convict who had served almost four years in the state penitentiary. Then, however, he did influence the direction of prison writing, more by personal example than through his already somewhat outdated trick-story technique. From this point on, prison writers began to see possibilities in fiction as well as autobiographical narrative, essays about crime and prison, and lyric poetry; they began to think of themselves as potential professional authors rather than just criminals with their own tale to tell. Of course, this process would no doubt have taken place anyhow, but for aspiring convict authors O. Henry was a supportive patron saint.

In the 1920s, novels and short stories by prisoners started to develop, especially after H.L. Mencken actively began to encourage convicts to submit their material to the *American Mercury*. This fiction of course varied widely in both quality and intention.

Some of it was romantic and escapist, like Howard D. Bolling's novel *The Mystery of the Cumberlands* (Lynchburg, Va., 192?). Bolling was born and reared in the foothills of the Cumberland Mountains in Virginia. While traveling through Winona, Missouri, he was accosted without cause by the town marshal, who, pistol in hand and not identifying himself, demanded Bolling's surrender. Bolling pulled his own gun, killed the marshal, and was sentenced to thirty-five years in a Missouri prison. He wrote *The Mystery of the Cumberlands* in prison, partly to raise money to reopen his case. The novel is a strange and rather fascinating tale of a wild, mysterious boy named "D," born to a strong, heroic mountain woman. "D" grows up to become a kind of savior-adventurer not only in his native Cumberlands but in Africa as well.

More typical fantasy was churned out by Jack Callahan, who describes the facts of his own life as a gangster, a prisoner, and an author in *Man's Grim Justice: My Life Outside the Law* (New York, 1928). Callahan makes little pretense to moral reformation as he narrates his own lurid adventures. He seems especially to enjoy telling of a shootout in a boxcar where he and his pals kill three "bad niggers," the "notorious nigger, 'Brooklyn Shine,'" and "two other coons, 'The Riverside Shine' and 'Boston Yellow'" (131). Callahan writes hard-boiled prose with great skill, and he is not totally devoid of moral sensibilities, as shown in his concluding sketch, a brilliant and shocking description of the hideous execution of a Black prisoner in the electric chair, which comes out as a far more criminal act than Callahan's own killings. Because of Callahan's extraordinary frankness, the description of his own career as a writer of fiction is exceptionally revealing.

His first venture as an author was an autobiographical article "on how a bank burglar attained success in the automobile business" (286). He "pounded out" this article, giving it a suitable "inspirational twist," and then went wild with joy when it was published. He decides to become a "great writer" by creating stories about criminals. With straight-faced ironical humor about both himself and his editors, he tells of his early success:

> . . . I began my crook serial. I wrote myself into the story. I called it "The Philanthropic Bank Burglar." I was robbing banks and building hospitals with the money I got. I was a burglar with an ideal. Prisons were all wrong. Criminals should be treated in hospitals by psychiatrists and pathologists. I was sending all the money that I got out of the banks to a well-known pathologist. I was sending it anonymously and he was building a hospital with it. I had celebrated detectives on my trail all through the story and just about the time that they were going to capture me, the reader read "continued in the next installment." I had learned how to leave readers "hanging in the air" gasping for breath, and I was sure that I was a great novelist when the readers began writing me letters complimenting me on the "marvelous Philanthropic Bank Burglar."
>
> But I was not so good on endings. I killed the detective at the end of the story. One of the Editors said that wouldn't do, that I would have to change the ending.
>
> "We must have a moral in the story," he said, "and the moral of this story should be defeat. A burglar should never succeed."
>
> So I switched the ending. I had myself killed by the detective! Needless to say I didn't like that ending. I preferred killing the dick to being killed. (287–88)

This kind of fantasy fiction by convicts, in which a loser can imagine himself a winner, reached its full development almost half a century later, when it was no longer necessary to point toward the moral that crime doesn't pay. E. Richard Johnson, serving forty years in Stillwater Prison, Minnesota, for a hold-up killing, churns out hard-boiled crime novels at a rapid rate: *Silver Street* (1968), *Mongo's Back in Town* (1969), *The God Keepers* (1970); *Case Load-Maximum* (1971); *The Judas* (1971). In some the criminal-protagonist ends up like Callahan's philanthropic bank burglar. But in *The Judas,* the hero—and first-person narrator—is a professional killer who single-handedly wipes out the really mean criminals in Kansas City and lives to enjoy his trade. (Johnson writes a more honest kind of fiction in *Cage Five Is Going To Break* [1970], a novel of brutality and betrayal set on a prison farm.) The highest artistic achievement in this genre is almost certainly Edward Bunker's *No Beast So Fierce* (1973), which carries the fantasy of the world-defying criminal explicitly to a Nietzschean level; I shall discuss this novel and its significance in the final chapter.

Quite a different kind of fiction develops from the reformist tendency still dominant in prison autobiographical narratives of this period. For example, the bank robber Ernest Booth, who published his autobiography, *Stealing through Life,* in 1929, went on much later to write a protest novel against prison and the legal machinery of which it is a part, entitled *With Sirens Screaming* (1945).

Booth, along with Robert Joyce Tasker, author of *Grimhaven* (New York, 1928), Victor Folke Nelson, who wrote *Prison Days and Nights* (Boston, 1933), and the prolific Jim Tully, were all encouraged by H.L. Mencken; their sketches and tales appeared frequently in the *American Mercury* between 1925 and 1933. Five sections of *Stealing through Life* appeared first in the *Mercury,* including the lead piece for September 1927, "We Rob a Bank," a marvelous description of his own feelings during a bank stick-up and getaway. Then a couple of years after the publication of his autobiographical narrative in book form, Booth made one final appearance in the *Mercury,* "Ladies in Durance Vile" (April 1931), fine sketches of life in the women's section of Folsom Prison. The last sketch points forward to his novel. It tells of an eighteen-year-old woman unwittingly trapped as the "accomplice" of her youthful husband, whom she had known only three days, because "under California law *all* accomplices, re-

gardless of how far they were removed from the crime, are equally
guilty with the principals."[16] Mary is serving life for a murder her
husband committed during a bank robbery she knew nothing about;
he is due to be hanged in the same prison. Booth describes the
final day, with the prison awash in a "ghostly grey fog" that
"drifted off the bay and shrouded the tops of the walls":

> From my hunched-up position on the railing I glanced up at the
> lighted window with the vent. The leaf was out. The window
> showed two figures pressed against it. Mary, also, had seen the
> warden pass.... I visualized that girl up there in a room filled with
> silent women. She, too, was waiting.
> The huge weight of the trap dropped with ponderous decisive-
> ness. Through the salt-bitter air that thud came with a sickening
> hard finality. More minutes dragged through my benumbed mind.
> Again the warden appeared, now walking rapidly through the
> fog, as though he would lose in it a pursuing ghastliness.... A
> gentle murmur rose in the cells. The prison stirred. Life moved
> again in the women's department. I heard the whirring of
> sewing-machines. At the window there was no shadow. The leaf
> had been replaced in the vent.
> Down through the awakening life there came the brown autum-
> nal voice of Grace: "Get to work girls! Get at your tasks!"
> Suddenly her voice rose in harshness: "Mary, go on in and get to
> work! Go on! Go on! There's nothing more to wait for. It's all over!"
> Then through that thin pane of glass and out into the heavy fog,
> there came Mary's cry: "All over?" And all the bleakness of the
> endless years before her was in her final anguished scream: "Over?
> God no! It's just *starting*!" (402)

Booth transmutes this material, but still uses it for reformist
purposes, in *With Sirens Screaming*. In this earnest and somewhat dated novel, a young World War II veteran and his
seventeen-year-old sweetheart unwittingly commit a crime just
by traveling together. She is held as a juvenile delinquent. He is
imprisoned on a morals charge, escapes, commits a crime, becomes involved in a prison riot, is convicted for another crime that
he did not commit, and is sentenced to capital punishment, as
Ann, his lover, here tells in protest against his fate and the system which determined it:

"Mark is unjustly condemned to die. Actually, he has not committed a crime. Trying to get married, we were treated like children. Mark escaped, so he could see my mother and get her to withdraw the charge against him. During a rainstorm he took an overcoat. For that he was given a life sentence. In Folsom Prison he was near by when a guard was cut with a knife. For that he has been tried and now the State will kill him. . . . All he wanted to do was marry me, live honorably, work hard, and be a credit to his parents and the country he has served."[17]

This protest in some ways is actually a retreat from the consciousness of much previous writing from prison, because it is directed primarily against the inflexibility of a legal system which victimizes an innocent individual, not a people or a social class. On the other hand, the novel can also be read as a forerunner of the protest movement against the oppression of youth, with even that movement's individualist anarchism and escape to a fantasy of life outside society. Faced with an implacably unreasonable society, Ann, unlike Mary, her model in real life, turns into a heroic figure of action. She pulls a gun in prison, and forces the warden to come with them to cover Mark's escape. She leads Mark to a well-stocked mountain cabin in an idyllic wilderness setting. At the end, the two lovers are preparing to live in this wilderness while the machinery of state, "with sirens screaming," is trying to apprehend them and all other youthful threats to the well-being of society.

The main ex-convict contributor to the *American Mercury* was Jim Tully, who published no fewer than thirteen stories and sketches in its pages between 1925 and 1933. Tully, born of a poverty-stricken Irish immigrant family in 1888, had become a "road-kid" at the age of eleven, and his adventures in the ensuing twelve years as a hobo, circus roustabout, prisoner, and professional prizefighter provided the materials for all his early books, which ranged from novels to autobiographical narratives, mostly falling someplace in between. *Emmett Lawler,* an autobiographical novel, appeared in 1922, but his real reputation began in 1924 with the publication of *Beggars of Life,* which described his initiation into the life of a hobo, his first arrests, and the lives and deaths of people on the fringes of society—tramps, jailbirds, and prostitutes.

Beggars of Life displayed all the main characteristics of the style and method Tully was to use in his subsequent twenty-four books: fast-paced, episodic, alternating between cynicism and sentimentality, tough and ostensibly detached on the outside but obviously filled with compassion, always aligned with the victims and misfits against organized society. Here, for example, is his description of a lynching in a western town:

I left the good woman's home and walked toward the centre of the town, carrying a "handout" which solved my eating problem for the day. As I reached the court-house square, a crowd yelled madly. They stood in front of the court-house jail yelling loudly at someone inside. Some broken iron bars hung from a third story window. Soon the end of a rope was thrown from the window to the waiting crowd below. Many men grabbed it. Framed in the window, with a rope around his neck, and men screaming behind him, was a negro, with eyes as big as eggs.

"Kill the nigger! Kill the nigger!" yelled many voices. "Pop his neck. Make it crack."

The negro's face writhed in fear, as women, men and children hurried from all directions into the square.

A terrific shout went up, and the rope was jerked by many men. The black body shot into space, whirled, and fell crashing into a tree. "Don't shoot," screamed a voice.

A man untangled the wriggling body, and, shaking and horror-stricken, it fell to the ground. They dragged the half-conscious negro to the business square, where a fire burned slowly.

He was placed upright above it, his armpits in heavy post-like crutches.

As the shoes were ripped off, the blaze burned his feet. He wriggled his body frantically as more fuel was placed on the fire and the flame shot upward. "Not too fast," yelled a voice. "Let him burn slow." The doomed Ethiopian's eyes rolled swiftly as the poles were knocked from under him and his body fell into the fire. A blood-curdling "Ouch, ouch, O God! Oh, ouch, O God, O God hab mercy."

"We'll mercy you—you black bastard," yelled a man.

The poles were made upright, and the negro's armpits were fitted into the crutch-like end of them. Wriggling loose, the black mortal tried to eat fire to end his agony. That boon was denied him. A club crashed his wrist. His head went on his breast. His eyes closed a moment, and as the blaze shot higher, they opened in awful pain.

The clothes burned first, and then the flame ate the hair from his skull. The ears charred and melted on his head. He moaned in prolonged and dying pain, "ooooo-ooch, oo-oh-oh-oh."

The burnt body fell from its moorings, and the poles dropped over it. Kerosene was thrown on the hissing fire.

Sick at heart, I turned away. Some children skipped the death-rope gracefully.[18]

At the end of the book, Tully assures us that "I am no reformer, but a weary writer who has been living in the memory of adventure" (336). In 1928, *Beggars of Life* was dramatized by Maxwell Anderson with the appropriate title *Outside Looking In.*

Tully's *Jarnegan* (1925) was a fast-moving novel about a supermasculine figure, something of a self-fantasy, who kills a man in a fist fight, is imprisoned, but eventually becomes a successful Hollywood director. *Circus Parade* (1927), consisting of fictionalized sketches of Tully's life as a roustabout in a traveling circus, was another sensation, chosen by the Literary Guild and banned in Boston. One of the tendencies in Tully's fiction is brought out in an extreme form in this book. Tully's sense of all his fellow outcasts as misfits and oddities leads to an art which always threatens to convert even the most sympathetic characters into caricatures. In *Circus Parade,* his misfits are actually turned into freaks, like "the female Hercules," the love-starved giantess who kills herself over unrequited love, or the "repressed but deeply emotional" beautiful young woman who converts herself into "the Moss-Haired Girl."

Shanty Irish (1928), a book dominated by the fine portrait of his Irish grandfather, describes Tully's impoverished childhood. *Shadows of Men* (1930) is, in Tully's own words, about "the tribulations, vagaries, and hallucinations of men in jail." *Blood on the Moon* (1931) brings the story of his life up through his career as a prizefighter and his decision to become a writer; it ends with the words, "In ten years my first book was published." *Laughter in Hell* (1932) is a novel about an Irishman who kills his wife and her lover. *The Bruiser* (1936) returns to Tully's days as a pugilist, and *A Hollywood Decameron* (1937) describes his life in the movie capital, where he went in the early 1930s, soon to become a publicist for Charlie Chaplin and ultimately to get rich doing articles for screen magazines. His final works included the novel *Biddy Brogan's Boy* (1942) and a series of short biographies of famous contemporaries, *Dozen and One* (1943), introduced by Damon Runyon, who describes Tully as at least "among the first five" of living writers.

During his days on the road, Tully spent a total of about five years in jail, almost all on vagrancy and similar charges. In other words, his "crime" was much like that of Bartleby, a refusal to fit into the workaday world of his society. This was not merely his crime but also the center of vision in his literary art. The category of literature I have established as a touchstone in this chapter about literature by criminals, the picaresque, is precisely the one in which Tully places his own literary achievement. Tully does not, however, see himself as a conventional picaresque novelist imagining the life of an outlaw and outsider, but as one of these beings actually opening up communication with polite society. As he puts it in the introduction to *Blood on the Moon* (New York, 1931):

> To those critics, however kind, who contend that I am a novelist trying to find myself, I will here answer for the first and only time. If I have not been able to invent a new medium in my picaresque books, I have at least been strong enough not to conform to one that is outworn.
>
> I did not study the people in these books as an entomologist does a bug on a pin. I was of them. I am still of them. I can taste the bitterness of their lives in the bread I eat today.

Tully's literary vision of the victim as the criminal is developed most fully in *Shadows of Men,* his book about life in jail. *Shadows of Men* opens with the chapter "Sapping Day" (which had appeared in the *American Mercury* in 1929), presenting in microcosm Tully's sense of a world divided between good citizens who are really vicious monsters, and their no-good victims, who are really good-hearted misfits. It takes place in Kansas, and Sapping Day is a ritualized mass brutalization of the tramps and vagrants:

Lined up on each side of the lane, hundreds of men awaited us. They were well supplied with clubs, stones, and long rattan whips.

At a signal we started to run.

On both sides of us were the leering and tobacco-stained faces of rustics, old, middle aged, and young. The lashing of long whips could be heard on naked skin. The hoboes grunted and staggered on. We, the despised and rejected, ran as if it were part of the day's work.

We had not gone far when two old vagabonds fell exhausted to the ground.

A group of rustics gathered about them.

Mud was thrown in their aged faces. They tried to ward off the brutality by holding their arms over their eyes. They were kicked in the sides. Hard hands slapped viciously against their hollow cheeks.

"We'll teach you, damn you, to stay away from honest men," a rustic in a rubber collar shouted. As if to better shield themselves from the fury, the two old codgers turned on their stomachs and buried their faces in the mud.

A farmer spat tobacco juice in their ears.

They took it in silence.[19]

At the end of the chapter "Sapping Day," Tully and the other vagrants are arrested on the charge of "having no visible means of support" and booked into jail, the scene of the main narrative. *Shadows of Men* concludes with a sketch restating the theme of the opening festivities in Kansas, "A California Holiday" (originally written in 1928 on assignment for the *American Mercury*), the hanging of an innocent convict in San Quentin, accompanied by all the solemn rituals of officialdom. From first to last, the book displays the victimization of the "criminal" by law-abiding society.

The vision of the loner, the outsider, the outlaw, the scapegoat persecuted and tormented by society is carried to its logical extreme in *Philosophy of the Dusk* (New York, 1929), an autobiographical and speculative narrative by Kain O'Dare, a professional criminal who had become a short-story writer. O'Dare, hanging from his thumbs in a midwestern penitentiary, being tortured to make him betray a fellow prisoner, perceives himself as reliving the experience of Christ:

My thumbs were being torn out of their sockets. I was dripping wet with sweat. Every bone in my body was aching. I was gradually slipping away into some vague world. Little flashes were appearing in the darkness. My mother was speaking to me. My sister was speaking to me. I was a child again. And I remembered a story that I had heard when I was a child.

It was the story of Christ nailed to the cross. Bleeding. Taking a repentant thief into paradise. I knew much how Christ must have felt, with his hands nailed high and his feet nailed low. And I knew in the bottom of my heart that Christ had never been a squealer, and that he would have helped John Gaber to escape so he could have reached the bedside of his dying wife. (155–56)

Not all prison writers saw themselves as loners or as part of an outcast class. In one of the most famous prison narratives of the 1920s, *The Twenty-Fifth Man. The Strange Story of Ed Morrell, the Hero of Jack London's "Star Rover"* (Montclair, N.J., 1924), Ed Morrell does describe his own experience of unspeakable torture in San Quentin and Folsom in terms very much like those used by Kain O'Dare, and he does dedicate much of his subsequent life to aiding prisoners. But Morrell's original crimes came from an identification with the very people Tully perceived as part of the hostile organized society, the working class and small property owners. Morrell had been involved with people who had been dispossessed by Leland Stanford's railroad and who were fighting back with night robberies of railroad funds. When his lover's father was jailed in this war, Morrell organized a successful jailbreak, during which a sheriff was wounded, leading eventually to Morrell's imprisonment as a lifer, first in Folsom and later in San Quentin. There he helped, as the "twenty-fifth man," to organize a prison mutiny, which was betrayed. During weeks of unimaginable torture, he experienced an almost mystical vision of his future mission in life, prison reform. Eventually pardoned, Morrell became an indefatigable worker for his "New Era Penology" and a writer of short stories on the side. *The Twenty-Fifth Man,* his major work, is introduced by George Hunt, the first governor of Arizona, who praises the courage of Morrell and the many others who had unsuccessfully fought back against the plundering of California by the railroad magnates.

The autobiographical narratives by prisoners in the 1920s were gradually leading toward a more radical social analysis. Toward the end of the decade, Charles Patrick Murphy, a lifer in the Idaho State Penitentiary who had previously published three books of autobiographical and other writing, brought out *Shadows of the Gallows* (Caldwell, Id., 1928), a lengthy and cogent analysis of crime, its causes, and the history of its punishment. Murphy perceived the so-called criminals as the people on the bottom, the victims of the real criminals, those at the top:

> For thousands of years the whip, the chain, the rack, the gibbet, and the sword, have been used to uphold the laws made by robbers, idlers, and by ambitious lunatics, to punish the "crimes" of the ignorant and the weak. (162)

The prison system rested solidly on the belief that convicts were not human beings, and this assumption permeated all aspects of the institutions, with only rare exceptions. So the spectacle of prisoners actually publishing books which were being received as literary achievements or intelligent social analysis or both was fundamentally threatening. These books posed the same kind of subversive threat that narratives by fugitive slaves had presented in the years between 1830 and 1860; for the practices of the modern prison system, and perhaps that system itself, like slavery, could not last if society recognized its victims as intelligent human beings.

In the economic boom times of the 1920s, however, there was not much opportunity for prisoners to link up with radical social forces in the society as a whole. Then came the Crash of 1929, and immediately a wave of suppression swept over the convicts trying to write from inside the prison to the people outside. This sudden shift of policy was described in 1945 by Herman K. Spector as merely a reaction to the success of prison writing in the 1920s: "Ironically enough, their flurry of success set off a counterflow of reaction and prohibition, during which California adopted the policy that convicts were in prison 'to be punished, not to make money.'"[20] Certainly the prison authorities did not want to see their inmates making money during the Depression. Did they also fear the lines of communication being opened between prisoners inside the walls and the millions of angry people on the other side? Whatever their motives, their new policy of suppression for a while had devastating results, as Miriam Allen De Ford describes in "Shall Convicts Write Books?," an article published by the *Nation* in late 1930: "... cells were searched all through *San Quentin*—not for narcotics or knives, but for manuscripts," and all those found were removed and presumably destroyed.[21]

The suppression was by no means entirely successful. A large breakthrough was made when Robert E. Burns's *I Am a Fugitive from a Georgia Chain Gang!* suddenly became a national sensation in 1932, the same year that scores of coal miners striking in Harlan County, Kentucky, were imprisoned for "criminal syndicalism," a year in which over a quarter-million acres of land in the United States were under cultivation by convicts.[22]

Burns had been launched into national prominence before he wrote his best-selling book; what made it so popular and influential was not only its horrifying revelations about convict labor but also the extraordinary circumstances of Burns's life. Before World War I, Burns had been a successful young accountant. He enlisted, served in a medical detachment at the front, and returned a fairly typical case of what was then called "shell-shock." Drifting into penniless desperation, he was more or less forced by another man to participate in a grocery store holdup which yielded $5.80. He was sentenced to six to ten years on a Georgia chain gang. A Black convict, who "had been in the gang so long and had used a sledge so much that he had become an expert,"[23] deformed Burns's ankle shackles for him; Burns slipped them off his emaciated legs and made a hair-raising escape, eventually ending up in Chicago. It was then 1922. By 1929, Burns was a prominent editor and businessman in Chicago. Then he was betrayed as a fugitive, and Georgia's successful request for extradition aroused a national storm of protest. He was sent to La Grange, the toughest stockade among the 140 chain-gang camps of the state, "a place shunned by everyone of Georgia's 5,000-odd felons" (142). There this well-educated, now widely respected white businessman and journalist comes to share the fate of the most brutally oppressed men in Georgia. He becomes part of a minority in what he calls "hell":

As I was locked in the bull pen, a guard changed the figures on a small blackboard to read:

White prisoners	33
Black prisoners	69
Total	102

I made the thirty-third white convict in the worst chain-gang camp of them all. (142)

Burns escapes once again. And like the fugitive slaves of the nineteenth century, he once again heads north. When *I Am a Fugitive from a Georgia Chain Gang!* was published in 1932, Burns was living a furtive existence under false names in New Jersey.

Burns precisely details the various forms of torture on the chain gang: the "jack," "a relic of the ancient Spanish Inquisition"; the sweat box, in which the prisoner can neither lie nor stand nor sit; the "pickshack," a ten-pound hinged steel bar locked on and around the calf of the leg in addition to shackles and chains; the "necklace," a massive iron collar with five feet of heavy chain; and of course the routine sadistic floggings. He describes the daily horrors of prison life: the crushing labor, the absence of any nourishing food, sleeping in chains, having to get permission to wipe the sweat off your face, rarely being allowed to wash, and so on. And just as foreign to Burns's accustomed life is the intimate contact with Black people, to whom this life is not at all uncommon. So Burns's narrative serves as a kind of surrogate, bringing many readers from his own social class and millions of other white Americans into touch with convict labor and, to some extent, with the Black culture developing within it.

Other prison narratives by white men had reported to their basically white audiences about Black songs. In *You Can't Win,* Jack Black on the night of his first arrest hears "a colored woman" prisoner "singing a mournful dirge about 'That Bad Stackalee'"; he tells us that he later learned "that this song is a favorite among negroes when in great trouble, such as being locked in jail, being double-crossed by a friend, or parting with their money in a dice game. At such times thirty or forty verses of 'Stackalee' invariably restores the laughing good humor and child-like confidence of the wronged one."[24] In *Shadows of Men,* Jim Tully describes a condemned Black convict singing a modern version of a song that we saw as a slave song recorded by William Wells Brown in *Clotel,* but Tully takes this singing merely as evidence that "the Negro" was facing "the meaningless futility of his chaotic life with the laughter of a fool":

> "Hang up de fiddle an' de bow,
> Lay down de shobel an' de hoe,
> Dey's no moah stealin' fo' pooh ol' Ned,
> He's goin' wheah de bad niggahs go."[25]

Burns, however, reporting from inside convict slave labor, the matrix of many Black songs, understands their true significance:

> Just as day was breaking in the east we commenced our endless heart-breaking toil. We began in mechanical unison and kept at it in rhythmical cadence until sundown—fifteen and a half hours of steady toil—as regular as the ticking of a clock.
> In the chain gangs, human labor has been synchronized as the goose step was in the German Army. When using pickaxes, all picks hit the ground at the same time, all are raised and steadied for the next blow with uncanny mechanical precision. So it is with all work, shoveling, hammering, drilling. The convict bodies and muscle move in time and in unison as one man. The tempo and speed is regulated by the chanting of Negro bondage songs, led by a toil-hardened Negro of years of servitude as follows:
> "A long steel rail," croons the leader.
> "Ump!" grunt all the rest in chorus as pickaxes came down.
> "An' a short cross tie," croons the leader.
> "Ump!" grunt all the rest in chorus as pickaxes come up.
> "It rings lik' sil-vah," croons the leader.
> "Ump!" goes the chorus as the picks come down.
> "It shin's lik' go-old," croons the leader.
> "Ump!" and all the picks come up.

And so it goes all day long, with the torrid rays of the blazing monarch of the skies adding their touch of additional misery.
This working in unison is called "Keeping the lick." (143–44)

Later Burns tells us that the usual "lick" was sixteen per minute, a very precise measure of a certain kind of musical time.

Burns by no means feels at one with his Black fellow prisoners. He not only habitually refers to them as "niggers," but when he protests against Georgia's violations of its own penal regulations, one of his complaints is that contrary to the law "whites and Negroes worked side by side" (176). Nevertheless, he has many passages of deep sympathy for the special oppression of the Black prisoners, and he understands that their servitude, unlike his own, is part of the history of a people. When two Black convicts flee in desperation, he perceives their predicament historically, even echoing Frederick Douglass's definition of their white pursuers as "beasts of prey":

Two illiterate Negroes, battling for freedom in the wilds of Georgia's swamps, hunted by white men like beasts of prey. For more than two hundred years the woods and swamps of Georgia have witnessed similar exciting scenes.
And even before that in the wilds of Africa the tragedy was enacted, the purpose the same, the result foretold. (160–61)

And he does not see the hell of convict labor as something unique to the South but as part of "Twentieth Century America, the land of ideals, human justice, liberty and progress" (147).

During this period, relatively little literature was published by women prisoners, partly because far fewer women than men were in prison and partly because their typical crimes—prostitution, shoplifting, drug addiction, begging, check passing—were merely part of the humdrum daily activity of poverty rather than the thrilling adventures of train robbery, bank stick-ups, professional forgery, and burglary. The real-life counterparts of Stephen Crane's "Maggie: Girl of the Streets" were not publishing their stories. If there were any happy hookers like Xaviera Hollander, they were certainly not convicts. And after all, even Moll Flanders had told her tale from the vantage of a now reformed—and wealthy—character.

One notable woman criminal who was something of an author was Bonnie Parker, but she wrote as a defiant fugitive, not a convict. Her famous doggerel ballad "Bonnie and Clyde," published by the Dallas *Morning News* on May 23, 1934, shortly after she and Clyde Barrow were shot to death in a police ambush, does illustrate one tendency in early twentieth-century prison literature, a mixture of rebellion against the state machinery with a sense of guilt and doom. As she puts it in some of the key stanzas:

> Now Bonnie and Clyde are the Barrow gang,
> I'm sure you all have read
> How they rob and steal and how those who squeal
> Are usually found dying or dead.
>
> There are lots of untruths to their write-ups,
> They are not so merciless as that;
> And they fight because they hate all the laws,
> The stool pigeons, spotters and rats.
>
> They class them as cold-blooded killers,
> They say they are heartless and mean;
> But I say this with pride that I once knew Clyde
> When he was honest and upright and clean.
>
> But the law pestered them, fooled around
> And kept locking him up in a cell;
> Till he said to me, "I will never be free,
> So I'll meet a few of them in hell."
>
> They don't think they are too tough and desperate,
> They know that the law always wins;
> They've been shot at before, but they do not ignore
> That death is the wages of sin.[26]

Quite different from Bonnie Parker, both as a criminal and as an author, was Agnes Smedley. Her crime was aiding friends from India in their struggle for independence from British colonialism. In 1918 she was arrested, charged with violating the Neutrality Law, and placed in solitary confinement in the Tombs for about nine months. There she wrote her first published narratives, *Cell Mates,* sketches of fellow women prisoners. This experience as a prisoner helped shape her future as one of America's most internationally respected writers of the 1930s and 1940s. Smedley's books about the Chinese revolution—*Chinese Destinies* (1933), *China's Red Army Marches* (1934), *China Fights Back; An American Woman with the Eighth Route Army* (1938), *Battle Hymn of China* (1943)—are just beginning to come back into acclaim in America after their suppression in the 1950s, but their international reputation has never waned. Her autobiographical novel *Daughter of Earth,* originally published in 1929, reappeared in 1935 with a long new section describing her imprisonment and its effects on her consciousness. Since the reissue of *Daughter of Earth* in 1973, many teachers of literature have come to regard it as the finest proletarian novel of the 1920s and 1930s, and a few make even larger claims for it.

The imprisonment of women convicts is the main subject of two autobiographical narratives published in the mid-1930s: the anonymous *Female Convict* (1934) and Edna O'Brien's *So I Went to Prison* (1938). These two books offer a startling, and most revealing, comparison.

Edna O'Brien is another one of those examples proving Julian Hawthorne's contention that prisons would not survive if enough respected citizens ever experienced them from inside. What makes O'Brien's narrative extraordinary is her sex. She had been vice-president and treasurer of a small manufacturing company. Then in the heady days of the late 1920s she began to branch out as a professional speculator on the stock market. Her first "radical" act was having a stock ticker installed in her office; in this man's world of business, "a ticker in a woman's private office was radical."[27] When the Crash came, she found herself unable to deliver some stock due to a friend, a wealthy woman doctor. She thought little of this until early 1933, when she was arrested for grand larceny, in a case making the front pages of the New York newspapers. Convicted in 1935, she served a year in the State

Prison for Women at Bedford Hills, New York. For her, the main torments of prison are merely the routine physical discomforts, the personal indignities, and the deprivation of her normal luxury and freedom. Nevertheless, she becomes a passionate opponent of penal imprisonment, wondering "Why do we keep deluding ourselves that herding people behind bars prevents crime?" (xi).

Female Convict is a far more powerful book. One of seven children, the anonymous narrator tells how she grew up in her family of ten "in two rooms on the top floor of a tenement," with "two grimy windows" through which seeped "the foul odors of the stockyards."[28] The physical prison conditions described by Edna O'Brien would have been a welcome relief from the childhood experienced by this woman. Her family "had but three beds for ten people," and "there was absolutely no privacy"; ". . . in order that my father or brother might sleep for their work the next morning, my little sister and I played on the roof or on the street until two or three in the morning" (12). They had "no electric lights, no bathroom, no heat":

> In the hall-way was a dirty sink with the only running water in the house. The only toilet facilities were in the back yard. The place was used by twelve families, some of them as large as our own. The yard was a rubbish pile, consisting of the garbage thrown from the windows of the tenements which looked out upon it. An ugly heap of refuse, sardine and tomato cans, beer bottles, whiskey flasks, old shoes and rags. A stable, a junk-yard and a box factory flanked our row of tenements. And across the street stood a kosher slaughter-house.
>
> A row of saloons and booze joints down the street kept the neighborhood in a constant uproar with rum-hound rows and drunken brawls. On Saturday nights the sidewalks were lined with drunks and tipsters. . . . Early every morning, at five o'clock, we were awakened by the bleating of sheep, and the cries of the cattle, as they were driven down the street to the slaughter-house. (12–13)

This is the norm of her prose: terse, precise, straightforward, unsentimental, clear, drawing its enormous strength from the reality of its remembered physical and psychological detail. It is a prose that flows naturally from her class experience, a prose that makes many of the would-be proletarian novels and plays of the 1930s seem hollow imitations. When she does generalize on the basis of her experience, it has the ring of truth, even when she uses language that has been purposely discredited, such as "the unabating exploitation of the masses." For in her next sentence she reminds us, "When I speak of the exploited class I speak from experience" (11).

There is nothing roundabout or abstract in her own understanding of both the causes of crime and the various schemes for punishing or eliminating it. She cuts directly through to the heart of the matter:

> Gangsters? They were grown as naturally in the alleys and gutters of our slum neighborhood as mosquitoes grow in a swamp. Now when I pick up a paper and read of one more noble crusade against gangsters, I smile—and understand. To whip up a crusade against gangsters is as ludicrous as to organize an army of mosquito-swatters while the swamplands where they multiply are left untouched.
>
> Society makes gunmen and then gets excited when their guns go off. (14)

"I understand," she adds, because "I saw how my own brother became a gangster."

Her father drank "to defend himself . . . against the hopeless cage of poverty which permanently imprisoned him. When drunk he was vicious." When Jack, her oldest brother, was nineteen, he returned home with the news that he had been laid off from the automobile parts factory because they had just installed new automated equipment. The result was the experience that makes her perceive the "criminal" as the desperate victim:

> That night my father happened to be drunk. When he learned of Jack's discharge he was enraged. He threw Jack out of the house and told him not to come back until he had another job. Jack was on the street without a nickel. He did the only thing he could think

of—went to a pool-room dive and slept that night on a pool-table. There he met a gang of unfortunate slum lads like himself—most of them farther down the road of ruin than he. Two months later Jack was caught in a hold-up and sent to Joliet for ten years.

Jack's story is the story of thousands of unlucky lads whom our social order labels criminals. (15)

Soon after, her father, who worked in the Gary steel mills, is "burned alive by a wave of fiery iron" (16). She is forced to leave high school. Before long, she is writing bad checks to survive. She is arrested, put in jail for six months awaiting trial, and is then sent to prison on a sentence of seven years maximum.

What oppresses her about jail is not, as it would be later for Edna O'Brien, primarily the physical conditions, though these are bad enough. What makes jail and prison qualitatively more hellish than the cage of her childhood poverty is the relationships among the human beings. This comes out initially as she sits on a bench at her first dinner, where she witnesses a racist incident that fills her with a profound "loathing for the place":

I squeezed in between a burly negress and a thin-faced, tired little woman. The latter gave a snarl of protest and poked me with her elbows.

The former was very friendly. "What's yo' name, honey?"

"Call me Eleanor," I replied.

"Mah name's Mary, dey call's me Black Mary. Whatta yo' all up for, Eleanor?" she queried.

"I guess you'd call it forgery," I replied. We became quite chummy. I rather liked Black Mary. Hers was a frank, friendly face....

The coffee-pourer for some reason had overlooked my companion, Black Mary. She held up her tin cup. "Give me some of dat dere chicory-soup, Mamie," said Black Mary, with a friendly grin.

"You dirty nigger, you got your coffee," said the woman with the pot in her hand, and as she passed behind Black Mary she gave her a vicious kick to emphasize it. Black Mary sat up straight with a cry of pain.

"Please, mam, don't do dat to me.... Ah ain't had a bit a coffee... ah swear ah ain't....

She didn't finish the sentence. The prison flunky came back and

gave Black Mary a resounding smack alongside the jaw with a
dirty towel she was carrying. With an oath, Black Mary leaped to
her feet. They closed in a furious, rough-and-tumble fight. The rest
of the prisoners began to cheer and yell, stamping their feet and
pounding the table with their tin cups.
"Bite her ear off, Black Mary," some of them cried.
Others yelled, "Kill that nigger, kill that nigger." . . .
The whole thing sickened me. I got up and left the table, my meal
practically untouched. I went back to my cell, with a loathing for
the place that burned in my heart like fire. (46–48)

When she arrives in prison, she is marched in company with
the other new "fish" to visit the warden's office. Her description of
this "sorry-looking crew," in "our gray prison dresses" without "a
scrap of underwear or a stocking in the gang," gives a brilliantly
vivid picture of the kinds of women confined as criminals in the
cages of the "penitentiary":

Directly behind Red-frotz [the matron] walked Laura, the Candy
Kid, seventeen year old shoplifter, prostitute and drug-addict, an
inveterate thief, pretty as a picture.
Then Rebecca, thirty year old Jewess, diseased, heavily sentenced after a fourth offence at shoplifting.
Next Old Lady Cuno, eighty-seven, arrested for begging, always
swearing in German and smelling like a fish factory.
Following her, Stephanie, the Czechoslovakian girl, with
swarthy complexion and large black eyes, with her deep guttural
voice, an all-around crook and shoplifter.
Then back of her, Dora Coningsby, drug-addict and prostitute,
with the needle-pocked body.
Next "Bugs," an old Irish woman who smoked a pipe and swore
like a trooper, and had a habit of spitting in your face if she was
angry.
Following "Bugs," Big Bertha, a burly dark-complexioned drug-
addict, with her mottled hair in curlers and skirts above her bare
knees.
Then Pauline, the most beautiful girl in the prison, klep-
tomaniac, graduate of Vassar, with the background of a fine family, up the second time for cashing bad checks.
Behind her, Lillian Johnson, six feet tall, pretty but a badly
diseased prostitute.

Then the Kid from Georgia, a nineteen year old girl taken from a sailor's dive, very badly diseased with red spots all over her body.

After her Rachel Endres, whose husband had framed her, then myself, followed by Ethel Kingsley, morose murderess, who had killed her husband in a row about another woman, and at the end of the rogue's gallery line Joan Barnum, bootleg queen, up for ten years for shooting a policeman.

Thus we lock-stepped down the iron stairs to the warden's office. (80–81)

Once in the office of the warden, she discovers one practical reason why the women were allowed to wear only their prison dresses:

"The first law of this prison," he continued, putting his hand on my shoulder, and gradually running it down my side, a smirk of sensual pleasure playing upon his leather-like countenance, "... is to obey at all times ... to obey your superiors ... to fit in to your surroundings without fault-finding or complaint. ..." His hand had now progressed below my skirt, and he was pressing and patting my naked thigh ... "because unruly prisoners are not wanted here and they are apt to get into trouble. ..." (83)

The main human relationship she has to cling to during her prison life is the love of the man who awaits her outside. At one point even this literally turns into a nightmare. One night she is pleasantly dreaming of her lover, when, as she describes in a splendid piece of narrative art, the dream becomes increasingly hideous until she awakes to find her body almost completely covered with cockroaches. Eventually she manages to escape from prison and rejoin her lover, who flees with her out west. *Female Convict,* like most of the nineteenth-century slave narratives, and like *I Am a Fugitive from a Georgia Chain Gang!,* thus comes to the reader from the mouth of a fugitive being hunted by the law.

Roger Benton, author of *Where Do I Go From Here? The Life Story of a Forger,* does not present himself as either a member of the same exploited class as the anonymous female convict or a more-or-less innocent individual caught in the clutches of circumstance. Benton was a highly skillful professional forger who had chosen that life after years as a professional gentleman on the safe side of the law. He is neither exploited nor oppressed until he becomes a prisoner. Partly because he makes no attempt to justify himself, Benton is able to assume a somewhat detached, almost neutral and objective role in the quest of his narrative, to define "crime" and its causes.

Benton served time in three prisons, including that stint as Eugene Debs's cellmate in the Atlanta Federal Penitentiary and a term at Sing Sing during the administration of one official universally praised by convict writers, Lewis E. Lawes (who wrote the Introduction to Benton's narrative). His most revealing term was his first, a stretch in the Louisiana State Prison at Angola. For there Benton was able to comprehend, for the first time in his life, the organization of his society from the bottom to the top.

Unlike Robert E. Burns, Benton shares not only some of the physical experience of his Black fellow convicts but also, in part, their perception of that experience. Burns had understood Black songs in terms of their survival value in convict labor. Benton goes further. As "the great steel door of the cell room" closes upon him, four Black convicts, and another white man, "one of the negroes began to moan a song almost to himself, so low was his voice":

> "O, Jail-House Key,
> Don't you never lock me in;
> O, Jail-House Key,
> Won't never be bad no more!"[29]

Unlike Jack Black, Jim Tully, and many other convict-authors who tell of Black prison songs as if they were part of an entirely alien, or even comical, point of view, Benton finds that the song "had struck a responsive chord" in his own mind (101). He is soon telling of other Black convicts' songs and their meaning to him:

Several of the Negro convicts had "boxes," that is banjos, and as I sat on my cot that first night . . . the voice of Mississippi Sam and the twang of his "box" suddenly changed the bleak, dour room into a hall and the ennui into entertainment.

> Ain't but one-a thing I done wrong, Baby!
> Ain't but one-a thing I done wrong, Baby!
> Ain't but one-a thing I done wrong, Honey!
> Stopped in Miss'ippi jes' a day too long, Lawdy!
> Stopped in Miss'ippi jes' a day too long!

Time after time Sam sang a song as appropriate to my own situation as that was. . . . In the implication of that fact is the great strength, it seems to me, of the wealth of folksongs made and sung by the Southern Negroes. . . . There is scarcely a human emotion or experience which has not been made into one of their tuneful ballads.

Another of Sam's favorites, which became one of mine, too, is one of the dozens of songs about "that lonesome road" which you will hear wherever southern negroes are. . . .

> Goin' down dat lonesome road,
> O,
> Goin' down dat lonesome road,
> An' I wont be treated dis'away;
> Springs on my bed all broken down,
> An' I ain't got no place to lay my head!

The "O" of the second line, was a long moan which had in it all the misery of the rest of the song. (103–4)

On one side, Benton relates to the cultural experience of both Blacks and illiterate white convicts. On the other side, he is confronted by the brutality described throughout prison narratives, but which he analyzes more deeply than his predecessors. For Benton's insights explain a great deal of perhaps otherwise inscrutable behavior, ranging from Claggart's hatred and Captain Vere's murder of the beautiful Billy Budd to the fact that throughout prison literature, right on to the present, we are constantly confronting the spectacle of guards and other prison officials making male prisoners take off their pants to be flogged. One of the worst beatings the infamous Captain Billy Sanders administers is to Jack, a kind of handsome-sailor convict toward whom the Captain felt some "friendship":

> . . . I know there was something twisted in Billy Sanders' emotional life. there were so many occasions in which he prefaced a flogging by announcing that his wife hadn't given him sexual satisfaction the night before, and he was going to make up for it now, that theories about sadism came back to my mind when I saw the results of Jack's beating and I wondered whether it wasn't Jack's hard luck that night that Sanders had always expressed a liking for him. Something more than punishment or even vengeance entered into that beating (183).

When another convict is deliberately murdered by the guards, who then have his body mutilated, Benton becomes "a murderer in my heart"; "I had never really known what hate was before" (193).

Benton assumes that at least some of his readers have as a main interest the discovery of what makes a person a criminal. He directly confronts these readers, representatives of law-abiding society, as he explains, in a passage echoing many dozens of prison narratives, his response to this murder:

> Every scrap of faith I had ever had in the fundamental rightness of Society, every desire I had ever known to be a recognized part of it, respected by its members, joining in its movements for law and order, vanished before the inpouring floods of bitterness and desire for violence which filled my heart and mind. If these men were representatives of that society, I wanted none of it; if this horrible thing which had just happened was an example of law enforcement, then to hell with the law. To the depths of my soul I was the enemy of all that I had seen and heard that afternoon and evening, and my fierce enmity could find expression only against the abstract thing, Society, and against its laws and its chosen representatives. All thought that I would "go straight" after I left prison was buried in the rough box which held Shorty's body. (193)

Benton's understanding does not stop on the psychological level, for he realizes that the underlying purpose of this prison is profit, that the Louisiana State Prison contains "one of the largest sugar plants in the world, producing a material proportion of the sugar output of the south through the almost Herculean labors of its convicts" (122). In a passage which recalls Melville's plea to the reader of *Moby-Dick,* "For God's sake, be economical with your lamps and candles! not a gallon you burn, but at least one drop of man's blood was spilled for it," Benton indicates the utilitarian function of the prison's brutality and sadism: "Torture and hate and death were the bitter raw materials out of which came Louisiana's sugar to sweeten the coffee of the world and the coffers of the state..." (200).

Earlier, Benton had given an overview of Angola and its historical background, showing his understanding of the special role of Black convicts:

> There were actually six camps at Angola, five of which were composed of men and one of women. Only in the women's camp were whites and colored mixed. Camps A, B, C, and D, were all colored and constituted by far the bulk of the population, furnishing the state with the cheap convict labor it so sorely needed to raise and harvest the mammoth sugar cane crop necessary to satisfy the hungry maws of its gigantic and profitable grinding and refining plant. Once you saw the operation of the plant, the terrific busyness of everybody during the grinding time—once you learned what the plant meant to the state in dollars and cents profit, you understood why it was so easy to convict and imprison a negro in the south, and gained a new understanding of the whole basis for the subjugation of Negroes. Although only forty percent of the entire population of Louisiana at that time was colored, five-sixths of the prison population was made up of negroes.... I learned at Angola that slavery did not cease with the Civil War and that the basis of class distinction in the south is an economic one. (118)

With the murder of Shorty, however, which takes place at Camp E, the white men's camp, Benton extends his perception even beyond the enslavement and imprisonment of Black people: "Thus would the sugar industry of the great state of Louisiana avenge itself upon one of its slaves who had tried to escape from slavery" (186).

At the end, Benton is "rehabilitated" in the sense that he has vowed never again to break the law. But he still does not know where to turn in his capitalist society, for he now sees little difference between a forger, such as his past self, and the "banker or broker" who gains money through "legal subterfuge," or, for that matter, between the murderer and the man who "sets up a factory in which men and women work for less than a living wage, under foul conditions which breed sickness and death" (307). Even with his own lengthy criminal record, he believes that he has done far less harm than "many a banker, broker, industrialist, politician, and even judge, leader of government, minister, lawyer, or doctor, who, while living completely within the law has sacrificed others for his material gain" (307). So he concludes, now out of prison for a year and living in deepening poverty and growing desperation, with the question of his title:

I haven't stolen yet.
Here I am "free."
Where do I go from here? (314)

The very year Benton published this book, 1936, another convict author, Chester B. Himes, was being released on parole after serving seven and a half years in the Ohio State Penitentiary. Himes's first stories had appeared in Black journals. By 1934 he had entered the major leagues, publishing stories alongside those of Hemingway and Fitzgerald in *Esquire*. These stories, as we shall see in a later chapter, took some of Benton's insights one level deeper, for Himes, writing as a Black convict, was projecting views of how Black prisoners appeared to white prisoners. Writing from the assumed point of view of white convicts, he was penetrating to a core of American reality to be laid bare historically three decades later, at the very moment America was to begin discovering Chester Himes as a major author.

By the mid-1930s literature by convicts had moved a long way from the confessional broadside of the eighteenth century and the picaresque adventure story of the nineteenth. All the types of prison literature developed in the preceding two hundred years would continue to have their successors, but there would be very little advancement in form and content for almost three decades. Robert Stroud, the "Birdman of Alcatraz," would publish his *Digest of the Diseases of Birds* in 1943. There would be dozens of narratives detailing the ongoing torture and murder in prisons throughout the nation. Chester Himes's long prison novel about Black convicts, finished in 1937 and originally entitled *Black Sheep,* would finally be published in 1952 as *Cast the First Stone,* now told from the point of view of a white convict from Mississippi. Caryl Chessman's *Trial by Ordeal* (1955) and *Cell 2455 Death Row* (1960) would once again help raise the question of capital punishment. There would be a novel by a Black convict, Paul Crump's *Burn, Killer, Burn!* (1962), in which the Black protagonist ends up tearing open his wounds in jail so he can bleed to death. There would be both confessions and lurid adventure stories by professional criminals, psychological self-examination and sociological analyses of prisons, poetry and fiction. But just as in many other areas of culture and social activity, it would not be until the mid-1960s that connections would again be made to some of the unfinished business of the 1930s. It would take *The Autobiography of Malcolm X* (1965), and the events that gave birth to that great personal narrative by a convict, to prepare us once again to understand the relations Roger Benton and Chester Himes were making in the mid-1930s among Black chattel slavery, convict labor, and the everyday life experienced in modern American society by the two main social classes, the workers and the people for whom they work.

Part III

The Present

CHAPTER 5

Two Novelists
of the American Prison

A. Malcolm Braly

Since the early 1960s, hundreds of books by American convicts have been published—autobiographies, poetry, political and social theory, plays, anthologies, novels. Many of these authors were civil-rights workers, antiwar activists, and revolutionaries imprisoned for their political crimes. But many more were "common" criminals—burglars, armed robbers, drug addicts, rapists, pimps, prostitutes—who became authors because of what they learned while in prison. We are only now beginning to recognize the historical significance of this body of literature by American criminals, and the question of its artistic significance is just being articulated.

One of the earliest in this group of contemporary criminals turned writers was Malcolm Braly. Braly was a burglar and armed robber, a four-time loser who spent almost all his early manhood, from ages eighteen to forty, in our prisons. He began writing fiction during his third term in San Quentin, and his first three published novels were all written behind bars: *Felony Tank* (1961), *Shake Him Till He Rattles* (1963), and *It's Cold Out There* (1966). *On the Yard,* his finest novel to date, offended the California Adult Authority, so Braly had to finish it surreptitiously while serving out a parole violation and wait until he was off parole in 1967 to publish it. *On the Yard* received enthusiastic critical acclaim. Kurt Vonnegut labeled it "the great American prison novel," a judgment few would dispute. Then Braly sank from view. His novels all drifted out of print. The first three, which had been brought out in paperback as Fawcett Gold Medal Originals, left few traces: hardly any reviews are recorded in the indexes; there were no critical articles; none of the three is listed even in the National Union Catalog of the Library of Congress; the physical copies of the books disappeared (Braly himself has only one copy of the original *Felony Tank,* bought on his last stretch in prison for two and a half cartons of Pall Malls, and it is missing two pages). Then in early 1976, a decade after his release, Braly published his autobiography, *False Starts: A Memoir of San Quentin and Other Prisons,* which was immediately recognized as a work of major importance; John D. MacDonald has called it "the ultimate revelation in the search for self." Later that year, Braly's first three novels were brought back into print, and in 1977, after being out of print five years, *On the Yard* was republished (by Penguin).

Ironically enough, it has taken the urban rebellions of 1964–68 and the prison rebellions still going on to create an appropriate audience for Braly's fiction, all of which portrays times before the mid-1960s, that turning point of recent American history. Braly's greatest achievements and his greatest weaknesses all relate to the fact that his consciousness was shaped in that earlier period. His reappearance in the literary world comes during the early stages of the debate about crime and art, imprisonment and creativity. In this setting, Braly recalls the public excitement at the first San Quentin art show, back around 1950, where his paintings won first prize. All this surprise at convicts being artists, he admonishes us, may merely reflect "the exaggerated regard we pay artists and the low opinion we hold of convicts."[1] There is a great truth here, but the kind of public interest Braly describes toward that art show is not the same as the public interest in prison art today. Thanks to what has happened since the mid-1960s, we now understand that prisoners have uniquely important messages to communicate, messages learned out of their own oppression but crucial to our comprehension of society as a whole and to our efforts to change it. The painting for which Braly won Best of Show was a self-portrait, showing himself "against a stand of Monterey pines, those same pines that every amateur artist in the Carmel Valley had turned into a cliché"; the prison Wit dubbed it "Shelley by the Seashore"; Braly agreed with the other convicts that this "self-portrait . . . was suitable only for reproduction on a candy box" (172, 177). There is a world of difference between this kind of art and Braly's writings, which are not some escapist image of a free spirit but the penetrating vision of an artist who learned his subject and the art necessary to communicate it by being defined as a criminal and caged as an animal.

False Starts, an astoundingly honest self-portrait, is indispensable to an understanding of Braly's fiction. For the fiction is what saved Braly's life, and his life is at the heart of the meaning of the fiction. Of course all novelists may be said to be creating in their fiction a kind of imaginative autobiography, and hopefully we have done away with that school of criticism, dominant in the 1950s, that made the lives of authors irrelevant to their art. But most authors are not imprisoned criminals writing books to be read by the society that locked them up. The central theme of *False Starts* is how one person became such a writer. Braly explores this theme with both a deep skepticism and an even deeper affirmation of the human potential. These qualities are not necessarily contradictory; both are part of one of the main messages here and in his fiction, that neither the criminal nor the artist is fundamentally different from the rest of us. (In a half-whimsical moment, he even repeats the suggestion made by the prison Wit that the greatest similarity between the criminal and the artist "is that neither wants to work" [170].) The boy who, like the protagonist of *Felony Tank* or Braly himself, breaks into a dry-cleaning plant to steal clothes and money cannot be set apart in a separate category, to have his identity summed up by the term "thief." Nor does this man who triumphs over his own weakness and the mindless power of the state want us to sum up his identity in the term "writer." The story of this person who grew up and found his identity in prison and in art is inherently a great and profoundly moving human drama. The devastating waste of those imprisoned decades and their triumphant creativity lead to a final affirmation startling in its simplicity and depth: "For myself, I would change nothing because it has all led me to become the man I hoped to be" (375). That man is one who was able to publish four novels, each a message smuggled out of prison to what he calls "the free world."

Felony Tank is the story of a seventeen-year-old boy trying to become a man. Doug Severson is running away, in every sense. Son of a construction worker, a man always on the move with the big jobs, which consume his essence while they furnish him the means to exist, Doug's "earliest memories were tied up with the smell and the feeling of furnished rooms, and the uncertainty of strange neighborhoods."[2] Doug is now drifting in a search for adventure, sex, glamor, respect, for some relationship which will define him as something other than a lonely "kid." He is vulnerable, posturing, afraid, and innocent of everything but crimes.

In his first night in a small southwestern town, Doug is caught burglarizing a store. He claims to be eighteen, so the police throw him into the felony tank. He escapes with two other boys, and in the three days that follow he is plunged into a swirl of shifting roles, achieves his sexual initiation, learns to love, sees one of his buddies killed, and is brought back to the jail, now facing much heavier charges, including, ironically enough, the felony of "escape." Braly used much autobiographical detail in *Felony Tank*: many of the physical details of Doug's burglaries, the impulsively desperate crimes of the three boys, the clumsy and not quite adequate first sexual experience, the clutching insecurity of youth are all described in *False Starts*. But the novel is not primarily autobiographical. It is an archetypal tale of a "kid" discovering an inner integrity as he loses his future.

What *Catcher in the Rye* does for the prep-school boy, *Felony Tank* does for poorer, even lonelier, and more ordinary boys. It is clearly a more universal book, arguably a truer book, and I believe a better one. Although the action is located in a period before the 1960s, the book is not dated. The town could be the set for *The Last Picture Show,* where one can imagine the scene as Doug's pals eat popcorn and "make out" with a couple of girls they pick up at the movies. These boys, however, are aliens and fugitives in the town, and their main goal at the theater is hiding out. They are not mere spectators of the movies but would-be bad men embodying the only attractive roles they see in this society, the ones projected on the screens.

Caught in a web of violence and betrayal, viciousness and carelessness, Doug refuses to reveal the identity of the woman who had, unknowingly, sheltered him, and, with full knowledge, brought him into the grown-up world in her bed: "He could sell himself, but not her" (198). It is this crime of resistance to authority, rather than his burglaries, his car theft and kidnapping, and his escape, which will probably bring him a heavy load of time. The 1961 first edition had a tacked-on happy ending; the latest edition cuts this, restoring the marvelous conclusion of an earlier draft.[3] Doug, stripped of his stolen suit, is left shivering in his underwear: ". . . he was ashamed that even the clothes he'd been wearing belonged to somebody else, and like fairy gold they'd fallen away, leaving him without a single thing he could call his own. Except himself."

In 1957 Malcolm Braly was paroled for the second time. Trying to make a new life at the age of thirty-two, he found himself drifting into the early Beat scene in San Francisco. He even occasionally joined jam sessions, with a rented flute, in North Beach clubs. In *False Starts* he looks back two decades to recall how it felt to dwell "in the hairy heart" of the Beat world:

> For a year or so we were a large social club holding a street carnival, all poets, the freest of lovers, singers of the only song, who were about to recreate an entire society. We were the ridgepole of the world, the essential happening, and we supported each other's pretenses and sheltered each other's defects, and most of these soidisant rebels were being supported with monthly checks from home. I wasn't and that soon made its own problem. (271)

Braly started popping speed heavily and began a run of burglaries. His self-destructiveness culminated in a spaced-out rampage through an office complex in Santa Barbara, netting him a total of eleven dollars. On the way home from that burglary, he made a terrifying discovery: back at the scene of the crime he had somehow dropped the eleven dollars—and, with it, a piece of paper containing his own address. He was to ponder the significance of this "slip" for many years. Then he numbly returned to the address he had provided for the police, and there they soon found him, down from his high. The second-longest period of freedom of his adult life—eleven months—was over.

Braly was once again returned to San Quentin: "I was classified as a Fourth Termer, one of a tiny hard core of apparently hopeless cases, and shuffled through the various entry processes like a case of condemned canned goods" (*False Starts,* 290). All that was left from his "brief vacation," his "short dance in the sun" (288), was his correspondence with the woman who embodied the most romantic of his dreams, Judy, his sixteen-year-old "Love Goddess of North Beach," who was lying in a hospital bed the night he was ransacking those offices searching for money to pay her medical bills. After several months, one of his letters to her came back stamped: "NO LONGER AT THIS ADDRESS." The next evening he began his first novel, a murder mystery set in North Beach.

This book, titled *The Young Dancer,* was Braly's turning point, the exact spot upon which his outward tag "thief" could be removed to be replaced by the tag "writer." It was a book written to be read not by the public world but by the people of his world, other prisoners. The most rewarding criticism he received was from his cellmate:

> When I finished a first draft, my cell partner asked to reread it, and I lay in the top bunk, staring at the bland cream ceiling, listening to the dry *whisk* as he turned the ms. pages. He read all evening, stopping only once to piss, and, finally, a little before lights out he finished and said, "You know, it's okay. It reads like a real book." (294–95)

The novel became in San Quentin "what we called a 'trip' book, one where you could blunk out and simply drift through the atmosphere of the North Beach nights, the sex, music and drugs, pulled along by some fairly unlikely events" (295). *The Young Dancer* has never been published. After finishing it, Braly wrote *Felony Tank,* which we know as his first novel. His second pub-

lished novel, *Shake Him Till He Rattles,* however, obviously has a
lot in common with *The Young Dancer,* for better and for worse.

Shake Him Till He Rattles attempts to be both an accurate
vision of that early Beat scene in North Beach and an exciting
action yarn with a Beat background. Braly obviously had not yet
attained, as he has in *False Starts,* enough psychological or historical distance from his own brief participation in that scene.
Shake Him, like *The Young Dancer,* is a kind of "trip" book, but
the decades that have passed will no longer allow us to drift
through the atmosphere of North Beach nights, the sex, music,
and drugs. The characters are self-conscious, and they posture not
only for each other but also for their readers, thus distorting the
vision and disrupting the action. Yet *Shake Him Till He Rattles*
does succeed in capturing some of the pretentiousness, the naïv-
eté, and the creative energy of that outburst which was to help
bury the 1950s. And despite a contrived happy ending, Braly
succeeds in dramatizing something of both the self-destructiveness and the contradictory will to live which he himself was experiencing as an individual and as part of our common history.

Shake Him Till He Rattles may most rewardingly be read as a
fictional projection of Braly's own predicament and its resolution.
There is a hero, Lee Cabiness, and a villain, Detective Lieutenant
Carver. No very subtle analysis is needed to see that Cabiness is a
kind of fantasy of self; he is the man Braly, many of his fellow
prisoners, and not a few of the rest of us would have liked to have
been, back in the late 1950s anyhow—a jazz musician with tremendous soul, a great lover, a loyal friend, a hero who spurns the
seductive wiles of a rich spoiled playgirl, rescues his true love
from the snares of a big-time gangster and pimp, and saves the
good people of North Beach by snaring the most villainous cop.
The picture of Cabiness hints of "Shelley by the Seashore," Braly's idealized self-portrait. But if Cabiness is the man Braly would
have liked to have been, at least in fantasy, his nemesis, Lieutenant Carver, may be the man Braly feared he might in fact be, the
self-loathing, self-destructive alter ego trying to imprison the
being who embodies his own creative potential.

The novel opens with Lieutenant Carver prowling through
North Beach like a "shark" in an unmarked police car. Everyone

he sees seems to be observing everyone else, "and he watched them all," trying to pierce "their flamboyant disguises" and "their lying poses." He longs to clean up all the filth of North Beach— sex, music, and drugs. Hearing a blast of music from a jazz club, his hand "twitched with disgust." He regards musicians as the worst of the North Beach vermin, "the original carriers of the Beat infection."[4] His most intense loathing seethes for Lee Cabiness and "the ecstatic singing" of his sax: "The thought of Cabiness smouldered in his mind like fire in wet rags, obscure and sullen" (9). To him Cabiness seems the living embodiment of all he most hates.

But what is it that Carver hates most, and why? He is sure that Cabiness is hooked on drugs, and aims to catch him. We soon learn, however, that it is Carver the policeman not Cabiness the artist who is the junkie, literally consuming his own body. What Carver projects onto Cabiness is the self he loathes. In reality Cabiness is what Carver is not, the creative artist, and it is this being that Carver is intent on destroying through imprisonment.

The point of view shifts to Lee Cabiness for the narration of the raid Carver leads on an after-hours joint. Put up against the wall for a shakedown, his "armpits were wet, and the insides of his palms slick with tension" (32). Behind him he hears Carver's voice pronouncing the order that gives the novel its title: "'. . . shake this guy till he rattles.'" But Cabiness is clean, and in the end, when everything is reversed, it is Carver who is left shaking himself till he rattles.

Though Cabiness is not an addict, he does routinely smoke pot and occasionally pop speed. Carver succeeds in setting him up and catching him with a couple of cans of pot. Carver has been entrapping other junkies and using them as informants, supplying their needs with what he keeps from stashes discovered in the line of duty. With Cabiness almost certainly headed for San Quentin, Carver now decides to eliminate his key informant, who has discovered Carver's secret addiction, by substituting envelopes of strychnine for the heroin he usually gives him as a payoff. He may also hope that some of these hotshots will be sold and find their way around North Beach, thus helping to clean up the place. Some do. Cabiness's best friend, shooting up for the first time, dies as soon as the strychnine hits him. Cabiness's true lover, who has been led into addiction by the pimp who has gotten her to turn tricks, also gets one of the envelopes. In the nick of time Cabiness arrives, saving her from a sudden death and rescuing her from a living one. The contrived happy ending has begun.

Though contrived and implausible on a literal level, this ending may represent the most profound psychological truths being dramatized by the novel. It presents in fiction the turning point that was actually being reached, in the very act of writing that fiction, in Braly's life.

Braly was perceiving that his creative self had a devious enemy, constantly plotting on a dark and secret level to trap and imprison him. That enemy was also a part of himself. It was that hidden force which was always destroying his freedom and his creativity, tricking him into blunders that would surely lead him back to prison. Who else had left that piece of paper with his own address at the scene of his last crime? "The prison," he tells us toward the end of *False Starts,* "was only my chosen instrument in the willful destruction of my own life" (364). If Cabiness is a version of Braly's creative self, is not Carver a form of his destructive self? If so, then the conclusion of *Shake Him Till He Rattles* can be seen as a kind of exorcism, in which Cabiness, representing the creative and loving artist, turns the tables on his secret enemy, leaving that self-loathing, vicious policeman locked up to die.

The reversal begins with Cabiness plotting against Carver. He sends the detective a tip that a huge stash of heroin can be found at a certain apartment, actually the home of Cabiness's friend killed by the hotshot. When Carver arrives, Cabiness steps from behind him and knocks him unconscious. Cabiness shakes down his unconscious enemy, finds his hidden supply of heroin, and washes it into the sink. He empties Carver's gun, and locks him in the dead man's small bedroom. Carver is now in prison. Cabiness knows that in eight hours Carver will be miserable; in sixteen, violently sick. Cabiness plans to finish him off merely by waiting and then calling the police to report "an addict kicking his life out":

Now Carver was hung in his own web. That was enough. Cabiness knew he couldn't give the hotshot back to Carver. The energy,

> the anger, the outrage that had first flashed the idea into his mind
> had blended into a weary understanding. Now he only wanted to be
> out of it. That was enough.
>
> He took the envelope over to the sink and slowly emptied it down
> the drain. Then in a sudden shock of rage and loss he crumpled the
> empty envelope and threw it against the wall. It bounced back at
> his feet, and he kicked at it savagely, sending it scratching across
> the floor.
>
> He sat down to wait. (168)

That piece of paper seems out of his control, bouncing back at him
like some perverse voluntary agent. Then Cabiness cannot control himself to follow his plan. The sounds of Carver's agony are
too much for him; he leaves.

When Carver recovers consciousness, he becomes as violently
sick as Cabiness had foreseen. As his body revolts against him, he
frantically searches himself for heroin. Cabiness, however, had
not taken into account Carver's ability to escape from his cell.
With a detailed knowledge of the skills his author had used in his
burglaries to break in, Carver forces the lock and manages to
break out, into the next room. Like his author, he meets his fate
on the other side of the forced door. There he finds the piece of
paper inadvertently left by Cabiness, the wadded envelope:

> Something about the dirty creases and the torn corner snapped a
> train of associations for him. He picked it up and carefully unfolded
> it. Then he tore it open and touched his tongue to the dusty paper.
> Stuff!
>
> There was a thin line of powder along the bottom crease, and
> trapped in the small pocket between the glued edge of the flap and
> the actual lip of the envelope there was a good fix. (171)

So Cabiness does not have to call the police or consciously give the
hotshot back to Carver. Carver destroys himself with the contents
of the carelessly left piece of paper. At the end, Cabiness is free.

When Braly betrayed himself with his dropped piece of paper,
he was sent back to San Quentin on an indeterminate sentence.
He served four more years. Then once again he was paroled, now

thirty-seven years old. This time as he entered the outside world, he was not just "a failed thief and a desperate fuckup" (*False Starts,* 309). *Felony Tank* had already been published, and *Shake Him Till He Rattles* was on its way out.

Before leaving prison, Braly had begun work on what was to become *On the Yard,* his major fiction, "a long collective novel" (*False Starts,* 330) woven out of the fragmented lives and myths of San Quentin. He knew that the Adult Authority, which had disapproved of what they had seen of *Shake Him Till He Rattles,* would never allow him to publish this book about prison itself, so he was careful never to leave the manuscript where one of the guards might start reading it. On parole, he had gotten a contract, with a large advance, to finish the book. Living outside Los Angeles, with life going reasonably well, Braly suddenly found himself with a zealous new parole officer, who threatened to violate him for driving a car, for having a woman spend the night in his apartment, or for writing anything he disapproved of. (In California there is no appeal from a parole violation; the agreement signed by all parolees states that "any parolee may be violated at any time with or without cause" [*False Starts,* 333].) When Braly had only six months left to serve on his parole, this new P.O. discovered the contract for the prison novel. "'Has this book passed the department censors?'" he asked.

"In an earlier version," I lied.
"And when will this be published?"
"I can't say, it's not finished. Probably not for some time, and certainly not before I'm off parole."
"Your parole can be extended." (*False Starts,* 345–46)

Braly had become serious with a woman, and he now asked his P.O. permission to marry. He was turned down. So he moved with her to San Francisco, thinking he would thus be able to shift his jurisdiction and obtain a different P.O. Three days after he mailed a letter to his P.O. in Los Angeles informing him of his new address, two parole reps arrived at his apartment to take him into custody for parole violation. With only a few months left to serve out his parole, Braly found himself back in prison, violated for three offenses: driving an automobile without permission, living with a woman, and leaving Los Angeles County without permission. For these crimes, the Adult Authority made him serve another two and a half years. During this final period in prison, he completed two novels: *On the Yard* and the only one of his books he never mentions in *False Starts, It's Cold Out There*.

It's Cold Out There, Braly's third published novel, should certainly not be read as autobiography. On the other hand, the book draws heavily on Braly's experiences during his previous parole. In *False Starts*, Braly gives us a direct portrait of himself as he stepped into "the free world" back then:

> I was now thirty-seven, close to two hundred pounds, beginning to gray. I was healthy, egocentric and there was little in my appearance to suggest how strange a man I had become....
>   I can now recover the simple arithmetic I ignored that day as I flew south along the Pacific coast—in the last twenty years I had been free ten months between Preston and the Nevada Prison, free eighteen months between my first and second jolts, and free eleven months between the second and third. A month better than two and a half years. For over seventeen years I had been trained to dependence on a system which had casually sustained my physical survival while it had, with equal casualness, starved my every other need. Most of what I knew of this vivid and richly varied outside world and those mysterious others, women, I knew from the stories I had heard from my fellows. I had studied the world through magazines and television, through advertising. For years I had watched one or two movies a week and read as many novels. (*False Starts*, 331–32)

Braly had begun his parole in an archetypal southern California apartment complex in a Los Angeles suburb. *False Starts* describes his difficulties coping with the practical details and penetrating the labyrinths of this new world. He realizes that "however harshly, the joint mothered us—fed us, kept us warm, treated our ailments—and now, away from home, I could hardly remember to pay the rent, and the gas bill and the phone bill, let alone take proper care of my teeth" (346). Even more treacherous were the mysteries of human relationships. He describes his clumsy affair with Lorna, a divorcee living in the next apartment, whose fantasies ironically include an image of him as the man "strong enough to protect her in this savage world" (340).

It's Cold Out There turns the art of caricature upon this experience. A clue to Braly's relation to his own art can be found in the work of a character in the novel, a cartoonist named Grover Alexander—"Grove" for short. When Braly describes Grove's favorite cartoon creation, he gives us something like a self-portrait of the artist doing a self-portrait:

> He drew plump, short-necked people with big, soft-looking noses and round eyes and eyebrows that angled up to suggest a chronic uneasiness. One character had come to seem the essence of the type, and Grove's best work centered around this living malaprop, who always stood, bland and faintly puzzled, pinned by his wife's incredulous scorn in the middle of some surrealistic goof. His chronic state was one of innocent perversity—he put the milk outside and the cat in the icebox, pulled flowers and left weeds, and appeared among his wife's bridge guests in his underwear, looking for the glasses he was already wearing.... Grove was fully aware of the element of self-portraiture in his creation.[5]

What this self-portrait is to Grove (who has neither wife nor cat), the protagonist of *It's Cold Out There* is to Braly.

That protagonist—named JD Bing—is a marvelous creation. He too is thirty-seven years old as he begins his parole in the Los Angeles area, and he too has spent almost twenty of these years in prison. He is a good man, simple but not simple-minded. Very large and powerful, he was known in prison as "Big One." In his search for survival, freedom, and dignity, JD veers between pathos and comedy as he stumbles through the treacherous mysteries of "the free world"—trying to sell encyclopedias, to become a lover, to fit in with the bizarre fantasies of a Los Angeles suburb.

JD is like a huge baby, pushed into that cold world out there after twenty years in his joyless but secure prison home. He now appreciates the value of "twenty years of free food" (35), of "clean socks every night" and "clean clothes three times a week" (64), of being accepted as part of an institution, of irresponsibility. In "the free world," he discovers with alarm, he must pay for everything. To JD, who "had never owed a bill before," an unpaid debt to a cheap hotel begins to rise in his mind "like the level of fire danger in a dry forest" (36).

Most of the other characters live somewhere on the edge of Los Angeles in a suburban apartment complex named the Bali Hai. There JD makes his one and only sale of encyclopedias, to a neighbor of the cartoonist Grover Alexander, an old man who also turns out to be a kind of artist. The old man is a fine craftsman who prints huge quantities of phoney checks for his son-in-law. He uses one of these forged checks to pay JD for the set of encyclo-pedias. While naïvely waiting for this check to clear his account, JD falls, unwashed, unshaven, and increasingly desperate, into the depths: a flophouse, charity meals in a mission, selling his own blood. When he finally realizes he has been stung, JD returns to the Bali Hai and extorts from the crooked son-in-law a five-hundred-dollar blackmail payoff. Now he can eat, wash, shave, sleep in a real bed, and even buy some fashionable clothes. He soon sports a stylish suit, his gigantic arms encased in French cuffs (bought because he was ashamed to admit he'd never heard of them) pinned up with paper clips.

Meanwhile, his sex life has begun. In another Bali Hai apart-ment, he accidentally opens a door, revealing a woman behind her husband:

> . . . he realized that the woman he had dimly seen was naked. She stood with a startled expression, her hands reaching to cover her-self. Suddenly the room seemed to heave, and something like heat lightning flashed in front of JD's eyes. His lips parted. He stared speechless and made no resistance as Haas shoved the door closed.
> *Jesus!* he thought. He closed his eyes, and the woman was as vivid in his mind as she had been in the flesh. . . . Except for one night in a burlesque theater two weeks ago, this was the first naked woman he had ever seen. (9–10)

At the very next Bali Hai apartment he calls on, he finds Kristie. Kristie is a caricature of Lorna, the divorcee living next door to

Braly, who had fancied him her savage lover. She too lives in a world of driving fantasies and guilt-ridden sex. She keeps a list of her men, defined by their roles, and receives viciously obscene phone calls that torture her with her own self-loathing. Like Lorna, her aggressive affairs with middle-management men wherever she works leave them conniving to get rid of her. When JD walks into her apartment, she has just been fired, with the collusion of her last lover, Nathan Holleran, vice-president of a company that manages NASA projects (ever since she joined the WAFs at the age of eighteen, Kristie has "worked near, if only on paper, flying things" [99]). Kristie's fantasies, unlike Lorna's, have already drifted over the line into insanity. Her obscene telephone calls are imaginary; her lovers are physical incarnations of imagined beings.

To JD, who hungrily watches Kristie in her dressing gown as he gives her his pitch for Universal Encyclopedias, she is simply the good lay he has been waiting for. To Kristie, however, "this handsome man had come to show her a collection of jewels she was considering buying" (12). She senses his excitement and takes it "as natural—a customer's man calling on a young and beautiful baroness" (12). As JD's voice drones on about the encyclopedias, he dissolves into a bare physical presence, an "anonymous maleness, a satisfyingly large and solid mass blurred on the edge of her vision but sharply recorded in her nerves" (13). He thinks she is just teasing him, and gets angry. She responds with a new fantasy: "The customer's man with the jewel collection vanished, and in his place a bandit leader stood watching her with lustful and contemptuous eyes" (13). Then "the bandit captain" seizes her: "It is rape, she told herself, and behind her closed eyes she seemed to look up into the intense blue of a Mediterranean sky, feeling the intricate irritation of the knotted grass beneath her back and the wind on her bare legs. She gasped and sobbed at the savageness of this attack" (14).

When this neo-Mediterranean product of the Hollywood dream factory vanishes, she finds herself "lying crushed beneath a door-to-door salesman who had neglected to shave that morning" (14). He now demands that she buy the encyclopedias; she argues that if he were "*any* kind of a man" he'd give them to her for free. Then she destroys JD's own fantasy, the main male role built up in prison (and elsewhere), of the brutal he-man lover:

> "Any kind of a man? I was all the man you could handle a few minutes ago."
> "Oh, take a bow, hero," Kristie taunted fiercely. "Take a big bow. You were like an ape, a slobbering ape."
> "Yeah?" JD said unhappily. "Maybe you'd like an ape. An ape ought to just suit you."
> "An ape doesn't talk. An ape doesn't sell encyclopedias." (15)

Before long, however, JD is back, he imagining himself the great lover, she, when she learns of his prison background, now elaborating a suitable role for JD, her "bandit chieftain, a man of swift and ruthless action, an ardent lover, yet a man familiar with fine things, as well as a man who was the confidant and secret advisor of kings and presidents" (160). JD will avenge her by attacking and robbing Nathan Holleran. JD plunges directly into his role. He lurks in Holleran's garage, and then attacks him with his bare hands, relying on his size and strength. But Holleran fights back. In the midst of this first and only attempt at strong-arm robbery, JD discovers that, like many big, strong men who are rarely forced to fight, "he didn't know how" (173). Holleran subdues JD and holds him at gunpoint while he calls in the private police who patrol his elegant neighborhood. Facing JD is now the vision that had been haunting him, the return to prison:

> If he had never been allowed to leave, he could have found ways to bear it, as the blind adjust to darkness, but to go back now would be like dying, or worse, a form of death where the mind continued to live on while the body decayed. (132)

We don't want this to happen to JD, and there might have been a good way of ending the novel less grimly. But Braly, who did go back four times, veers from the truth of the situation and contrives an ending which is little short of ludicrous. Holleran realizes that Kristie has put JD up to this, and so this wealthy corporate executive, still battered from JD's blows, sends the police away and lets JD go free. Kristie, meanwhile, is finally recognized as clinically insane, and it is she, rather than JD, who ends up institutionalized. At the end, she is locked in a room in an asylum, waiting for the imaginary phone to ring again so her mysterious obscene caller can tell her, in detail, of her rottenness.

There is much in *It's Cold Out There* that reminds me of Nathanael West at his best—the vision of the southern California dream factory, the dozens of almost identical apartment complexes "with names like Le Sabre, The Cavalier, The Pink Pussy Cat, The Flamingo" (7), the interactions of the characters with each other's fantasies, some of the emblematic minor characters. The finest of these is "the Scavenger," an old man who has been reduced to pure animal existence, and who flits through the action as a mere rummager through the garbage of California apartment courtyards, except for the fact that he too is a writer:

> He lived entirely on refuse, and the single characteristic, other than to cover himself, that distinguished him from any other foraging animal was his rudimentary sense of religion. Though he had, years before, gradually abandoned the painful struggle to communicate with anyone, he still retained a magical apprehension of the power of language, and among his gleanings of bread crusts, bones, and vegetable trimmings, he included pencil stubs, nearly exhausted ball-points, broken crayons, and odds and ends of paper and cardboard. (167)

"Crouched in the security of his burrow," he becomes an author, transforming the refuse of this society into a world of meaning:

> Often he wrote along the sides of larger cardboard boxes, turning the box around and around, so that sometimes an enormous sentence would spiral down from the top left-hand corner, filling all four faces, cutting through such bland communications as BAB-O CLEANSER, Disinfects and Deodorizes, 2 Doz. 14 oz. Cans. (167–68)

The Scavenger writes for himself a daily signboard, each with a different message: "THE CROSS IS THE MARK OF THE BEAST" (8); "WE ARE HIS TROUBLED SLEEP" (79); "THE GRASS-HOPPER SHALL BE A BURDEN" (187).

It's Cold Out There displays a chilly world in which buying and selling has become the fundamental human relationship. The characters, bumping into each other's dreams and fantasies without communicating, inhabit an environment where writing and other art have been reduced to the merchandise of a door-to-door salesman peddling universal knowledge, the grotesque self-portraits of a cartoonist, cryptic religious messages scrawled over advertisements, and colorful checks that come back stamped "FICTITIOUS" (45). One wishes that Braly had not buried parts of this vision under that phoney ending. But then *It's Cold Out There* may be considered the last of his apprenticeship novels. After this, he was ready to complete *On the Yard*.

That recurrent nightmare of the twentieth century, a world bounded by walls, a place where people have numbers instead of names, a society ruled by an omnipotent bureaucracy and its omnipresent police, first appeared in American prison literature, as we saw in the previous chapter, right after the turn of the century. The literary and movie versions of this nightmare, from Eugene Zamiatin's *We* to the film *THX 1138,* have always fallen short of the realities of the large American penitentiaries. *On the Yard* is a vision of one of the best known of these nightmare worlds, San Quentin, particularly in the 1950s and early 1960s.

In all of Braly's novels to date, he has used a shifting, multiple point of view. This is not always successful in the first three books, where it often makes us move away from characters just as they are beginning to come to life. In *On the Yard,* however, where Braly has mastered the ability to create living characters in a few pages, the multiple point of view succeeds in creating a brilliant mosaic of prison life. There is no single protagonist, and the stories of the different men interweave in complex patterns. In the early novels, especially *It's Cold Out There,* the fantasies, dreams, and roles of different characters sometimes collide and determine each other's fate. This vision is perfected in *On the Yard.*

Although there is no central character in the usual sense of that term, there is one character who forms a center for the action, a schemer whose web includes all the lines of fate traced in the book. This is inmate Oberholster, still called Billy by his mother, but known on the yard as Chilly Willy. In *False Starts,* Braly writes that "our ideal convict" was "a zombie of coolness"— "hard, smart, utterly certain" (246). This is the role played by Chilly Willy, chief manipulator of the yard, who controls the importation of nasal inhalers used as the main source of speed, runs the big betting syndicate, loans cigarettes, the prison currency, at 50 percent interest, hires torpedoes to collect any bad debts, and disdains all human relationships except power over others. One of the main stories in *On the Yard* is the tale of how Chilly Willy ends up "blowing his cool."[6]

Chilly, like Braly, had been involved with crime from his youth, beginning with the burglary of a store. A few months after his release from reform school, he "staged a string of armed robberies with two other boys," covering three states and ending in a running gun battle, not totally unlike Braly's own youthful spree. Like Braly and his two companions, Chilly and the other two boys "were sent to prison in the state of their arrest, and upon completion of that sentence they were extradited home in chains to be tried for the robberies they had committed before they left" (193). Chilly is paroled at age twenty-four, "a two-time loser with almost seven straight years of reform school, county jail and prison behind him. He had never held a job. He had never had a girl friend" (193). When he is sent back to prison, he is classified as a "habitual criminal." I do not mean to suggest that Chilly Willy is an autobiographical character, any more than several of the other prisoners who are shaped partly out of Braly's experience. Chilly's character is certainly not a self-portrait, conscious or unconscious. But it is significant that of all the prisoners, Chilly's life in externals most closely resembles Braly's. Chilly is the man whom Doug Severson, the youth in *Felony Tank,* will hopefully not grow up to be.

The man most hated by Chilly Willy is Paul Juleson, one of those who has lived a respectable, lawful, apparently successful life only to become branded a "criminal" for a single act that takes just a few moments in the decades of his existence. Juleson, like Braly an abandoned child, had "planned in his orphan dreams" to "use marriage as a beachhead for his assault on some community" (222). His marriage, to a deeply innocent and romantic young woman from a large Italian family, "had been a picture wedding" (220). But his wife turns out to be not the person of his fantasy: "He had superimposed a dream over her face. And the dream hadn't even been his own, but one he had borrowed" (219). She has her own fantasies and roles to play. Like Kristie in *It's Cold Out There,* she "had rehearsed for life in movie houses and in front of the television set" (222). So Juleson turns out to be just "an ordinary man who beat his wife for all the ordinary crummy little reasons" (158). Except that she hemorrhages internally from one of these beatings, and Juleson thereby becomes a murderer, and a prisoner.

Juleson thinks of himself as different from the other prisoners, whom he regards as "animals" (47). He is quiet, bookish, outwardly dignified. His own strategy is "to do his own time" and keep free of the other inmates of "the prison zoo" (47). Despite all their superficial differences, Juleson and Chilly resemble each other in telling ways, ways that will prove fatal for both. Each considers himself a being superior to the other prisoners, and each is determined to remain aloof from any intimate relationships.

In a moment of weakness, Juleson decides to borrow a carton of cigarettes from Chilly, who monopolizes the prison trade, at the usual payback rate of three for two. He finds himself unable to pay. Chilly, who has penetrated Juleson's self-deceptions, revels in the chance to destroy his posturing and drag him down to the level of those he disdains: "'You walk this yard like you were wading through shit, like you were caged with animals. But then you wanted something the animals had, and you held your nose and asked for it, and you got it. Now you don't think it should cost you anything'" (140–41). Chilly gives the order for Juleson to be beaten by his main goon, Gasolino, a beefy killer half-crazed from sniffing carbon tetrachloride.

Juleson rejects the prison officials' offer of protective custody, stubbornly refuses to snitch on Chilly, and prepares to confront his fate on the yard. He challenges and fights Gasolino, who runs away when a guard starts shooting. Gasolino, driven by shame, now drinks carbon tet and, "his guts . . . falling out his ass" (157), dies in agony—like Juleson's wife. The reversals are intense and ironic: Juleson attains his human dignity by abandoning his superiority to the other prisoners and accepting their code, by leaving his precious books to fight with blind instinct, by committing the same kind of violent act that had hurled him into this purgatory; and this very act will cost him his life.

Chilly Willy now looks for a replacement for Gasolino. One conveniently presents himself in the form of "Stick," who seems to Chilly just another "gunsel" looking to make a quick reputation, leader of a gang known as the Vampires. The Vampires seem a large gang, judging by the number of drawings of their symbol the prisoners have been encountering lately. But actually Stick, a tall, skinny nineteen-year-old, is the only one left of his original group of three, which is not, in his frenzied mind, a gang at all, but the core of a revitalized Nazi party of which he is destined to be the Fuehrer. Stick's plans are far deeper than Chilly's. What he wants from Chilly is an assignment to the night list at the gym, so that he will be able to make a legendary escape, clad in the elaborate Nazi uniform he has been secretly patching together, in a balloon that his cellmate has been artfully constructing for years. Stick accepts from Chilly the job of taking care of Juleson, who now in his mind becomes "the Hit." He elaborately plans the attack as a grand military adventure, and, appropriately enough in the library, slips up behind Juleson, who has just now recovered his dignity as a person: "The first blow was solid, directly across the dome of the head. The Hit's knees buckled and the book slipped from his hand and dropped to the floor" (227). Chilly is somewhat surprised to learn of Juleson's death and finally realizes, since this was not a gang attack, that Stick must be a loner.

Stick gets his reward, his gym assignment. He murders his cellmate, stuffs the huge balloon and his contrived Nazi uniform into a duffelbag, makes his way to the roof of the gym, secures the balloon and attaches its mouth over a ventilator shaft, and then calmly sets a fire in the room below. The hot air from the fire

gradually fills the balloon. The fire bursts into the crowded gym-
nasium. During the tumult and panic, several of the lives traced
by Braly interweave and we witness a revelation of their inner
meanings. Meanwhile, Stick is floating ecstatically over the
prison walls (like the airborne vision in the beginning of *The
Triumph of the Will*). Eighty-six men are killed in the fire. Stick
is easily recaptured, clad in his resplendent uniform, permanently paralyzed from a broken back suffered when his balloon
plummeted to earth. Unlike Stick, his cellmate never seriously
intended to escape in his handmade fantasy, and one of the seams
was just tacked in to be ritually resewn.

Meanwhile, some of the prison officials had been planning Chilly's undoing. They have assigned him a cellmate, despite the
standing order, finagled by Chilly, that he is never to have one.
The cellmate is a young drag queen, known back in Tracy, a
prison for young inmates, as "Candy Cane." Chilly becomes the
envy of the yard, but he, his total cool still intact, sneers "'that's
not my game'" (184) and works, unsuccessfully, to have Candy
Cane taken away. Of course everybody knows who ordered the
attack on Juleson, and Chilly is brought in for questioning. The
goon squad humiliates him by merely demonstrating their total
power over him. They force him to see through his own pretenses,
to recognize that "any power he had gathered was illusionary"
(234). When he returns to his cell, his shell partly cracked, his
attitude toward Candy changes. Chilly now is forced to consume
his own product, the speed-soaked cotton from the inhalers, in
order to evade the real world, and he shares these with Candy.
"She" easily seduces him. Soon the whole yard realizes that
Chilly is "finally blowing his cool" (258), hanging around in his
cell "laying up with that sissy and a tube of cotton" (272). Chilly,
for the first time in his life, discovers that he is a human being
capable of pleasure and something like affection; he comes close
to having an intimate and loving relationship with another person. But that's not what it looks like on the flash pictures that are
suddenly popped of them, or how it seems as they both are subjected to a brutal "proctological examination," ostensibly to determine which one was "pitching" and which one "catching."
Chilly ends up reduced to the scared kid he had hidden inside

himself as the authorities write home to his mother to inform her that "your son has been apprehended in the performance of a homosexual act" (278–79).

These are just a few of the characters whose lives constitute the half year of San Quentin existence re-created in *On the Yard*. In some senses the central character on the yard is not Chilly Willy, who thinks he controls everything, but Society Red, who does nothing and to whom nothing ever really happens. Red's true home is the prison, and his brief paroles have been mere sprees, likened to those of an old timer in the military between reenlistments. The book opens with a blues stanza:

> Born in this jailhouse
> Raised doing time
> Yes born in this jailhouse
> Near the end of the line

Then comes the first sentence: "Society Red was the first man on the yard that morning." At the end, Red overhears "two kids, just brats," whispering about the big score they are going to make as soon as they get paroled:

> Some third kid had clued them to an old broad who lived alone, and kept a half-million cash in a shoe box under the bed.
> Red shook his head in sour wonder, trying to remember how many times he had heard of this same shoe box.

Red has the very last word, just after he hears this fantasy, when another old timer asks, " 'What else is new?' " " 'Nothing,' Red said."

This is both the greatest strength of the book and its greatest weakness. Braly magnificently describes the deadening sameness of prison, the fantasies that make possible life within it and that cause the extinction of many of these lives, the society of losers who play at being winners, the mindless power of the system and the impotent creativity of its victims, the ways in which the inmates reproduce the exploitative relationships of the capitalist society which has entrapped them, the diversity and potential of the thousands of lives concealed within the prison uniform. With few exceptions this is all presented as though it were timeless and unchanging, except in superficial detail.

One exception is the belief that "a new inmate was emerging, the waste product of a new society" (274). This is "a growing breed of career convict, largely alcoholic check writers" who could be trusted to minimum security jobs; "Sometimes they ran off, but their escapes seldom amounted to more than drunken sprees where they ran wild for a few weeks with someone's checkbook or credit cards before they were caught and returned like runaway boys" (274). They are not, however, fundamentally different from Society Red.

Another view of change is one described explicitly in *False Starts*. Just before his 1962 parole, Braly sensed that Quentin was changing:

> The yard was abuzz. Seven inmates had been killed in the last ten days, and the smart heads said it had been because a bunch of gunsels had fallen out over a big heroin deal, but that the joint was filling with a violent spirit, and the morning before I went to the board I saw Conejo Rojos beaten to death by militant Indians armed with baseball bats.... The blacks were angry. The Indians were angry. The gunsels arriving from Tracy were anxious to make reps as tough dudes. There was a different spirit in Quentin. The blacks said, Why struggle and suck ass to make parole when they send you right back to the same mess that first put you in the Man's hand?
> The Cynic said, You keep buttoned up and get back to camp. This joint is beginning to go hard rock. (328)

Then when he is returned to Quentin after his parole violation:

> I hit the yard. It looked the same, but a few things were different. There were rumors of strikes and riots, and I talked to one man who was suing the state for peonage because they forced him to work without pay. The Warren Court had filled everyone with writ

fever. Twice a day the hardrocks and the psychos formed in a wavering line the length of the yard while an MTA issued them tranqs. They were now gentle as rabbits. But the blacks were salty and there were no tranqs for their problems. (*False Starts,* 355–56)

This is a misunderstanding of the historical situation, a misunderstanding that represents the greatest weakness of *On the Yard.*

What gives *On the Yard* its vitality and its profound truths is Braly's ability to get inside the heads of many different kinds of prisoners. There is no single self-portrait. But Chilly Willy, Paul Juleson, Society Red, even Stick, and many others—each contains a part of Braly's own consciousness and experience, and each is thoroughly convincing. Braly becomes the collective voice of all these prisoners. But this ability breaks down when Braly attempts to render the lives and feelings of Black prisoners, all of whom remain unconvincing stereotypes. The most completely rendered scene with Blacks shows them participating in a caricature crap game. However, Braly also gives us one brief glimpse of a group of "ten Negroes with shaven heads" who "called themselves Simbas" (152). *Simbas,* of course, is an African word for lions, and these men are apparently Black nationalists. They never reappear. But toward the end, Braly indicates symbolically that their organization is just a somewhat more up-to-date substitute for Stick's Nazi gang of Vampires, with all its destructive fantasizing. He describes the fate of one of the old Vampire drawings, now being replaced by its symbolic equivalent:

Now the drawing was beginning to weather and fade, and it had been partially overlapped by a new figure, a four-legged animal of indeterminate kind, though clearly possessed of slanting eyes, and an entire mouthful of teeth, bared in a crude but vigorous display of ferocity. Scrawled beneath this animal was the single word: *Simbas.* (283)

The Black nationalism developing in American prisons in the early 1960s was neither a new form of Nazism, nor just another gang, nor a mere fantasy. It was to become the most important single force changing life in prison and the literature emerging from prison, and a crucial historical movement within American society as a whole.

Because he has failed to comprehend the historical significance of the changes going on both in the prison and on the outside, Malcolm Braly remains—so far—limited in range as a novelist, despite all his profound insights. It has yet to be seen whether he can use what we have learned since 1965 about our lives before then or after. Even in *False Starts* he shows few connections between his own experience in the forty years of his chronicle, 1925–65, and the monumental changes taking place in the world. Part of this may reflect the isolation of the world in which he spent most of this period, cut off by walls, guards, and machine guns from what he sardonically refers to as "the free world." But those prisons in which he lived were very much part of that "free world." Since then, we have seen the consciousness formed in prison participating deeply in the changing reality of our society. Malcolm X, who was assassinated in 1965, is still the dominant figure in those hundreds of books being studied on both sides of the walls. This is not to ask Malcolm Braly to have the same vision of the world as Malcolm X, but to recognize and include the significance of that vision in his own.

As a California convict, Braly was Number A-8814, a number so low it made him feel more and more like a "curiosity" left over from some earlier time. One view of his art comes from a later generation of prisoners. Number A-71991, Philip T. Brylke, Jr. of the California Prisoners' Union, writes in his Introduction to the 1972 Fawcett reissue of *On the Yard*: "The convict of the '70's has torn away the thin veil of programed 'rehabilitation' and is facing his rejectors with the demand for dignity whatever the cost. Braly has detailed and defined yesterday's pathos, now we must live with today's rage."

B. Chester Himes

The novels of Chester Himes, together with the American critical responses to them, provide a kind of miniature social history of the United States from World War II through the days of the Black urban rebellions of the 1960s. Himes has been not only one of the most neglected of major modern American authors, but also one of the most misunderstood. In fact, it took those Black rebellions to make any significant number of critics realize that Himes *is* a major writer.

When Himes was paroled from the Ohio State Penitentiary in 1936, after serving seven and a half years of his twenty-year sentence for armed robbery, he finished the manuscript of his long prison novel, then titled *Black Sheep*. For fifteen years, he tried unsuccessfully, off and on, to find a publisher. One company verbally accepted the book, but when Himes showed up to sign the contract, he discovered that the decision had been overruled from higher up.[7] Meanwhile, he had published two naturalistic novels about the lives and struggles of Black workers striving for human dignity in the racist jungle of America, *If He Hollers Let Him Go* (1945) and *Lonely Crusade* (1947). The critical response was predominantly liberal, with condescending praise for the power of Himes's prose and imaginative vision, coupled with a regretful scolding of his excessive violence and hate. Typical was a review of *If He Hollers* by William Lynch in the *Saturday Review,* which argued that in the novel "Prejudice is met only with prejudice," and reasoned that the "only result is a blind weltering hate which can lead in the end to the rawest kind of violence."[8]

Finally the prison novel was accepted and published, in 1952, now entitled *Cast the First Stone* and told from the point of view of a white man from Mississippi. The novel details the hellish alienation of prison, then shows the redemption of the protagonist as he is finally able to love another human being, a fellow convict. Although one or two reviewers understood the book, most were more disgusted by the love in this book than by the rage in *If He Hollers* and *Lonely Crusade.* The reviewer for the *Saturday Review,* who confesses that he had never heard of the author before, is deeply disturbed by the book's "preoccupation with homosexuality," as if this were a fault of the novel rather than of our prison system. Though the love between the two men is not consummated physically, except for a very asexual kiss just before their final parting, this reviewer objects to their relationship being called a "friendship," for "it bears no resemblance whatsoever to any friendship I've ever noted or experienced."[9] The reviewer for the *New York Times Book Review* is even more insensitive both to the sufferings of American convicts and to the truths wrung from these sufferings. He states contemptuously that the book "has the curiously authentic quality of reading exactly like the autobiography of one of those penitentiary lawyers very often thrown up by prison life. Such men are glib, reasonably literate, authoritative in a superficial way, full of self-pity and whining mannerisms; they are the propounders of highly complicated systems of thought invariably based on irrational, deeply neurotic premises. . . ."[10] Within three months of these reviews Himes emigrated to Europe, where he has remained in his own kind of exile ever since.

The next two novels to appear were excruciating probes of Himes's experience outside prison. *The Third Generation* (1954), largely autobiographical, attempts among other things to come to terms with the tortured, ambiguous relationships among Himes, his father, and his mother. *The Primitive* (1955) is an agonized exploration of an archetypal, mutually devastating relationship between a Black man and a white woman. Although based directly on his own love affair with Vandi Haygood in 1952,[11] this relationship symbolizes even more than the most familiar sexual psychopathology of American historical experience. The names of the two lovers—Jesse and Kriss—would seem to have a fairly obvious symbolic significance; this religious symbolism, as I shall show, has its roots in Himes's earliest stories, written in prison.

These first five novels are all more-or-less autobiographical, and they span the range of Himes's American experience, from his childhood as the son of a Black professor in Mississippi, through his years in prison and his later work in Los Angeles shipyards during World War II, to that destructive love affair with a white American woman shortly before he left the country. Then he switched suddenly, it seemed, from the highly personal, often confessional mode of these novels to an entirely new genre. Or rather, as some critics in the last few years have pointed out, he created a new genre. This was the Black hard-boiled detective novel, set in Harlem and featuring that tandem of tough Black plainclothes cops, Coffin Ed Johnson and Grave Digger Jones. At this point the critics began playing a new tune: Himes was no longer a serious writer; he had given up any pretense to significant fiction; he had descended to writing potboilers.

Between 1957 and 1969, eight of these Harlem detective novels appeared. All but the first—*For Love of Imabelle*—and the last—*Blind Man With a Pistol*—were published in France before they appeared in America. The second and third in the series, *Il pleut des coups durs* (1958) and *Couché dans le pain* (1959), were published, before too long, in America as *The Real Cool Killers* (1959) and *The Crazy Kill* (1960). Here they found a lukewarm reception, to say the least. Some of the next novels in the series were not published in Himes's native land until five to seven years after their French publication. (Another of his books, *Une affaire de viol,* 1963, has yet to be published in English.)

The events of 1964–65 dramatically changed the response to Himes in America. *Retour en Afrique,* published in 1964, just before the first of the "long, hot summers," was brought out in 1965 as *Cotton Comes to Harlem* in the United States, where it received notable critical attention and where, in 1970, it was made into a motion picture. *Pinktoes,* originally published in Paris by Olympia Press in 1961, appeared in America in 1965. The following year saw the first American publication of *Run Man Run* (published in France as *Dare-Dare* in 1959) and *The Heat's On* (published in France as *Ne nous énervons pas* in 1961). Then in 1969 came the last of the Harlem detective series, at least to this date, *Blind Man With a Pistol,* the first of Himes's books to be published originally in America since 1957. After that, Himes seems to have gone through a period of summing up, represented by *Black on Black* (1973), a retrospective collection of short writings spanning his career from 1937, the year after he got out of prison, to 1969, and his autobiography in two volumes, *The Quality of Hurt* (1973) and *My Life of Absurdity* (1976).

The critical reaction to Himes has also transformed radically since that train of events touched off in the Black ghettoes in 1964–65. In 1966 John A. Williams, long an ardent supporter, was able to publish Himes's essay from the 1940s, "Dilemma of the Negro Novelist in the U.S.A.," in his anthology *Beyond the Angry Black*. Important revaluations of Himes soon followed:

"Race and Sex: The Novels of Chester Himes," a chapter in Edward Margolies's *Native Sons* (1968); "The Thrillers of Chester Himes," an essay by Margolies correcting his previous dismissal of the detective novels (*Studies in Black Literature,* Vol. 1, 1970, pp. 1–11); a brief but incisive analysis of these detective novels in Catherine Juanita Starke's *Black Portraiture in American Fiction* (1971); Raymond Nelson's important essay on these same detective novels, "Domestic Harlem: The Detective Fiction of Chester Himes" (*Virginia Quarterly Review,* Vol. 48, 1972, pp. 260–76); a special issue of *Black World* (Vol. 21, March 1972) devoted to Himes; and in 1976 the first two books on Himes, James Lundquist's *Chester Himes* and Stephen Milliken's *Chester Himes: A Critical Appraisal.*

Himes's achievement as a writer of fiction, indeed his very existence as an author, comes directly from his experience in prison, which shaped his creative imagination and determined much of his outlook on American society. If one goes back and reads Himes's first works, the short fiction he wrote as a convict in the Ohio State Penitentiary in the early and mid-1930s, one discovers the matrix of his vision, with all its contradictions and power, and his key images and symbols, even those thought to be unique to the Harlem detective novels.

Himes himself recognizes, in words strikingly similar to those of Malcolm Braly, that he was shaped by prison:

> I grew to manhood in the Ohio State Penitentiary. I was nineteen years old when I went in and twenty-six years old when I came out. I became a man, dependent on no one but myself. I learned all the behavior patterns necessary for survival, or I wouldn't have survived, although at the time I did not realize I was learning them.[12]

Yet Himes is now unable himself to explore the exact nature of this prison experience and its effects on him, apparently because these effects were too deep and too intertwined with his unconscious. As he puts it in this extraordinary passage in the very first paragraph of *The Quality of Hurt:*

I knew that my long prison term had left its scars, I knew that many aspects of prison life had made deep impressions on my sub- conscious, but now I cannot distinctly recall what they are or should have been. I find it necessary to read what I have written in the past about my prison experiences to recall any part of them.

The most extended statement about his prison experience is of course his prison novel, *Cast the First Stone*. But in one of the paradoxes characteristic of the life and work of Chester Himes, this novel, though profoundly autobiographical, is told in the first person by a white prisoner from Mississippi. In its original form, when it was entitled *Black Sheep,* it had apparently been told in the third person about a Black prisoner. Whether Himes changed the protagonist and the point of view just to get it published, as maintained by James Lundquist,[13] is not so certain. Significant sections of the book are reworkings of those stories he originally published in *Esquire* between 1934 and 1936, and those stories were told from the point of view of white prisoners (though in the third person). Himes's motives are certainly not so clear to Himes. In fact, by 1972 he can no longer comprehend, if he ever did, why he narrated his prison experience from that point of view in *Cast the First Stone*: "I had made the protagonist of my prison story a Mississippi white boy; that ought to tell me something, but I don't know what—but obviously it was the story of my own prison experience."[14] Then in 1976, he seems to take an opposite view: "My publishers wished to imply that the story in *Cast the First Stone* was the story of my life and problems and I wanted to state outright that it had nothing to do with me."[15]

And then one further paradox. This experience, which lasted for seven and a half crucial years of Himes's early manhood, which left scars too deep to be touched, which remains beyond Himes's own present comprehension, was, he tells us, nothing new at all: "Nothing happened in prison that I had not already encountered in outside life."[16] Although this may be the paradox of the history of Black people in America, that does not resolve it psychologically for Himes.

The contradictions Himes expresses about his prison life cannot be resolved. Indeed, these contradictions are the very life of his fiction, with all its seething tension, appalling violence, macabre comedy, bizarre shifts in plot, and agony relieved only by occasional hints of some future apocalyptic redemption. To understand these contradictions, the best place to begin is in the fiction Himes wrote and published while still a convict.

In March, April, and May of 1933, there appeared in *Abbott's Monthly and Illustrated News,* a Black journal published in Chicago, a novella by Chester Himes entitled *Prison Mass.*[17] The story reveals a great deal about that young convict author that does not appear in his autobiographical writings four decades later or even in *Cast the First Stone,* and it illuminates from within the sources of the visions which constitute the mature fiction.

Prison Mass is a deeply religious story set in the Catholic chapel of a prison, where a Christmas mass is being celebrated. The tone is quiet, restrained, earnest, almost hushed with a reverence befitting the scene. The story begins with a humanistic overview of the prisoners, who represent the "gamut of men," and ends with an explicitly Christian exaltation of their human dignity. The convicts are, with relatively few exceptions, guilty of crimes; they include every kind of criminal from "soft-eyed embezzlers" to "granite-eyed killers," from kidnappers and "fair-faced thrill seekers" to "obese bankers" and "oily-haired politicians." They range the extremes of human intelligence and moral decency. They come from all parts of the world and all races: "Some were white, some were red, some brown, some black, some yellow. Some were Americans, some were Europeans, some Indians, some Mexicans, some Malays, some Chinese . . ." (March, 36). In short they represent humanity itself, and Himes's attitude toward them is one of expansive—though by no means naïve—compassion.

The main characters are three Black men sitting next to each other in the middle of the congregation: "One had attended Mass to borrow money. One was drawn, like a moth to flame, subtly fascinated by the altar lights. One had attended to pray" (March, 37). Obviously they constitute a microcosm of the Black prisoners. The first is a cynic whose "habitual scoffing and jeering" at everything and everybody has earned him the name "Signifier." Although Signifier on the surface personifies crass selfishness and almost brutish opportunism, and although he sneers at all decent behavior, he is "square with his friends, generous to his fellow convicts in some ways," and underneath it all even he is moved by some vague religious impulses.

The second Black convict, who comes to the Christmas mass because he is fascinated by the lights and the pageant, is appropriately known as "Brightlights." Without any doubt Brightlights is a self-portrait, and as such gives us a detailed image of at least one way Himes perceived himself when he was a young convict and a beginning author. Like Himes, Brightlights has broken vertebrae, must wear a steel back support, and is officially designated a "cripple." Both Himes and Brightlights had spent some time in college, and each has a blind brother who has recently graduated from college. Like Himes, Brightlights is serving a twenty-year sentence for the armed robbery of an affluent couple in their suburban home; the details of that robbery are almost identical to Himes's description of his own crime in *The Quality of Hurt*. Brightlights was caught in precisely the same foolish way as Himes, and he has the same self-loathing for his failure to escape: he agonizes over the memory of trying to sell the stolen jewelry in a pawn shop in a midwestern metropolis, "chatting with the jeweler until the law came in and plucked him like a ripe tomato" (April, 50). Just like Himes, Brightlights was then hoisted by his manacled ankles over a door in police headquarters, and while dangling head down, beaten mercilessly by the police with their pistols. At the end of the story, Brightlights returns to "his work, his writing, his bid for the lime-light, fame" (May, 62).

Brightlights is an intellectual who philosophizes about religion. He regards Signifier's cynicism as mere foolishness, speculates about the kind of divinity to whom the thousands of human creeds might be equally acceptable, and allows himself to be hypnotized by the ritual of the Christmas mass. But he is prepared to commit himself to a kind of "damnation" in order to follow his chosen path, to be a writer. He realizes that "the secret reason he had taken up writing" is essentially a new form of the drive that had led him to the fast life of gambling and crime, a "passionate

longing for the bright lights, for the lime-light, for adulation"
(May, 61). As he delves into his motives, he becomes like some
character out of Hawthorne, his eyes reddening with the glare of
hell:

> He had wanted the renown more than the money; wanted to see his
> name on the pages of the popular magazines, wanted others to see
> his name. "I shall pass beneath this earth no common shade." That
> was his motto now—I shall be no *forgotten man*. What was impor-
> tant in life? From his burning thoughts came the answer—
> ambition, achievement, fame. A smile curved the corners of his
> lips, and for the moment, a dull, red glow suffused his eyes. (May,
> 61)

The third Black man sitting in this group is known as "the
Kid." He had been an innocent boy who had taken the murder rap
for his brother. The Kid, now doing a life sentence, has just heard
that his mother is dying, and much of the story is an exploration
of the depth and significance of his faith in Christ. The Kid himself is the innocent scapegoat who has taken another's crime upon
himself. Like Christ, he is crucified by his society in the midst of
the crucifixion of actual criminals—including a representation of
Himes himself. He is apparently Himes's first version of the
Black Jesus who is to appear with increasingly intense symbolic
significance until we reach the possessed and demonic world of
Blind Man With a Pistol.

The Kid (who in some ways resembles Billy Budd), though "an
idealist by nature, enthusiastic, impulsive, trustful, therefore
easily hurt," is also capable of great violence and is now kept "in a
company of incorrigibles in a cell to himself" (March, 62). But at
the end his fate, like that of all the convicts, is still in the hands of
a gentle Christ. *Prison Mass* concludes with an explicit statement
of religious affirmation, a vision of the contrast between the
harsh brutality of this prison and the brooding compassion of a
divine savior:

> A guard lieutenant said: "Start 'em off."
> A guard said: "Forward march." Other guards repeated the or-

der. The companies began to move through the crisp, cold December morning.

A few flakes of vagrant snow were drifting slowly through the air, groundward. The skeletons of the trees were outlined against the bleak sky. A cat scampered across the dirty snow.

The high, stone wall rose in the distance like gray, storm clouds, cutting off the sunshine.

And Christ in heaven looked down on this day in commemoration of His earthly birth, eyes bright with immortal pity, over the lot of man. (May, 62)

The Christian orthodoxy of this early fiction by Himes shows that the Christian symbolism of the late fiction is not mere literary decoration or hyperbole. Brightlights is the portrait of the artist as a young man, but this self-portrait is itself a seething mixture of contradictions between the jeering Signifier and the pious Kid. We can surmise how Himes's later experience, his deepening knowledge that his main punishment was not for being a criminal but for being a Black, together with all the resulting pain described in *The Quality of Hurt,* turned his youthful religious yearnings into the infernal visions of his mature fiction. As the priest in *Prison Mass* preaches: "Is this Babe of Bethlehem not a God? Then is the history of the world and of man incomprehensible, and an unintelligible falsehood!" (April, 50). The first glimpses of a hellish society compounded of "unintelligible falsehood" are to come very soon.

However, the next story to appear in *Abbott's* still has the mingling of reverence and doubt, with that peculiarly hushed air, which characterizes *Prison Mass.* This is "I Don't Want to Die," a brief tale in the October 1933 issue, about a twenty-four-year-old Black man, imprisoned since the age of nineteen (like Himes), dying of tuberculosis in the prison hospital. At the end, as his desolate and hopeless life on earth finishes in the dissolution of his body, one of his hands is held by a priest, the other by his best friend, a fellow convict:

And then he left them, went out there to some Valhalla, one hand clinging tightly to the hand of a priest who offered him the salvation of God, the other hand clinging tightly to the hand of a

thief who offered him nothing but friendship, he went out without
ever knowing which offer was greatest.[18]

Himes's stories about prison life published in *Abbott's* concern
the experience of Black convicts and are told from a point of view
close to their own. In August 1934, *Esquire* published the first of
his stories to appear outside Black periodicals, "Crazy in the
Stir." Himes was to have two more stories accepted by *Esquire*
before his parole in 1936, "To What Red Hell?" (October 1934) and
"The Visiting Hour" (September 1936). (After his release, *Esquire*
accepted six more stories by Himes, published between 1937 and
1959.) In those first three *Esquire* stories, Himes shifts to the
experience of white convicts and tells their tale, in the third person, from a point of view close to them. All three stories focus on
tough convicts, are narrated in something of the hard-boiled style
of Jim Tully, and show the crippling, literally paralyzing, effects
of prison on even these hard guys.

"Red," the protagonist of "Crazy in the Stir," is an ex-Marine, a
boy raised in the alleys and "dirty gutters" of the Bronx, a combat
veteran of the trench warfare of World War I and the U.S. im-
perialist adventures in Nicaragua and China. Boiling with rage
and frustration, he paces down to "Black Bottom," the section of
the prison dormitory where the Black convicts bunk. At this point
Himes gives us an extraordinary perspective.

In Chapter 3 of this book I outlined the development and significance of the songs created by Black slaves and convicts. In
Chapter 4 I discussed the awareness of these songs found in the
works of some white convict authors. What Himes provides, first
in "Crazy in the Stir," then a bit more in "To What Red Hell?,"
and throughout *Cast the First Stone,* where it forms a kind of
choral counterpoint to the alienation of the protagonist, is the
insight of a Black author imagining white convicts as they respond, for the first time in their lives, to living with Blacks and
hearing their music in the prison environment where it was
created.

To Red, like Captain Delano in *Benito Cereno,* "the Negroes"
are "black, stolid animals."[19] He paces down to Black Bottom on

his first visit just to "see what the hell they were doing." There he finds what seems to him a collective, mindless experience:

> Georgia Skin . . . A group of black faces . . . Cards spinning face-upward in the yellow glare . . . Soft, intense curses rising like thick smoke . . . A black boy strumming a uke, feet patting time . . . Another cutting a step . . . A circle of swaying bodies . . . Hands clapping in rhythmic beat . . . Animated faces . . . (114)

Red recoils in disgust and contempt, thinking that only he is capable of consciousness and the torture that comes from an awareness of time:

> Chiselers! Petty larceny! Most of 'em in for stealing a ham or strong-arming some hunky laborer. Some in for carving up their women. The days passed and they didn't know it. Time meant nothing to them. (114)

Then he observes two men singing a traditional religious Black song, sharing a Bible and a friendship. He is even more repelled:

> A voice came out from between two beds.
> "Oh, de little black train's a'coming; Oh, de little black train's a'coming . . ."
> A chunky black man and a lean yellow one were sitting side by side on a bed with a Bible between them chanting the repetitious drone.
> Red thought: Probably in for rape, both of 'em. Singing to a white man's idea of God. Don't know what the hell it's all about. Don't wanta know. Just an emotional release, a substitute for sex. (114)

Writhing in his own entrapment, sensing even more keenly now his extreme alienation, Red turns away, wishing he could see a man die, just to break the monotony, the sameness of the passing days.

Storming back to the white section of the dormitory, he agonizes about his past, curses God, and knocks down a man who bumps into him. He hears the guard being called and hurries away, to find himself, like an automaton, down in Black Bottom again:

> The darkies had a "strut" on ... Instruments clanging ... A saxophone wailing. Red looked for the saxophone, saw a black boy blowing a hair comb. Slender bodies swaying to the hot rhythm ... Feet shuffling, patting ... A brown boy bucking a step, cap pulled low over his eyes ... White teeth gleaming in black faces ... Yellow faces were ivory masks in the shadowed corners ... Soft voices were a steady beat of sound ... *Laughter!*
> The noise bubbled like hot tar in Red's mind.
> But what the hell? The darkies were happy, they laughed. Nothing could hurt them. (117)

At this point Red's infernal torture has not sufficiently sharpened his perception. He still does not understand what he is hearing.

But on his third visit to Black Bottom, his mind now rapidly collapsing in upon itself, Red hears the truth in the music that wails over the laughing voices, a music born and developed in endless imprisonment:

> A wail rose above the laughter, poignant, stirring with the anguish of a race that has learned to suffer—"*All-l-lll night lo-o-ooo-OOONG, ah set'n, ma cel-l-ll an' mo-o-o-aaa-AAANNNnnn!*" (117)

At this point the significance of Red's name is revealed: "Red chaos was his mind." He is being slowly burned alive in the hell of this prison.

Although a penniless victim of his own society, Red had one inheritance from the masters of the land, the same attitudes toward Blacks shared by the masters of Frederick Douglass. When he moves from seeing them as mere "black, stolid animals" to sharing their fate, while remaining alienated from their culture, he ends buried under a vision of bars collapsing around him, crushing him in the insane inferno of his own mind.

In "The Visiting Hour," another alienated longtime convict tries, with almost no success, to suppress his desperate, thrashing lust for freedom long enough to communicate some love to his suffering wife. Expending her life in efforts to get him pardoned, she finds herself spending the precious few moments of her visit being abused by him for not doing enough.

By far the most interesting of these three stories is "To What Red Hell?," which is based on Himes's experience in the conflagration that swept through the ancient Ohio State Penitentiary, killing over three hundred convicts and severely burning many more. Here the internal vision of hellfire has a fitting counterpart in the objective world.

The flames are "devils' tongues" spreading an inferno through the hell created by some men for other men. Some of the prisoners become heroes, braving the flames again and again to carry men trapped in blazing cellblocks to some hope of life. Others go to the opposite extreme of human behavior, looting the pockets of the dead and dying of small change or packets of Bull Durham. Some men get drunk; some run to send telegrams home; some plan an abortive campaign of "Passive Resistance" to the reestablishment of authority. The protagonist can do none of these things. Paralyzed in the grip of some bewildering force, he can only wander in an aimless daze, merely observing the world revealed by the holocaust.

He is much like Red of "Crazy in the Stir"—a tough white convict, a loner, a combat veteran of World War I—though he has the more ironic name of Blackie. The decisive moment of the story comes when Blackie confronts one of the heroes, a Black convict bringing out "a live one":

A big Negro called Eastern Bill loomed suddenly in the door with a limp figure draped across his shoulder. The unconscious figure strangled suddenly and vomited.

Blackie looked at the slimy filth, felt his stomach turn over inside of him. He heard a voice say: "Get a blanket and give a hand here." His lips twitched slightly as a nausea swept over him. He said: "No can do," in a low choky whisper and walked over toward the chapel.[20]

This passage reappears, rewritten in the first person, eighteen years later in *Cast the First Stone*.[21] More significantly, the image of a protagonist frozen, unable to act, in an agony of paralysis, is to reappear again and again in Himes's autobiographical works, both fiction and nonfiction, from Bob Jones's inability, at the final moment, either to rape the white woman or to kill the white man in *If He Hollers Let Him Go* through all the confessions of inaction in *The Quality of Hurt* and *My Life of Absurdity*. The frozen moment in the pawn shop, when Brightlights, like Himes, was unable to flee, and the convulsive paralysis of the protagonists of "To What Red Hell?" and *Cast the First Stone*, who are unable to be either heroic or merely helpful, are at the center of this tortured imagination. The spell is broken only by those two men of ruthless action, Coffin Ed Johnson and Grave Digger Jones, and then the results are no less painful.

Blackie cannot comprehend his own condition:

> Didn't know what the hell was the matter with him, getting sick like a convent girl at a cess-pool. He really wanted to go up in that smoking inferno where heroes were being made and angels were being born. But he couldn't, just couldn't, that's all. It wasn't a case of being afraid . . . Hell, he'd been on the Marne—he'd seen liquid fire rolling across no man's land—he'd seen men carrying their guts in their hands . . . But he couldn't go up there on that sixth tier of hell and bring down a puking stiff on his shoulder for love nor money. He just couldn't do it! (100)

So Blackie walks in a "gray daze" to the chapel.

There he finds a convict standing in the vestibule "cursing God with a slow, deliberate monotony" and other men shooting craps on the floor of the aisle. He hears "a slow run on the bass keys of a piano" and sees "the red glare through the frosted glass." When he looks toward the stage he perceives a symbolic scene which has usurped the beatific ritual of *Prison Mass*:

> Somebody had rolled the cover from the grand piano over in the corner and a curly-headed youth was sitting on the stool, playing Saul's Death March with slow feeling. A pencil streak of light, coming through a cracked door, cut a white stripe down the boy's face. He saw that the boy's cheeks were wet with tears.
>
> Then the slow, steady beat of the bass keys hammered on his mind like a cop's fist. He said: "Don't you know people are dying outside?"
>
> The youth looked around and said: "Sure," without stopping. "I'm playing their parade march into some red hell." (101)

This scene, which, like much of "To What Red Hell?," is somewhat revised and then incorporated into *Cast the First Stone,* prefigures the deepening sense of the absurd that characterizes Himes's autobiographical novels and Harlem detective series. The images of Christianity now become increasingly identified with those of death.

Blackie backs out of the chapel, stumbles through swiftly shifting scenes of chaos, and encounters "black-robed priests flitting here and there among the dead" like "black ghouls." Then he finds a "black boy" looting money from the underwear of the corpse of another Black convict, whom he claims was his lover. "Blackie swung a hard, wild haymaker at the shiny, black face," misses, and flies sprawling over the "soft, mushy" corpse. He frantically scurries away through "the dense crop of corpses," his feet slipping on leg bones, and finds himself standing in front of the Catholic chapel, which is being systematically looted. Inside, the remaining Christian icons and paraphernalia now form a mere island of illusion. Blackie enters and experiences a conversion out of faith which is to last Himes throughout his writing career:

> He went on up the stairs into the Catholic chapel, leaned against the wall beside the bronze basin of Holy Water just inside the door. Candles were burning on the white altar, their yellow flames tapering up toward the polished bronze crucifix... A well of peace amid chaos.
>
> He notices the curved backs of several fellows bent over the railing before the Images of the Saints. He caught himself reciting: "I

believe in God, The Father Almighty, Maker of heaven and earth ..." Then he thought of the prone, gray figures on the cold ground outside; of the smoke and flame and confusion. He felt a sneer form on the bottom side of his lips next to his teeth ... "I believe in the power of the press, maker of laws, the almighty dollar, political pull, a Colt's .45 ..." (101, 122)

Twenty-three years later, Himes begins his series of Harlem detective novels, featuring that pair of ambiguous heroes, those men of action, those tough Black cops with their names of death—Coffin Ed and Grave Digger—who beat and shoot their way through the mayhem that surrounds them. It has been observed that Himes's detective novels move toward a negation of that genre. Raymond Nelson argues that since "the faith in the ability of men to discover truth" is "a basic precondition of the detective genre," Himes's sense of "maniacal" contradictions "simply cannot be contained" within this form.[22] Others approve of Himes's creation of a kind of antigenre emerging out of the detective novel. All readers of the series would have to agree with Nelson's description, whether or not they accept his evaluation. Although in the earlier novels the specific crime usually gets "solved" in the sense that we discover who was the immediate agent of its commission, the action introduces increasingly senseless, absurd, incomprehensible events and behavior. At the end, unlike that in the more traditional detective stories, we are left with more mysteries, more confusion, more loose ends, less control of crime and disorder, than when we started. And in *Blind Man With a Pistol* the original murder is never solved, more bizarre crimes appear every few pages, and at the end crime and disorder are becoming universal. Before showing how these detective novels relate to Himes's writings as a convict and how I believe they contribute to an understanding of literature written by American convicts since 1964, I should like to suggest how they fit in with the overall history of detective fiction.

In Chapter 4, I argued that the principal literary form of the capitalist epoch, the novel, originated in the form of extended prose narratives of the lives of criminals, and that literature about crime and criminals is central to bourgeois culture. Prior to the American and French Revolutions, this literature was concerned almost exclusively with the criminal, and was often told, in a picaresque mode, from his or her own point of view. The narrative of the detective appears only after the consolidation of bourgeois power. The bourgeoisie, having emerged from its origin as an illegitimate, even outlaw, class, now begins to view the question of crime and criminals from the point of view of the establishment, of law and order. The key figure here of course is François-Eugène Vidocq, the ex-convict who founded both the first official detective bureau, the *police de sûreté,* in 1809, and the first private detective agency, in 1832. The narratives attributed to him (probably falsely)—*Mémoires de Vidocq* (4 vols., 1828–29), *Les Voleurs* (1837), *Les Vrais Mystères de Paris* (1844)—are the fountainhead of modern detective literature. The word "detective" appears first in the English language in 1843 (*Oxford English Dictionary*). In the 1840s Edgar Allen Poe created the archetypal detective story in which a lone man of genius, relying on his intellect, deftly solves mysteries which puzzle the populace and confuse the authorities. These "tales of ratiocination," like the later adventures of Arthur Conan Doyle's Sherlock Holmes, represent the era when the bourgeoisie, together with its cultural values, is in unchallenged supremacy. Threats to the bourgeois world order appeared with World War I, the Russian revolution, the developing economic crises of the 1920s, the worldwide capitalist crash that followed, the emergence of fascism, World War II, and the global era of revolution and national liberation movements that has been developing ever since, especially among nonwhite peoples. In these decades of disintegration for the capitalist world hegemony, a new type of detective fiction has emerged, in which the purported upholder of law and order fights crime less and less through rational intelligence, more and more through fists, brass knuckles, guns, electronic eavesdropping, bombs, broken bottles, or any other available means of proving that occasionally crime doesn't pay. This is the age of Mickey Spillane, *Badge 373, Death Wish, French Connection,* and the detective fiction, as well as the life, of E. Howard Hunt.

The most seminal influence in the development of the hard-boiled, rough-and-tough school of detective fiction is of course

that former Pinkerton detective, Dashiell Hammett, whose masterpiece *Red Harvest* appeared, appropriately enough, in 1929.
Hammett's craft developed, along with many other writers of this
school, in the main organ of hard-boiled detective fiction, the pulp
magazine *Black Mask,* especially in the early 1930s. During this
period a convict in the Ohio State Penitentiary, an aspiring young
author named Chester Himes, subscribed to *Black Mask.*[23] So
Himes's interest in detective fiction did not suddenly emerge, as
he suggests in *My Life of Absurdity,* in 1957.[24] Far more significant, Himes—as a former criminal, as a convict, and as a Black
man—was in a position to develop the contradictions of this
proto-fascist detective fiction to their full logical absurdities.

Himes's Black killer-detectives protect the people of Harlem by
enforcing upon them the law and order of white capitalist
America, doing this with a brutal and often literally blind violence their white colleagues can no longer employ with impunity,
often committing more crimes than they solve. They embody
what they represent, the ultimate stage of social disorder mas-
querading as order. For in their blindness and rage, they are
always in the process of discovering that the real criminals are
the masters of American society, and that the people Coffin Ed
and Grave Digger are attacking are their own brothers and sisters, daughters and sons. And all this is shadowed forth in a story
Himes published in 1933, while still a convict, almost a quarter-
century before the first of his Harlem detective novels.

This story is "He Knew," published in *Abbott's,* December 2,
1933. It is told, in the third person, from the point of view of a pair
of hard-boiled Black detectives, John Jones and Henry Walls, as
they follow an assignment on a December night in a waterfront
district of "dismal warehouses and squalid tenements."[25] The
white precinct captain has explained, " 'I'm putting you two men
on this job because it's a Negro neighborhood and I believe that
it's Negroes who are pulling these jobs. You fellows are plodders
and it's plodders we need.' " Walls has "splotched, yellow, mulish
features." Jones is a "tough dick," with a "harsh black face."
Like Coffin Ed, he has two sons and a teenaged daughter.

The climax comes in a scene with some revealing similarities to
the key event in *For Love of Imabelle,* the first of the Harlem

detective novels. In *For Love of Imabelle,* Coffin Ed and Grave Digger confront some gangsters in a waterfront warehouse; one of them hurls acid into Coffin Ed's face, temporarily blinding him and permanently turning his face into a hideous mask (he is subsequently known as Frankenstein, and he bears great resemblance to Stephen Crane's "The Monster"); Coffin Ed blindly empties his .38, accidentally hitting a light-switch, thus plunging the room into total darkness; now in double blindness, he begins "clubbing right and left with the butt of his pistol," and accidentally knocks Grave Digger unconscious; more blind mayhem ensues.[26] In "He Knew," Jones and Walls have a shootout in a pitch-black warehouse with a gang of young hoodlums, killing three of them. When the white cops come and light is restored, they all bend over the bodies. One of the white cops wonders what the father of any of these dead young men would feel like. Jones knew—hence the title—because two of them are his own sons.

"He Knew" is the imaginative core of one of the main themes of the Harlem detective series, the infinite forms of violence perpetrated by Blacks on Blacks, forms embodied by the two detectives as much as by the criminals they hunt. In *The Real Cool Killers,* there is even an echo of "He Knew" as Coffin Ed kills two teenaged Blacks whose little gang includes his own teenaged daughter. But these two Black cops—Grave Digger more consistently than Coffin Ed—do know who the real enemy is. In this same book, Grave Digger actually does some real old-fashioned ratiocinative detective work to solve the original murder they were sent to investigate, discovers the murderer—and then conceals her identity. For he has recognized her as one of those occasional Black persons in Himes's fiction who strike out successfully, even if somewhat blindly, against the oppressor, in this case a wealthy white sadist who comes to Harlem to whip young girls.

This heavily loaded image of the shootout in the dark crisscrosses in Himes's late fiction with the equally heavily loaded image of the Christian church. For example, toward the end of *Cotton Comes to Harlem* we find ourselves in a scene somewhat like the Catholic chapel of *Prison Mass,* "To What Red Hell?," and *Cast the First Stone,* except that now it is illuminated neither by the bright lights of the Christmas mass nor by the flames of the inferno outside, but by the fires ignited in everything and everybody hit by the tracer bullets streaming out of the .38s of Coffin Ed and Grave Digger:

> [Coffin Ed] saw the top of a head coming around the front bench on the center aisle and threw a tracer bullet at the round mop. He saw the bullet go through the bushy hair and penetrate the front of the platform supporting the rostrum and the choir. The scream was commencing as he ducked.
>
> A figure with burning hair loomed in the flickering red light from the burning organ with a .45 searching the gloom and Grave Digger peeped. The shotgun went off and splintered the back of the bench in front of him and the church quivered from the blast....
>
> The burning shape of the body issuing these screams fell atop the broken leg, on the floor between two benches, and Grave Digger pumped two tracer bullets into it and watched the flames spring up. The dying man clawed at the book rack above him, breaking the fragile wood, and a prayer book fell on top of his burning body.[27]

The fires of hell which surround the chapel in "To What Red Hell?" are now in its midst, and Blackie's last article of faith—the gun—has triumphed over the symbols of a lost divinity. The scene finishes with details that recall, through complete contradiction, the hushed, reverential ritual of *Prison Mass,* presided over by a Christ looking down with "eyes bright with immortal pity, over the lot of man":

> ... light from the burning gunman on the floor lit up the figure of the gunman with his head on fire crouched behind the end of a bench ahead.
>
> On the other side of the church Coffin Ed was standing with his pistol leveled, shouting, "Come out, mother-raper, and die like a man."
>
> Grave Digger took careful aim between the legs of the benches at the only part of the gunman that was visible and shot him through the stomach. The gunman emitted an eerie howl of pain, like a mortally wounded beast, and stood up with his .45 spewing slugs in a blind stream.... Coffin Ed shot him in the vicinity of the heart and his clothes caught fire. The screaming ceased abruptly as the

gunman slumped across the bench in a kneeling posture, as though praying in fire.

Now the entire platform holding the pulpit and the choir and the organ was burning brightly, lighting up the stained-glass pictures of the saints looking down from the windows. (203)

Cotton Comes to Harlem was published in France (as *Retour en Afrique*) in 1964, on the eve of those massive Black urban rebellions of 1964–68. There was to be a very long pause before the next, and as it now seems, the final novel in the Harlem detective series, *Blind Man With a Pistol,* would appear in 1969. In fact Himes published no novel at all during this period of the rebellions. In 1965 Himes met another ex-convict, Malcolm X, and found that he thoroughly agreed with all his politics (but not with his religion).[28] Two weeks later, Malcolm X was assassinated. Then in 1965–66, an America in upheaval began to discover Chester Himes. In 1968 Martin Luther King was assassinated. The following year appeared *Blind Man With a Pistol,* whose subject is explicitly the Black rebellions, the political and religious leadership of the Black community, the disintegration of the power Coffin Ed and Grave Digger are supposed to enforce, and the beginnings of an apocalypse.

Blind Man With a Pistol is perhaps Himes's ultimate vision of a world with neither religious nor secular principles of order, a world without hope, a world gone mad. In his preface, he indicates that the governing metaphor applies directly to the leadership of the Black community, for "all unorganized violence is like a blind man with a pistol." In no way is this to be read as a condemnation of armed struggle. Himes in recent years has consistently maintained the principle enunciated in *My Life of Absurdity* in 1976: "Deep in the heart of every American black person is the knowledge that the only way to fight racism is with a gun" (27). Nor is the blind man with a gun entirely ineffective, as Himes demonstrates at the end of the novel. He merely incarnates unguided spontaneity in action, with both its potential for liberation and its massive self-destructiveness.

Coffin Ed and Grave Digger have one main official job in *Blind*

Man With a Pistol: they are supposed to find out who is starting the riots. Just as Himes's first tale of two tough Black detective cops was entitled "He Knew," this one might be entitled *They Knew,* for this is the only mystery in the book that Coffin Ed and Grave Digger can solve. They explain in detail to their white superior officer, Lieutenant Anderson, the identity of the criminal:

> "Some folks call him by one name, some another," Coffin Ed said.
> "Some call him lack of respect for law and order, some lack of opportunity, some the teachings of the Bible, some the sins of their fathers," Grave Digger expounded. "Some call him ignorance, some poverty, some rebellion. Me and Ed look at him with compassion. We're victims."
> "Victims of what?" Anderson asked foolishly.
> "Victims of your skin," Coffin Ed shouted brutally, his own patchwork of grafted black skin twitching with passion.[29]

So instead of pursuing this job, Coffin Ed and Grave Digger rampage through Harlem trying to find a murderer, someone who slit the throat of a white man who had come up there to buy young Black men for sex. They have only one clue, the dying man's last gurgling words, which indicate that he knew the murderer by the name of "Jesus Baby." This murder, like the others that follow because of the two detectives' misguided zeal, remains unsolved. Despite their ruthless and brutal search, Coffin Ed and Grave Digger must report that "they had found no trace of Jesus Baby" (171). But those of us familiar with Himes's prison writings can guess his identity: he is "the Kid" of *Prison Mass,* that 1933 novella imagining the Christ as a young Black prisoner.

Though the Kid was innocent, he was also capable of great violence. In his own agony, he incarnated the possibility of an avenging Black Jesus. While Coffin Ed and Grave Digger are pursuing their fruitless quest, a new religion is being launched on 116th Street, east of Lenox Avenue in *"The Temple of Black Jesus."* There, in "a urine-stinking hallway," presides the "gigantic black plaster of paris image of Jesus Christ, hanging by his neck from the rotting white ceiling":

> There was an expression of teeth-bared rage on Christ's black face.
> His arms were spread, his fists balled, his toes curled. Black blood
> dripped from red nail holes. The legend underneath read, THEY
> LYNCHED ME. (82–83)

At the end, Coffin Ed and Grave Digger have no function left.
They are using their guns now merely to shoot the rats pouring
out of a building that is being demolished as part of "urban re-
newal." At this point the blind man with a pistol emerges from
the subway underground. In his blind rage, he fires, accidentally
killing the white policeman who had a bead on him. The other
white police quickly converge on the blind man and gun him
down, as he clicks away with his empty pistol. Coffin Ed and
Grave Digger, those two men of violence and action, become mere
spectators, as passive and impotent as the paralyzed figures who
haunted Himes's prison fiction. Like wildfire, a rumor spreads
through Harlem: "WHITEY HAS MURDERED A SOUL
BROTHER!" And Himes's last completed novel ends with these
words:

> An hour later Lieutenant Anderson had Grave Digger on the
> radio-phone. "Can't you men stop that riot?" he demanded.
> "It's out of hand, boss," Grave Digger said.
> "All right, I'll call for reinforcements. What started it?"
> "A blind man with a pistol."
> "What's that?"
> "You heard me, boss."
> "That don't make any sense."
> "Sure don't."

Is this 1969 scene the end of the road for Himes's two Black
detectives, with their final role being that of their enslaved and
imprisoned ancestors, putting on the slavemaster or the chain-
gang boss? What might come next, either in the bizarre logic of
the Black detective novel or the historical logic of the events
reflected in *Blind Man With a Pistol*? The next logical stage after
this spontaneous, inchoate, unorganized violence is a conscious

attempt at revolution, as Himes recognizes. So he "began writing a book called *Plan B,* about a real black revolution in which my two detectives split up and eventually Grave Digger kills Coffin Ed to save the cause."[30] But the Black revolutionary organizations generated by the spontaneous Black rebellions were at this very moment being annihilated by the U.S. government, intelligence agencies, secret police, and local police forces. Himes soon found that his novel *Plan B* "was gradually heading for disaster."[31] After all, as he had said in response to the reviews of *If He Hollers Let Him Go* in 1945, his fiction merely reflected the existing realities of American society and was not offered as a blueprint for change.

There was one work, however, written in 1969 and published as the concluding story in his retrospective collection *Black on Black,* which reaches back to the images of his earliest prison fiction and uses them to project an apocalypse of the future. In this parable, Himes is finally able to exorcise the image of the Catholic church—by converting it into the sanctuary of armed Black rebellion against all those forces that overwhelmed Blackie with cynicism in "To What Red Hell?": ". . . the power of the press, maker of laws, the almighty dollar, political pull, a Colt's .45." This story is audaciously entitled "Prediction."

"Prediction" is set on the main street of a big American city. Six thousand white policemen are on parade. Although billed as a parade of unity between the races, "only the white race was on view and it seemed perfectly unified. In fact the crowd of all-white faces seemed to deny that a black race existed."[32] There is not a single Black person in sight. But there is a Black character in this parabolic fantasy. He is the janitor of the city's big Catholic cathedral, which sits on the main street, along the parade route. He is the last incarnation, at least to date, of Himes's Black Jesus.

Today the Black janitor is invisible, for he is hiding within the chamber which holds the public poor box of the cathedral, connected with the street only by a coin slot through the stone wall. He sits straddling the coin box, holding "a heavy-caliber blued steel automatic rifle of a foreign make." He waits, at the end of "four hundred years," with "all the time in the world." All the mystification of religion has been replaced by a sense that he himself, as a lowly Black human being, embodies all hopes of the salvation of his people:

> It required a mental effort to keep from making the sign of the cross, but he knew the God of this cathedral was white and would have no tolerance for him. And there was no black God nearby, if in fact there was one anywhere in the U.S. Now at the end of his life he would have to rely on himself. He would have to assume the authority which controlled his life.... consoled only by the hope that it would make life safer for the blacks in the future.

The massacre that follows is described with the characteristic Himes touch for detail so grisly that it verges on the comic. The reality of flying pieces of brains, bones, and guts brings the fantasy to life. Rows of police officials are mowed down. A riot tank is dispatched to end this "macabre comedy." But "the riot tank didn't know where to look for him," and "in its frustration at not seeing a black face to shoot at it rained explosive 20-mm. shells on the black plaster of Paris mannequins displaying a line of beachware in a department store window." The forces of law and order continue to generate the apocalyptic disorder:

> On seeing bits of the black mannequins sailing past, a rookie cop loosed a fusillade from his .38-caliber police special. With a reflex that appeared shockingly human, on hearing itself shot upon from the rear, the tank whirled about and blasted two 20-mm. shells into the already panic-stricken policemen, instantly blowing twenty-nine of them to bits and wounding another one hundred and seventeen with flying shrapnel.

Eventually, the assassin is discovered in the Catholic cathedral. After the tank "stared a moment as if in deep thought," it quickly reduces "the stone face of the cathedral to a pile of rubbish." But the entire symbolic event has cut too deep, giving an "almost fatal shock" to "confidence in the capitalistic system": "In the wake of the bloody massacre the stock market crashed. The dollar fell on the world market. The very structure of capitalism began to crumble."

During the three and a half decades that had passed since he composed *Prison Mass* as a convict in the Ohio State Penitentiary, much had happened to alter Chester Himes's outlook. But there is also an underlying unity in the imagination and the art of this man whose last words in his 1976 autobiography are "that's my life— the third generation out of slavery."

CHAPTER 6

From Malcolm X to Attica and Beyond: Contemporary American Prison Literature

Although hundreds of books by American prisoners and ex-prisoners have been published since the early 1960s, the mere fact that prisoners are creating literature is nothing new. Many important figures in European and American literature have been incarcerated as criminals: Socrates, Boethius, Villon, Thomas More, Cervantes, Campanella, Walter Raleigh, Donne, Richard Lovelace, Bunyan, Defoe, Voltaire, Diderot, Thoreau, Melville, Leigh Hunt, Oscar Wilde, Jack London, Agnes Smedley, Maxim Gorky, Genet, O. Henry, Robert Lowell, Bertrand Russell, Brendan Behan, Chernyeshevsky and Dostoevsky, Stalin and Solzhenitsyn, Christ and the Marquis de Sade. There is certainly nothing unusual about activists and writers being imprisoned as criminals, and, as we have seen, quite a few imprisoned criminals have become authors.

But the literature emerging today from the prisons of America constitutes an unprecedented phenomenon. The quantity itself is so vast that it makes for the first qualitative distinction: this is a coherent *body* of literature, not just works by individual criminals and prisoners. Second, this literature includes some of the most influential and revealing documents of contemporary American culture, such as *The Autobiography of Malcolm X,* Eldridge

233

Cleaver's *Soul on Ice,* George Jackson's *Soledad Brother* and *Blood in My Eye.* Third, the dominant voices in this literature are those of ordinary criminals who have become literary artists through their prison experience. The three authors just cited were imprisoned for burglary (Malcolm), rape and possession of the "dangerous drug" marijuana (Cleaver), and armed robbery (Jackson). The fourth distinguishing characteristic of this literature comes from the formative role of Afro-American culture.

The influence of Black culture on contemporary prison literature comes from a combination of causes. Afro-Americans were always, at least from the time of Emancipation, the majority in southern prisons, and there, as we saw in Chapter 3, a Black convict tradition of song emerged directly from slavery to become a powerful cultural force not only among Afro-Americans but in American society as a whole. Now, however, Afro-Americans are also the largest coherent group of prisoners throughout the middle Atlantic, northeast, midwest, and west coast, often constituting a majority in the prisons of these areas. This is due to the Black mass migrations from the rural South to the urban and industrial centers, combined with the high residual urban unemployment since 1930, except during World War II and the Korean War. The situation of Afro-Americans within U.S. society as a whole is generally reproduced in microcosm within the prisons; that is, they are on the very bottom along with other nonwhite peoples. But there the primary fact of Afro-American experience—imprisonment—is shared by other groups and individuals on the lower levels of U.S. society. Finally, and I think most important, the national liberation movements of nonwhite peoples around the world have changed the perspective of Black people in general, not the least Black convicts, who now include many veterans of the Korean and Indochina wars. For all these reasons, Afro-American culture has come to shape both the form and the content of contemporary American prison literature, making it something fundamentally different from any previous literature.

I do not mean to suggest that contemporary American prison literature can be considered a literary genre. It consists of novels, plays, poetry, essays, letters, songs, autobiographies, etc. Yet despite the wide range of generic forms, there are certain unifying and predominant formal characteristics, determined not only by the background of the writers but also by their intentions. Though these intentions are by no means all identical and are often, in fact, mutually contradictory, they mostly function in the same arena of struggle. To comprehend the artistic achievement of this literature, we must approach it with an aesthetic radically different from most aesthetics applied in the university and the university-dominated cultural media. In truth, it may not be going too far to say that the prison and the university provide the contradictory poles defining the field of aesthetics, as well as some other areas, for in our society the two main competing intellectual centers may be the universities and the prisons.

I am in no way implying we should apply a *lower* aesthetic standard to prison literature. The truth is that literature by prisoners has to overcome great prejudices among most college-educated readers, even when it does conform to theories of art promulgated on the campus. An ironic demonstration of this turned up in the long article on the Attica rebellion in *Time* magazine (September 20, 1971). The *Time* writers, attempting to display the primitive quality of literature by the Attica prisoners, picked as their one example "a poem written by an unknown prisoner, crude but touching in its would-be heroic style." The poem *Time* quoted was none other than the famous sonnet "If We Must Die" by the great Jamaican-American poet Claude McKay, which one of the prisoners had apparently copied from memory. (An even deeper irony, as Stephen Henderson has pointed out, is that this very poem, written in revolt against Anglo-American racial oppression, was recited by Winston Churchill to rally England during World War II.)[1] Totally beneath the notice of *Time* was the splendid poetry written by the Attica convicts themselves, a sampling of which is available in *Betcha Ain't: Poems from Attica* (ed. Celes Tisdale, Detroit: Broadside Press, 1974).

Contemporary American prison literature is of course not the culture of some people separate in time and place. It is very much part of American culture. It cannot be lumped in some timeless category of "prison literature," as though prisoners of all times and places constituted a society. The experience of being imprisoned does always have some common features, no matter what the particular historical or individual situation. But if we compare a work like George Jackson's *Blood in My Eye,* which attempts to solve the main theoretical problems of revolutionary strategy in America by applying the lessons learned in prison, with, say, Boethius's *The Consolation of Philosophy,* we see at once that the historical differences are primary, though both authors wrote while lying in prison waiting to be killed. I would argue that even Genet, many of whose *themes* are common to contemporary American prison writings, has a radically different outlook; this is shown in his introduction to Jackson's *Soledad Brother,* where Genet, despite some fine insights, fundamentally misreads Jackson's message as being antiwhite, whereas Jackson, both in his writings and in his prison leadership, was trying to forge revolutionary class unity between Blacks and whites (Sartre makes precisely the same error in his introduction to Fanon's *Les Damnés de la Terre*).

Contemporary American prison literature can be dated from *The Autobiography of Malcolm X.* Malcolm has a unique place in the social thought of the Afro-American people. One of the many Black "common criminals" awakened by the Nation of Islam since the late 1940s, Malcolm advanced beyond the mid-1960s Muslim ideology, to make crucial discoveries about himself as a Black man and as a criminal in America, about his people, about the history of America and its alternatives for the future. These discoveries still define the frontiers of both prison literature and much of our subsequent experience as a nation-state.

As we saw in Chapter 4, one conventional form for a convict's personal narrative was to begin by exploring his or her conversion to criminality, and then, by chronicling individual experience in crime and in prison, to arrive at some understanding of both the self and the society that had shaped that self. This was not, however, an established form for Black convicts, whose art was restricted almost entirely to song and other oral forms. But even before there were many Black convicts, as we saw in Chapter 1 the slave narrative had created the first distinctive genre of written literature within the American nation-state, by exploring what it means to wake into consciousness as a Black slave imprisoned within the boundaries of America and bound by its laws into mere animal existence and perpetual servitude. *The Autobiography of Malcolm X* is, as far as I am aware, the first extended autobiography by a Black common criminal and convict. Like many other convict narratives, it is recorded and organized by a writer, in this case Alex Haley, someone who shares with the narrator the common historical experience of the Afro-American people. The book is cast in the conventional form of the convict narrative, not of course because of literary influence but because that is the form most appropriate to—and somewhat determined by—the experience. At the same time, however, it also uses the form of the slave narrative, for much the same reason. *The Autobiography of Malcolm X* joins and unifies the main lines we have been tracing.

The first chapter of *The Autobiography,* like the beginning of many slave narratives, shows the destruction of the author's family by the surrounding white society. Entitled "Nightmare," it opens with a scene of hooded Ku Klux Klansmen, brandishing guns, riding around their house in Omaha in 1925, threatening Malcolm's mother, then pregnant with him. When Malcolm is four, white terrorists burn down his family's home in Lansing, Michigan. This is his "earliest vivid memory," a "nightmare night" of "pistol shots and shouting and smoke and flames."[2] When he is six his father, an organizer for Marcus Garvey's Universal Negro Improvement Association, is killed; "Negroes in Lansing have always whispered that he was attacked, and then laid across some tracks for a streetcar to run over him" (10). In 1937, at the age of twelve, Malcolm is taken away from his mother.

About three years later, Malcolm moves to Boston, gets a job as a shoeshine boy, and drifts into the world of the hipster. One of the famous scenes of this period is the description of his first "conk," "my first really big step toward self-degradation: when I endured all of that pain, literally burning my flesh to have it look like a white man's hair" (54). In 1941, at the age of sixteen, he enters the "life" of Harlem, soon becoming a drug addict and a typical zoot-suited hustler, pimping and pushing dope. Four years later he returns to Boston, sets up a burglary gang, and is eventually trapped, with a piece of stolen property, by a jeweller—just like Chester Himes in 1929.

Malcolm brilliantly describes his drift into criminality, rendering with rich and living detail the hustler's Harlem. This section has by itself come to be regarded as a classic narrative. Although superficially resembling the picaresque and confessional narratives of many other American criminals, it is set off from these by Malcolm's later role, the one in which he as author is addressing us. Like Frederick Douglass, Malcolm is writing with a consciousness of himself as an activist having a historical mission and destiny. As he tells us:

> I want to say before I go on that I have never previously told anyone my sordid past in detail. I haven't done it now to sound as though I might be proud of how bad, how evil, I was....
>
> Today, when everything that I do has an urgency, I would not spend one hour in the preparation of a book which had the ambition to perhaps titillate some readers. But I am spending many hours because the full story is the best way that I know to have it seen, and understood, that I had sunk to the very bottom of the American white man's society when—soon now, in prison—I found Allah and the religion of Islam and it completely transformed my life. (150)

When Malcolm entered prison on a ten-year sentence in 1946, at the age of twenty, he "had not even started shaving" (151). He went in as a criminal so hardened that his fellow convicts nicknamed him "Satan," the title of the first of the two chapters narrating his life in prison. He was virtually illiterate and almost entirely ignorant of everything but the fast life of the streets and the personal events that had led him there.

His first teacher was Bimbi, a Black "old-time burglar" in the Charlestown State Prison of Massachusetts. Bimbi lectured about "historical events and figures," expounded on Thoreau, and taught Malcolm "that the only difference between us and outside people was that we had been caught" (154). In 1947, Malcolm got his first communication from the Nation of Islam, and in 1948 he was transferred to the Norfolk Prison Colony, a model penitentiary with an extraordinary library. There he received a typed message sent to him personally from Elijah Muhammad:

> The black prisoner, he said, symbolized white society's crime of keeping black men oppressed and deprived and ignorant, and unable to get decent jobs, turning them into criminals. (169)

Malcolm decided to learn how to read with understanding and to write with clarity. He began by copying his entire dictionary page by page, and then proceeded to devour the prison library, concentrating on books of world and American history. When he walked out of the Norfolk Prison Colony in August 1952, after almost seven years of imprisonment, Malcolm was a devout Muslim, a formidable intellectual and scholar, and a few years from becoming one of the most influential political leaders of Black America. At the time of his assassination in 1965, he was a man of great national and international importance.

By unflinchingly probing his own deepest degradation and then showing the successive stages of his own consciousness, Malcolm was able to reveal the upside-down structure of the U.S. political economy and the culture that makes it seem rational, just, and enduring. He was the first common criminal to create a great literary work based on a vision that has become more commonplace since the events of 1972, that the biggest criminals in America control it and that the people in prison are merely their most brutalized victims.

After the assassination of Malcolm, prison literature acknowledged him as both its political and spiritual leader; he is conventionally compared to Moses, Jesus, even Allah. Etheridge Knight, who has written several poems about Malcolm, cut through to the essence of his role in "It Was a Funky Deal," a poem about the assassination:

> You rocked too many boats, man.
> Pulled too many coats, man.

Saw through the jive.
You reached the wild guys
Like me.[3]

Bobby Seale embodies Knight's message. Seale begins *Seize the Time* with a chapter entitled "Who I Am." These are his very first words: "When Malcolm X was killed in 1965, I ran down the street." After throwing bricks at police cars, he cries like a baby, and finally makes a vow: "Fuck it, I'll make my own self into a motherfucking Malcolm X, and if they want to kill me, they'll have to kill me."[4] In *Soul on Ice,* Eldridge Cleaver has a key chapter entitled "Initial Reactions on the Assassination of Malcolm X," in which he shows that Malcolm spoke directly to the majority of Black prisoners, including himself, who already were no longer seeing themselves as "criminals" but as "prisoners of war."[5] *Look For Me in the Whirlwind,* the collective autobiography of the New York Panther 21, has an entire section describing how Malcolm changed the thinking, and the lives, of its authors. A convict in Malcolm's alma mater, Norfolk Prison in Massachusetts, sums up the meaning of Malcolm's life and death in his poem "Black Thoughts '71 (malcolm)." This poet, Insan (Robert S. Preston), unfolds the "math lessons" that have led him to move from the day of Malcolm's assassination toward a future in which the victims become the force destined "to destroy empires &/build nations." The main lesson is not to deify Malcolm but to understand that he incarnated what was divine in the most oppressed people. It was Malcolm himself who

... got me to thinking that
if he wasn't the supreme being himself,
AllahGodMunguJehovahRama
(after someone pulled my coat &
told me that he was a man the same
as me. it messed me around but i
got it together).
& what he was i am
capable of being plus some.[6]

Malcolm X obviously did not fall from the moon, and the growth of his consciousness was neither isolated nor accidental. He was very much a person shaped by the swiftly developing upheaval in the world and in America, as he kept reiterating. The year of Malcolm's breakthrough to an internationalist vision, 1964, was the watershed year of our present history. It was the year of the first of those "long, hot summers" which were to culminate in April 1968, in that week of simultaneous Black revolt in 110 American cities, just after Martin Luther King, with his long record of criminal convictions by various states, was disposed of in the same manner as Malcolm X, John F. Kennedy, Fred Hampton, and George Jackson. In 1964, LBJ personified the collapse of democratic illusions, the United States first admitted armed attacks against North Vietnam, and significant organized opposition to the Indochina War began. It was also the year of the beginning of a separate white student movement, easy to date from the Free Speech Movement at Berkeley that fall, led by many of the veterans of Mississippi Freedom Summer.

There has been a reciprocal, and intensifying, relation between life inside and outside the prison walls. Tens of thousands of politically motivated young people, including white draft resisters and Black youth swept off the streets in the 1964–68 rebellions, have been sentenced to prison. A high percentage of the leading activists in the civil-rights movement, the Black, Chicano, Puerto Rican, and Indian liberation movements, the antiwar movement, and the developing revolutionary movement have been incarcerated, at least briefly; some have died in prison; many are still there. Quite a few of these activists, such as Angela Davis, Bobby Seale, Sam Melville, Jack Cook, Barbara Deming, Howard Levy, David Reed, John Sinclair, T.J. Reddy, David Harris, Daniel Berrigan, Philip Berrigan, and Huey Newton, have written books showing the influence of their prison experience. These activists also have brought political ideas from outside into the prisons, in turn helping to move the prison toward revolutionary thinking or even actual rebellion. The leadership of some of the Panther 21 in the 1970 Tombs rebellion and Sam Melville's role at Attica in 1971 are striking examples.

At the same time, the experience of arrest and at least temporary imprisonment has become more widespread throughout
American society. Most obviously, any involvement in political
protest activity is now likely to lead to arrest; more than twelve
thousand antiwar protestors have been arrested in a single demonstration in the nation's capital. But far more widespread is the
routine arrest for ordinary crimes. In 1975, the most recent year
for which official statistics are now available, the annual number
of *reported* criminal arrests, far less than the actual total and
excluding routine traffic arrests, passed 9,273,600 and was
rapidly climbing.[7] Furthermore, even affluent, respectable white
citizens now commonly have experiences formerly reserved only
for the classes thought of as actually or potentially criminal:
routine searches of personal belongings, police pat-downs or even
body searches in public buildings, no-knock raids and warrantless
police entries into private homes, police demands for identification papers, fingerprinting (which appalls many foreign visitors,
since this practice in most countries is still limited to criminals).
There is no longer such a clear demarcation between the criminal
prisoner-author and the law-abiding citizen-reader. Even the line
between Black convicts and white professors of literature is not
quite so inviolable, as we learn in Leslie Fiedler's *Being Busted*
and *Attica Diary* by William Coons, a college English instructor
who served fifteen months in Attica for possession of LSD.

Now we have two overlapping groups of prison authors: the
political activist thrust into prison, and the common criminal
thrust into political activism. The distinction between these two
groups tends to dissolve as the definition of crime, from both sides
of the law, becomes increasingly political. For instance, in which
category do we put Tamsin Fitzgerald (author of *Tamsin,* ed.
Richard Condon, New York: Dial Press, 1973), who was imprisoned in 1969 when she, then eighteen, and her twenty-one-year-
old lover attempted to hijack a plane to Cuba so he would not be
drafted to fight in Indochina? Or Hurricane Carter, who was incarcerated at age eleven, remained locked up in reform schools
and prisons until the age of twenty-four, except for three months
on the streets and two years in the army, then rose to fame as a

prizefighter, made a widely quoted public statement supporting the right of Black people to defend themselves with guns against police during the urban rebellions, was promptly harassed by several police departments and speedily framed for a triple murder, and did not write his astonishing autobiography, *The Sixteenth Round* (New York: Viking Press, 1974), until he had served several years of his resulting triple-life sentence? Or the poet and essayist John Sinclair, a leading white revolutionary arrested, in the words of the official indictment, for "possession of two marijuana cigarettes," who wrote while serving two and a half years of his ten-year sentence on this charge?[8]

Two Black poets discussed in this chapter embody the two extremes, the prisoner who becomes a writer and the writer who becomes a prisoner. One is Etheridge Knight, who, shortly before his release from Indiana State Prison in 1968, summed up his life very simply: "I died in Korea from a shrapnel wound and narcotics resurrected me. I died in 1960 from a prison sentence and poetry brought me back to life."[9] The other is T.J. Reddy, who had a university education and was already a published poet of some distinction before he was imprisoned. In fact, the judge who sentenced Reddy, like the judge who sentenced Imamu Amiri Baraka in 1968, explicitly cited his poetry as a reason not to lower bail. The judge claimed that the purpose of Reddy's poems was "to mold people's minds to malicious ends." This is literary criticism with a vengeance.[10] The poetry of these two "criminals," Etheridge Knight and T.J. Reddy, displays how the lives of individual Afro-Americans and the collective history of Black people in America determine the central content and define much of the form of contemporary American prison literature.

What is the essence of the experience of imprisonment? The answer to this question obviously has something to do with the general question of human freedom. If we look at most prison writings of the past, we find that the prisoner-artist typically approaches his or her loss of freedom as both an individual matter and as emblematic of something universal in the human condition. Hence the famous lines from Richard Lovelace's 1642 prison poem, "To Althea, from prison":

> Stone walls do not a prison make,
>   Nor iron bars a cage;
> Minds innocent and quiet take
>   That for an hermitage;
> If I have freedom in my love,
>   And in my soul am free,
> Angels alone that soar above
>   Enjoy such liberty.

As we saw in Chapter 4, the earliest writings by American convicts stressed their imprisonment as an individual, even an exceptional, fate: *I* am now unfree. *I* am a branded outcast. *I* was a sinner and am now being punished. *I* am an example to deter others from crime. *I* am a professional criminal who has lived a fascinating life. With the development of the modern prison system in nineteenth-century America, some convicts began to perceive themselves as part of a social subclass—prisoners. Then, especially in the first third of the twentieth century, some convicts conceived of prisoners as part of the main exploited and oppressed social class, the proletariat. Afro-American prisoners began from a different position, with a different perspective.

From the point of view of the Afro-American experience, imprisonment is first of all the loss of a *people's* freedom. The questions of individual freedom, class freedom, and even of human freedom derive from that social imprisonment. From this point of view, American society as a whole constitutes the primary prison. The Afro-American experience started in chains in the prison of a slave ship. "What Next," a poem by T.J. Reddy dedicated to Gustavus Vassa, author of the first widely printed slave narrative, dramatizes that primal imprisonment:

> thick sticky spit
> surrounds
> still Black mouths
> seasalt stains
> Black skins
> already covered with mud
> silent halfdead eyes
> look on in disbelief

shoulder to shoulder
suffering Black eyes
look deep past
each other's waste
wondering what next
will call the cough
of a Black life up,
or sputter out
the safest bloodsong
the swiftest bloodsong
the swiftest and sweetest
way to die

not as a slave... drown overboard
not as a slave... starve
not as a slave... swallow the tongue
not as a slave... kill the children
not as a slave... the beauty of horror
down
down
down
in the belly of a wooden beast's
indigestion
choking on the morbid air
breathing over and over again
each other's waste
wondering to death
what next[11]

What *was* next? As soon as the captives arrived in America, the boundaries of the prison expanded to become the boundaries of American society. Beyond the prison lay Canaan, the slave's code name for the most accessible foreign country. Malcolm X relates his own prison background to American society in these terms: "Don't be shocked when I say that I was in prison. You're still in prison. That's what America means: prison." In his introduction to *Black Voices from Prison* (New York: Pathfinder Press, 1970), Etheridge Knight explicates Malcolm's statement: "From the time the first of our fathers were bound and shackled and herded into the dark hold of a 'Christian' slaveship—right on up to the present day, the whole experience of the Black man in America can be summed up in one word: prison." Knight compresses this

vision into a brilliantly ironic jewel of a poem, "The Warden Said
To Me the Other Day." There he stands, a prisoner, assuming
that old Black slave stance—scratching his head, dropping his
jaw, outfoxing the master:

> The warden said to me the other day
> (innocently, I think), "Say, etheridge,
> why come the black boys don't run off
> like the white boys do?"
> I lowered my jaw and scratched my head
> and said (innocently, I think), "Well, suh,
> I ain't for sure, but I reckon it's cause
> we ain't got no where to run to."[12]

Knight, a convict late in the twentieth century, here reiterates
the same state of imprisonment experienced by that anonymous
Georgia peon, born during the Civil War, when shackled Black
convicts are first brought to work on his native plantation: "I felt
like running away, but I didn't know where to go."[13] Bobby Seale,
who was transformed, in the Chicago courtroom of Judge
Hoffman, into a living symbol of Black imprisonment, his arms
and legs bound, his mouth gagged and taped shut, said it is just a
question of whether you are in "maximum security"—which is
called prison—or "minimum security"—which is called being
free. This is how the Black convict Ellsworth R. Johnson opens his
poem "Alcatraz":

> Six feet of chambered stone
> The nation gives us for a home.[14]

Hurricane Carter refers to the United States as "a penitentiary
with a flag."[15]

What crime had the African people committed to be imprisoned? Obviously none at all. Hence the Afro-American people
quickly arrive at a further conclusion: the real criminals must be
those who uphold what is called law and order in America. As

Frederick Douglass put it in the 1845 *Narrative,* "I could regard them in no other light than a band of successful robbers, who had left their homes, and gone to Africa, and stolen us from our homes, and in a strange land reduced us to slavery." The nineteenth-century slave narratives, which were part of a militant abolitionist movement, could express this view frankly. But for most of the twentieth century, the art of Black prisoners could express such insights only with disguise, through indirection, in songs to be sung primarily to themselves.

Take, for example, the most famous Black prisoner-artist before Malcolm—Leadbelly. Huddie Ledbetter served two long terms in Texas and Louisiana, finally got out in 1934, then recorded songs until shortly before his death (as a pauper in Bellevue Hospital) in 1949. Few of his songs contain any explicit political message, though his vision of America does sometimes slip through, especially in his late songs. In "Bourgeois Blues," for instance, the nation is represented by Washington, D.C., which Leadbelly labels "a bourgeois town." Leadbelly describes his fruitless search for a place to live, then wails, in a classic blues mode, "Home of the brave, land of the free, / I don' wanna be mistreated by no bourgeoisie."[16]

Contemporary prison literature returns to the explicitness of the slave narrative, as in George Drumgold's poem, "These Prison Walls": "They say we're the criminals, a threat to society / But in truth they stole us, so how can that be?"[17] But this literature goes much further than the slave narrative, for it speaks as part of a profoundly more revolutionary age. Now, in the epoch of worldwide national liberation struggles, the Afro-American vision moves from the understanding of being colonial victims to a sense of national—and international—war against colonial enslavement.

In contemporary American prison literature, the central theme is America, prison house of the Black nation. But—and here is the crucial point—this consciousness, developed through the Afro-American historical experience, and brought to its highest level in the narrative and poetic art of prisoners, has now transcended the experience of one people. On one side is its internationalism; it perceives itself and is seen around the world as part of a global revolution of Third World peoples. On the other side, it has broken through to a class perception of U.S. social reality, and hence has deeply influenced not only white inmates but much of the white populace. It is no accident or fad that millions of white Americans have been profoundly affected by works written by Black convicts. For the most distinctive feature of the history of *white* America is Afro-American slavery and the subsequent role of Black people within the United States.

Afro-Americans are a people created within the United States, and it was their unpaid labor, producing the main cash export commodity of the 1830–60 period, that provided the principal capital base for the political economy of modern America. Imprisonment within chattel slavery provided a viewpoint from which one could perceive that the real criminals in capitalist society are those who live off other people's labor. When Frederick Douglass was hired out by his master, he asked himself why he must surrender his earnings to his owner, and his answer implicitly extends to all wage slavery:

> And why? Not because he earned it,—not because he had any hand in earning it,—not because I owed it to him,—not because he possessed the slightest shadow of a right to it; but solely because he had the power to compel me to give it up. The right of the grim-visaged pirate upon the high seas is exactly the same.[18]

So from the very beginning the Afro-American people have been in the best position to understand the basis of American political economy, and their understanding has advanced stage by stage as they have moved from rural chattel slavery in an agrarian economy to peonage and wage slavery in developing capitalism to become now the core of the three main sectors of the working class: (1) the industrial proletariat, particularly in the auto, steel, rubber, and meat-packing industries; (2) the service proletariat, ranging from mass transportation in New York, Chicago, Philadelphia, and San Francisco to the office buildings of the federal bureaucracy in Washington; (3) the vast and growing army of the permanently unemployed, which forms a distinctive feature of decaying monopoly capitalism and which provides the main population of the jails and prisons.

Part of the present decaying economy is the prison system itself, the latest version of chattel slavery, superseding the chaingang labor and peonage of the 1930s. The huge American slave labor camps known as prisons constitute an enormously profitable industry. In fact, the Federal Prison Industries, Inc. is "far and away the most profitable line of business in the country. Profits on sales in 1970 were 17 percent... the average for all U.S. industries is 4.5 percent."[19] Prisons constitute the fifth largest industry in California. According to official California statistics for 1968—the last year California released this kind of statistic—some prisoners produced well over $14,000 revenue each per year. By 1974, the highest wage for a California prisoner was up to $3.40 a week; using a conservative estimate of inflation, this prisoner must have then been bringing in about $20,000 a year.[20] And remember that fewer than 10 percent of the people in our jails and prisons are there because they had a trial and were convicted of a crime.[21]

It is not just the political economy that is stripped bare by the Afro-American experience. From this point of view, it is also possible to comprehend some of the main cultural and psychological characteristics of American life. For example, the sexual problems characteristic of each stage of our history have been analyzed most keenly in literature by Afro-American "criminals." There is an unbroken line of development from *Incidents in the Life of a Slave Girl* by Linda Brent, whose crime was refusing to submit to the perverted sexuality of her master, through that turn-of-the-century Georgia peon whose wife was taken away to service the sexual needs of his masters, through Malcolm X, who worked as a pimp in Harlem, guiding wealthy old white men to ogle and participate in their most diseased sado-masochistic fantasies with Black women and men, to Eldridge Cleaver's own sexual aberrations, which led, in *Soul on Ice,* to his incisive exploration of the psychopathology inherent in the stereotyped sexual roles imposed by American culture on the Black man, the white woman, the white man, and the Black woman.

People who have become literary artists because of their imprisonment tend to write in an autobiographical mode. The reason is obvious: it is their own personal experience that has given them both their main message and the motive to communicate it. The works of today's prisoners, though predominantly autobiographical, are rarely intended as a display of individual genius. Whereas the literary criteria dominant on campus exalt what is extraordinary or even unique, with "originality" as the key criterion, most current autobiographical writing from prison intends to show the readers that the author's individual experience is not unique or even extraordinary, but typical and representative. This presents some problems, for how can a single author prove that his or her own experience is commonplace? By reading ten or twelve autobiographies, we can corroborate the general truthfulness of each. But this clearly entails other problems, both aesthetic and practical.

A splendid achievement in the autobiographical mode is *Look for Me in the Whirlwind: The Collective Autobiography of the New York 21* (Black Panthers framed and later acquitted). The authors of *Look for Me in the Whirlwind* solve the aesthetic and practical problems of the individual autobiography by creating a collective autobiography of not only themselves but their people. As each life is interwoven with all the other lives, the bits of individual experience come to form a living epic. The decisive events in the life of each author are juxtaposed, giving an overwhelming sense of truthfulness, heroism, and inevitability of their collective commitment to the liberation of their people.

The *Me* of their title is not the same as the first-person singular found in the title of so many personal narratives by white convicts: *My Life in Prison* (1912); *I Am a Fugitive from a Georgia Chain Gang!* (1932); *Where Do I Go from Here?* (1936); *So I Went to Prison* (1938); *My Shadow Ran Fast* (1964); *My Chains Fell Off* (1966); *Monkey off My Back* (1972); *Doing My Own Time* (1972); *Castrated: My Eight Months in Prison* (1973). This *Me* is not an individual, but a people conceived of as a single entity, living in the past, present, and future. The collective authors take their own identity from the prophetic words of a past Black prisoner, and use his quoted words, in both their title and their opening epigraph, as a projection of this identity into the future:

"Look for me in the whirlwind or the storm, look for me all around
you, for, with God's grace, I shall come and bring with me countless
millions of black slaves who have died in America and the West
Indies and the millions in Africa to aid you in the fight for Liberty,
Freedom and Life."

Marcus Garvey, writing from Atlanta
Prison, February 10, 1925.[22]

Here we encounter head-on the conflict between the aesthetic
dominant in the prison and the aesthetic dominant in the university, which can see little value in such a book. *Look for Me in the
Whirlwind* does not ask us to admire the creative genius of each
individual artist, but to see each artist as merely representative
of a collectivity. We are not to look for the unique and the original, for ambiguity and countless types of irony, for architectonic
structure or the self-conscious solipsism of a Nabokov or a Borges.
We are to look for what is common, clear, purposeful, useful. We
are not supposed to sit around admiring the authors, but to get up
and put their message into action.

The most collective autobiography of the American prison is
not any single work, but the body of poetry by Black prisoners.
This poetry incorporates the common oral and musical tradition
developed in the songs of Black slavery and extended through the
songs of Black peonage and imprisonment. Integral to present-
day Black convict poetry is the history and theory of poetics outlined in Chapter 3, including the primal role of rhythm in human
life, the collective creation of poetry, music, and dance, and the
historical development and function of these arts in Afro-
American culture.

The poetry now being written by Black prisoners recapitulates
the history of Afro-American music and song, tightly integrates it
with a poetic analysis of the development of the United States as
a society, and extrapolates toward a liberation both in poetic form
and social life. T.J. Reddy, for example, experiencing, like his
ancestors, kidnap and enslavement, leads us back through the
underlying source and meaning of poetry toward the moment of
creation, then forward toward freedom. In "A Poem for Black
Rhythmeticians," he renders human history in the course of poet-

ry's rhythms, beginning in humanity's African womb:

> The drum is the heartbeat
> Of mother Africa
> As she shapes life and
> Gives birth
> To the world

The drum, that amplifier of our own heart, is linked to words from our brain, and it pounds out the rhythms of day and night, of the labor of the tribe and of its councils, of making love. The rhythms themselves then come to express meanings projected by talking drums:

> The drums sounded the warning
>   Oppressors are coming
>   Oppressors are coming
> And when slavers discovered
> How much we communicated
> With music they could not understand
> They took up our drums
> But not our rhythm

Reddy traces his ancestors as they pound out the songs of slavery and imprisonment on the plantations and the blues that pick up the rhythms of urban poverty. In the final stanza he breaks through the walls of his prison with the long heavy beats of:

> Now for freedom is not too soon
> Now for freedom is not too soon

The poet Lanners L. X, writing from Folsom Prison, yokes the explosive contradictions inherent between the origins of Black music and its present functions in "A Black & Blue Experience":

```
mister music man
duke of orchestration
composer of not only
                    time rhythm
& melody
        but
the harmonies
of a slave culture
as well
from hell it came
                    echoes of harlem
heard by souls/ears
blues/jazz
            it's called . . .
kings & queens
finger pop toe tap
            & shake their
ahhhhhhhhhhhh heads
to the moans & groans . . .
400 yrs. of labor pains[23]
```

In "Tribute to the Avant Garde," H. Fowler, writing from Comstock Prison in New York, hears the "Black Liberators of Music" giving the beat and meaning to an apocalyptic hurricane.[24] "Listen To Your Heartbeat," a poem written by James Lang in Norfolk Prison, Massachusetts, tightly compresses the whole tale. Lang begins in Africa and traces the songs sung in the

```
Holds of
Frigates
Plying the North Atlantic,
Engaged in the
"Black Gold" trade that
Was the cornerstone of
Mercantilism, Capitalism/Americanism.
```

Then he relates this poetry to the Black rebellions of the eighteenth and nineteenth centuries and carries it forward to the present and future:

Toussaint, Christophe and Desalines
Rocked Haiti with some of that
Good ole 18th Century Rock 'n Roll
And they (still keeping time to the beat)
Rolled the Little Corsican's
Inflated Empirical dreams
Back to the hills from which they came;
Nat, Denmark and Gabriel
Assembled their troops
To the same strains,
Then they took their shot.
Now, we got
Curtis and Ra
And Rahsan Roland Kirk
And Sisters Kim, Aretha, Elaine and Nina
(Bird, Trane, "O" and the Lady
Were saying it, too,
Before overexposure—To a blinding snowstorm—
Wasted them/But they weren't wasted)
Wicked Wilson, Leon Thomas, Lou Donaldson and Pharoah
    Sanders.
LISTEN! ! !
They talkin' at
YOU,
They tryin' to *tell* you somethin'.
Got the message?
It say—
OUR DAY HAVE COME.[25]

In the immediate background of contemporary Black prison poetry is the body of work songs developed by Black convicts on chain gangs and prison farms. To understand what this poetry owes to its tradition—and how far it has come from that tradition—compare the traditional convict work song about a Black Bad Man, "Po' Laz'rus" (discussed in Chapter 3, p. 113) with a modern treatment of a Black Bad Man, Etheridge Knight's poem "Hard Rock Returns to Prison from the Hospital for the Criminal Insane." Knight's rhythms (plus the rhythms of the group that plays behind him on the tape made in prison and available from Broadside Press) are liberated from that chopping beat of the work song, providing a much broader range of expression (the name of Knight's Bad Man, "Hard Rock," is actually a complex pun on both the prison experience and funky jazz). Knight is free to shift the scene of conflict away from some remote mountain directly into the prison, where the Bad Man's adversaries are the guards (the "screws"). Knight doesn't have to mince matters about Hard Rock's character: there is "the jewel of a myth that Hard Rock had once bit / A screw on the thumb and poisoned him with syphilitic spit." The elimination of the Bad Man is itself extremely topical, being performed not with a .45 but with advanced psychosurgery techniques developed in our universities. Knight is able to bring his message directly home to his audience of fellow inmates. In his introduction to the taped reading, he jokes around about the "twenty guys" who "have already told me that I was talking about them"—that is, they all like to think of themselves as the baddest. Knight is warning them about their fate. But Knight must also veil his message somewhat, because underneath he is telling the men to stop the old projection of their desires for resistance and rebellion onto some legendary figure in the past or in some mythic version of themselves:

Hard Rock was "known not to take no shit
From nobody," and he had the scars to prove it:
Split purple lips, lumped ears, welts above
His yellow eyes, and one long scar that cut
Across his temple and plowed through a thick
Canopy of kinky hair.

The WORD was that Hard Rock wasn't a mean nigger
Anymore, that the doctors had bored a hole in his head,
Cut out part of his brain, and shot electricity
Through the rest. When they brought Hard Rock back,
Handcuffed and chained, he was turned loose,
Like a freshly gelded stallion, to try his new status.
And we all waited and watched, like indians at a corral,
To see if the WORD was true.

As we waited we wrapped ourselves in the cloak
Of his exploits: "Man, the last time, it took eight
Screws to put him in the Hole." "Yeah, remember when he
Smacked the captain with his dinner tray?" "He set

The record for time in the Hole—67 straight days!"
"Ol Hard Rock! man, that's one crazy nigger."
And then the jewel of a myth that Hard Rock had once bit
A screw on the thumb and poisoned him with syphilitic spit.

The testing came, to see if Hard Rock was really tame.
A hillbilly called him a black son of a bitch
And didn't lose his teeth, a screw who knew Hard Rock
From before shook him down and barked in his face.
And Hard Rock did *nothing*. Just grinned and looked silly,
His eyes empty like knot holes in a fence.

And even after we discovered that it took Hard Rock
Exactly 3 minutes to tell you his first name,
We told ourselves that he had just wised up,
Was being cool; but we could not fool ourselves for long,
And we turned away, our eyes on the ground. Crushed.
He had been our Destroyer, the doer of things
We dreamed of doing but could not bring ourselves to do,
The fears of years, like a biting whip,
Had cut grooves too deeply across our backs.[26]

Knight's "For Freckle-Faced Gerald" is more brutal and more poignant. It deals with the rawest fact of life in our prisons. The fundamental punishment inflicted upon prisoners in America is the deprivation of normal sex, which turns the prisons into sexual hells. All the other aspects of prison life—the loss of the freedom of movement, the brutality of armed police, atrocious food and medical care, squalid surroundings, the arbitrary authority of the state in daily life—all these are common features of life in the ghetto, the barrio, and many poor white neighborhoods. But what is unique about prison is that sexual deprivation. The result is a society where the only sexual relationship generally available is coerced homosexuality. Whereas everybody pretends to be Hard Rock, nobody wants to acknowledge any resemblance to freckle-faced Gerald. Knight, in his taped introduction to this poem, jokingly professes that "there are not too many guys here with freckled faces."

Now you take ol Rufus. He beat drums,
was free and funky under the arms,

fucked white girls, jumped off a bridge
(and thought nothing of the sacrilege),
he copped out—and he was over twenty-one.

Take Gerald. Sixteen years hadn't even done
a good job on his voice. He didn't even know
how to talk tough, or how to hide the glow
of life before he was thrown in as "pigmeat"
for the buzzards to eat.

Gerald, who had no memory or hope of copper hot lips—
of firm upthrusting thighs
to reenforce his flow
let tall walls and buzzards change the course
of his river from south to north.

(No safety in numbers like back on the block.
two's aplenty. three? definitely not.
four? "you're all muslims."
five? "you were planning a race riot."
plus, Gerald could never quite win
with his precise speech and innocent grin
the trust and fists of the young black cats.)

Gerald, sun-kissed ten thousand times on the nose
and cheeks, didn't stand a chance,
didn't even know that the loss of his balls
had been plotted years in advance
by wiser and bigger buzzards than those
who now hover above his track
and at night light upon his back.[27]

Knight's poem is excruciatingly intimate, but it also expresses a
broad political vision. Though the immediate agents of Gerald's
rape are the buzzards in prison, his fate is part of a systematic
plan, "plotted years in advance / by wiser and bigger buzzards."
The victim, defined as the criminal, literally lies crushed at the
bottom of American society.

T. J. Reddy's first book of poems is entitled, with a play on his
twenty-year sentence, *Less Than a Score, But a Point.* Throughout this volume there throbs a dialectic between death, in the
form of capitalism's unending variety of prisons, and life, in the
form of the poetry of its victims. Sometimes this is explicit, some-

times stated only by conflicting rhythms, with a prosaic, even legalistic, phrasing pitted against Afro-American music and experience. As he says in "What Color Is Life?," "I come to paint sound."

In "Dr. Death the Community Physician," Reddy paints in sound and image a composite portrait of the various forms of white dope pushers, including the surgeon and the politician. The first line beats the sound of death in a ponderous syllabic sprung rhythm: "The white death dust dopes our eyes." The poem moves relentlessly toward the final description of the capitalist politician:

> Dr. Death the political magician
> Needles Black neighborhoods
> Selling death for a profit

In "One Day Ten Minutes a Thousand Years" the prison blots the sight of the human face allowed its weekly visit:

> One day a week in a steelpaneled room
> I look through greasestained
> Thickglass window
> and try to wipe the smudge
> Away from the face I see
> The face that looks back and sees
> the smudge on me

"Judge Poem," the deftly titled story of the judge who sentenced him, sets the rhythms of Reddy's heart against those of the judicial decrees:

> Judge Snepp snips snaps at my heart
> Labels me tactician, conspirator, overeducated revolutionary
> Beyond rehabilitation

The judge's words represent one pole of the rhythmic dialectic. Many of the poems, especially the longer ones, have a disquieting discursive quality, threatening to lapse into prose. This is not unintentional. For Reddy himself is not an African tribesman or a field slave or an old blues musician or an assembly-line worker. The tension between the prosaic and the musical is part of Reddy's own alienation, and the institution that first alienated him was not the prison but the university. So even in a cage with other inmates, he feels a bit like an outsider. One of his finest poems, "Running Upon a Wall," wryly expresses this double alienation. Attending a "Negro university as a colored track student," he finds himself, jogging,

> Going around in circles and getting
> Nowhere at different places
> All the time
> I ended up in a Black slum

There, the eyes of weary Black folk seem to tell him where to run for help:

> Run fool run
> Run fool run
> Run fast as you can for help to that place
> Written across the front of that sweatsuit
> You are wearing

But back there he finds himself "as isolated as the slum," slowly learning that the business of the university is not to help the ghetto but to control it.

Prison actually links him more directly to his people, as he shows ironically in "Black Children Visit Modern Jail." Black schoolchildren are brought in lines to see an example of a fine modern facility, the lines of cages where Reddy and the other inmates, 85 percent Black, are on exhibit. He yearns to teach them the truth of their own imprisonment, "captives / of classrooms learning ignorance," perhaps like him becoming "'criminal'" for "stepping out of line to be free."

Less Than a Score, But a Point describes a sterile wasteland, not fabricated out of an elitist poet's contempt for common people, but manufactured by a system that crushes human beings first into slave ships where "suffering Black eyes / look deep past / each other's waste," and finally into prisons where men have "orgasms in toilet paper," and into the room of a prostitute where she pays for her children's Christmas tree with "sticky spills down her thighs." But it is a book of affirmation, even of celebration. Reddy admits the judge's charge:

> Judge said I am something of a romantic
> And, yes, I confess I am
> I love life, I love love.

So far in this chapter we have been looking almost exclusively at the works of Black convicts. But, as I said earlier, Afro-American consciousness in prison reaches way out beyond the experience of Black prisoners. Even the term "Black" sometimes comes to signify a *class* point of view. For example, Etheridge Knight included in his early collection entitled *Black Voices from Prison* the personal narrative of Louis Bean, a white inmate. Knight explains:

> Louis Bean is a white boy—a "po' white" boy. And his "Testa-ment" is also the truth. He tells of running away from home, of spending time in juvenile institutions, and of finally picking up the gun—the unequivocal *No*. On the prison scene, Louis Bean is known as somewhat of a nigger-lover because he realizes that the poor whites are exploited and enslaved along with the blacks, and that ego-satisfying prejudices do not fill empty bellies or balance the scales of the oppressor's justice.[28]

This is a relatively recent and by no means universal develop-ment in the outlook of white prisoners. The autobiographical literature of white prisoners in the eighteenth and much of the nineteenth centuries typically focused on the lone individual, first in the confessional mode, then predominantly in the picaresque mode. Prison literature from 1860 through the 1930s showed a growing consciousness of class oppression, and a few works, such as Roger Benton's *Where Do I Go from Here?*, even began to display an awareness of the relation between the bondage of the Afro-American people and the servitude of the white working class. But this, like much political and social consciousness developed in the 1930s, was largely expunged in the late 1940s and the 1950s.

As I attempt to define the presently emerging tendencies in literature by white convicts, I do not want to create any false impression that it is, like literature by Black convicts, essentially unified and largely revolutionary in outlook. First, even the earliest modes of perception and narration still survive. A very recent autobiography, *Where the Money Was* (New York: Viking, 1976), by the famous bank robber Willie Sutton, describes his criminal adventures, his imprisonments, and his escapes in the same picaresque manner employed in *A Narrative of the Life, Adventures, Travels and Sufferings of Henry Tufts* (1807), the eighteenth-century horse thief. Although Sutton boasts that he "loved" robbing banks, he claims that this is a "very moral book," and that "the message it imparts is that crime doesn't pay"; he hastens to add, however, "but writing about it does." The wide interest in literature by prisoners, largely a result of the intense politicization of the prisons in the mid-1960s and the wave of rebellions that has been going on ever since, ironically has led to the publication of books by prisoners of the past who reject today's consciousness. For example, the aptly titled *Lonesome Road* by George Harsh, who not only served twelve years on a Georgia chain gang but then later was a leader in the "Great Escape" of prisoners of war from Stalag Luft III, ridicules the political thrust of recent prison literature, though he does concede that "there is one law for the rich and another for the poor."[29]

In fact, most literature by white convicts still maintains as individualistic a viewpoint as earlier prison literature. It is, nevertheless, part of that coherent body of contemporary prison literature; together with the writings of Black prisoners, it forms a single dialectic. Within that dialectic, the principal unfolding contradiction is between a collective revolutionary consciousness based on Black historical experience and the loneliness of the isolated convict ego, branded and cast out, seeking either to reintegrate with the social order or to defy it in anarchic rebellion.

The emerging contradiction can be seen in an early form in the poetry of the late William Wantling, whom Walter Lowenfels has called "the best poet of his age." Though white, Wantling's path to becoming a criminal and a prisoner was almost identical to that of Etheridge Knight: "When I was in Korea they gave me my first shot of morphine. It killed the pain. It was beautiful. Five years later I was in San Quentin on narcotics."[30]

A master stylist himself, Wantling was almost obsessed with the ways in which being determines the form of what we call beautiful and the ways in which humanity breaks through the physical forms in which it is incarnate or imprisoned. He compresses these two visions into the brief philosophic lyric, "Nothing Human Is Alien":

> artist, dare you doubt
> that if Woman gave
> birth in litters you would
> find in multiple breasts the beauty
> & mystery unceasingly provided by the female
> form?[31]

Therefore, on the one hand he expresses individual human creativity transcending the prison itself. In *"from* Sestina to San Quentin," he is even able to transfigure San Quentin in his poetic imagination:

> Do you remember now?
> How the grey and green walls rose invincible about us?
> How we raised our eyes to the sheer heights climbing to a final
>   pinnacle perspective
> Until high, high off over our heads we saw the
> Sun-stricken gun-towers, the archer-turrets of ancient castles?

And how, scudding by the turrets, scudding through the
    child-blue sky
Great puffed balls of popcorn clouds went tumbling by, the
Chaste being chased by reflected crimson from a dying sun?

Do you remember how the gulls went wheeling and crying their
    shrill plaintive cries?
How they spun down in tightened spirals to spy upon us and climb
    again?
How their wings pounded the air until, catching a rising
Current of warmth they spread their wings wide and were free,
    free and still, serene, hanging
Poised and then swiftly gliding as the chance quick current
Drifted them off over the deep blue waters of the bay?[32]

On the other hand, the brutal daily facts of San Quentin life
threaten to overwhelm his human creativity. In the poem entitled
"Poetry," he takes the kind of view of San Quentin we get in
Malcolm Braly's *On the Yard* and *False Starts,* carries it to an
extreme, and allows it to redefine his poetic form:

I've got to be honest, I can
make good word music and rhyme

at the right times and fit words
together to give people pleasure

and even sometimes take their
breath away—but it always

somehow turns out kind of phoney.
Consonance and assonance and inner

rhyme won't make up for the fact
that I can't figure out how to get

down on paper the real or the true
which we call life. Like the other

day. The other day I was walking
in the lower exercise yard here

at San Quentin and this cat called
Turk came up to a friend of mine

and said Ernie, I hear You're
shooting on my kid. And Ernie

told him So what, Punk? And Turk
pulled out his stuff and shanked

Ernie in the gut only Ernie had a
metal tray in his shirt. Turk's

shank bounced off Ernie and
Ernie pulled his stuff out and of

course Turk didn't have a tray and
he caught it dead in the chest, a bad

one, and the blood that came to his
lips was a bright pink, lung blood,

and he just laid down in the grass
and said Shit. Fuck it. Sheeit.

Fuck it. And he laughed a soft long
laugh, 5 minutes, then died. Now

what could consonance or assonance or
even rhyme do with something like that?[33]

Many of Wantling's poems express outrage at the injustices within American society, at its foreign wars of conquest, at what was done to him personally. But unlike the literature by Black convicts, Wantling's poetry ultimately finds his only victory in the almost existential transcendence by the individual, anarchic poet over organized society. This is a projected transcendence by the artist of his life, perhaps of art over life, as he puts it in "Who's Bitter?":

when Judge Lynch
denied probation

& crammed that 1 - 14
up my ass
for a First offence
I giggled

when Dr God
stuck 7 shocktreatments
to me
for giving my chick
in Camarillo
2 joints
I laughed aloud
now
when the State of Illness
caught me bending over
2 jugs of Codeine
cough medicine
& charged me w/Possession
and Conspiracy
I shrieked
in idiot joy

a bit worried
they all inquired
—What are you Wantling?
—A goddam Masochist?
I, between hilarious gasps
O howled—No,
—I'm a Poet!
—Fuck me again![34]

Wantling was not by any means untouched by the rising tide of Black nationalism in prison, but his response, as in " 'But See How Cunningly the Trap is Baited . . .,' " is to define the world as a gigantic San Quentin in which "the Muslims & / the Nazis firebomb each other's narrow cells," while sensible inmates try to do their own time:

the best advice is what any old Con will tell you:
"Walk slow, drink a lot of Water"[35]

For Wantling, the criminal is merely a victim of society and of all political forces, a victim whose only victory lies in becoming an artist. For Edward Bunker, the criminal achieves victory over society by fulfilling his own character to the utmost, something which Bunker has achieved more successfully in art than in life.

Bunker first gained wide attention with his article "War Behind Walls" in *Harper's Magazine* in early 1972, which blamed violence in prison on "the flower of Black racism," a flower that was "blossoming, virulent and paranoid."[36] He warned the respectable readers of *Harper's* that unstoppable "race war" had begun in California prisons, and this could be "a precursor for society as a whole."[37] The problem, according to Bunker, was "the mutative leap in black militant rhetoric," which was based on the belief that Black convicts are "political prisoners." The typical Black convict "feels that he has never been a part of this system, but is still in slavery, and consequently the white laws do not apply to him"; this, according to Bunker, causes a "psychological truncation" where "nothing is left but hate."[38]

Bunker's views do not reflect what had taken place in Attica five months before his article appeared, what was then happening in the California prisons, where even white convict groups originally formed to implement white supremacy, such as the Polar Bear Party in San Quentin, were uniting with Black and Chicano revolutionary organizations, or what was to happen later, such as the hunger strike begun on June 21, 1976, at Lucasville Penitentiary in Ohio, by six white convicts, all members of the Nation of Islam and part of a group of sixty-four Muslims, white and Black, who issued a statement denouncing U.S. capitalism, which had "programmed us as criminals":

> You taught us to steal, your very history revealed that it was all stolen to begin with. You run an ever-constant brainwashing program at us, teaching us to lie, to cheat; you taught us that it was an honor to kill as you splashed your history books with the blood of those you oppressed and robbed.[39]

While Bunker's views do not reflect the political reality of today's prisons, they do unconsciously reveal the psychological core of a body of literature by and about criminals stretching all the way back to the origin of the bourgeois novel in the picaresque narrative. Bunker's warning to the readers of *Harper's* about Black convicts is a modern version of Guzmán de Alfarache's warning to the captain of his galley about the planned mutiny of his fellow galley-slaves, a warning designed to achieve his own release from bondage. Bunker's projection of self-consuming hatred upon Black convicts is in reality an expression of his own desperate, wildly individualistic quest for personal worth, a quest which forms the substance of his brilliantly executed novel, *No Beast So Fierce.*

No Beast So Fierce, which is presently being made into a motion picture (*Straight Time*), appeared in 1973 and, together with the *Harper's* article, helped Bunker win parole. On a formal level, it is one of the finest achievements of prison literature, and, indeed, of that much larger body of literature about criminals. In content, it represents one kind of culmination for that obsession with the criminal characteristic of the bourgeois novel in its picaresque beginnings and in its current hordes of urban thieves and murderers, western outlaws, and jet-set spies.

The philosophical and historical designs of *No Beast So Fierce* are very tightly integrated. As in many, perhaps most, novels, freedom is the main theme. Here the quest is to be totally "free"—from prison, from restraint, from environment, from society, from conventional morality—and the hero achieves his freedom, in isolation, by existentially choosing his own predetermined destiny in a world of international and internecine warfare. The book is set in 1964, that turning point of our recent history, and in the background of the action are the television reports of the Vietnam War.

No Beast So Fierce is formally divided into three parts, each unfolding from an epigraph chosen with fine precision. Part One opens with lines from Blake's "London," expressing the hopes for human liberation arising in the late eighteenth century during the era of the American and French Revolutions:

> In every cry of every man,
> In every infant's cry of fear,

> In every voice, in every ban,
> The mind forg'd manacles I hear.

The hero—and he is a hero—Max Dembo, professional armed robber, is awaiting parole from a California prison. The prison is just what one would expect from reading the *Harper's* article. Blacks and whites are polarized into warring factions. Max has to sneak a walk with his one Black friend, Aaron Billings.

Released from prison, Max has much the same experience as JD in Braly's *It's Cold Out There*. With a shock, he receives "freedom's full impact."[40] Totally alone, his new-found freedom is "freedom to the point of being in a void" (29). All other people seem "happier in their invisible fetters," for they have "destinations born of choice and linked with past choice" (29). Struggling to meet the heartless demands of an officious parole officer, to secure his first legitimate job, to find new human associations, he finds himself being forced back into his old circles and his original destiny. He then makes an existential choice; exercising his new "freedom," he wilfully chooses what he was already destined to be:

> I was going to war with society, or perhaps I would only be renewing it. Now there were no misgivings. I declared myself free from all rules except those I wanted to accept—and I'd change those as I felt the whim. I would take whatever I wanted. I'd be what I was with a vengeance: a criminal. My choice of crime and complete abandonment of society's strictures (unless society could enforce them against me) was also my truth. Someone else might have chosen to gain as much power as possible. Crime was where I belonged, where I was comfortable and not torn apart inside. And though it was free choice, it was also destiny. Society had made me what I was (and ostracized me through fear of what it had created) and I gloried in what I was. If they refused to let me live in peace, I didn't want to. I'd been miserable that week of struggling— miserable in my mind. Fuck society! Fuck that game! If the odds were vast, fuck that, too. At least I'd had the integrity of my own soul, being the boss of my own little patch of hell, no matter how small, even if confined to my own mind. (105)

This is a logical choice for a white convict who does not comprehend the social message of Black convicts. After all he cannot, like the Black criminal, identify with "his people," because, considered as a whole society, they are his tormentors, and the creators of this Frankenstein's monster.

Part Two opens with a passage from Nietzsche concluding with the words "I will." So we have now moved into the heyday of the bourgeois epoch, and Max implements the most extreme philosophy of nineteenth-century capitalism. He becomes a self-made man, in fact a superman of crime, leading a bold gang of armed robbers, including his Black friend Aaron, whom Max rescues from prison. At the end of this section, Max is ready to execute his biggest job. The very last thing he hears from the society at large, coming at the very close of this section, is the TV report from CBS Election Central "declaring Lyndon Baines Johnson a landslide winner" (215).

Part Three opens with a quotation taken from the years of capitalism in decline:

> Do not go gentle into that good night.
> Rage, rage against the dying of the light.
> Dylan Thomas

The big job is betrayed. Max's friends are killed. He leaves his woman as he flees. But he still has the money, the big haul, and his "freedom."

Then, as a desperate fugitive wildly driving east across the country, he picks up a hitchhiker, who turns out to be the new kind of criminal, a young man "running from the draft, not because he was afraid to fight but because he believed the war was senseless, wrong" (273). This idealistic youth turns out to know more about one technical aspect of crime than Max does. He explains to Max how to get to Canada and there obtain the one great liberating document he needs—a passport.

This obviously symbolical passport arrives on New Year's Eve, and on the first day of 1965, Max, in his new identity, escapes with his wealth to Portugal. In the Epilogue, Max describes the lonely, peaceful life of his four-year exile. Now he is prepared to return, as the successful master criminal. His last words are:

> They might get me this time.
>   Fuck it! (283)

Edward Bunker has thus traced the course of criminal fantasy in the bourgeois novel from *Guzmán de Alfarache* to the 1970s.

Those white convict-authors who do not accept the Black definition of crime in America, and who do not see themselves primarily as victims of class oppression, usually reach a conclusion that can be summed up as "I did it to myself." This characterizes the writing of many convicts whose views were formed prior to the mid-1960s. Although Braly's brilliant psychological autobiography *False Starts* displays the archaic barbarity of our prison system, it is primarily the tale of how one man triumphs over what he perceives as his own worst enemy, himself. One of the most accomplished white artists of that earlier generation of prisoners, Merle Haggard, dramatically reveals the limiting effects of this focus on the self as the criminal.

Haggard is of course the most popular country and western singer and song-writer in America. His family were Okies, driven during the Depression from the dust bowl to the promised land of California, where they became migrant workers. Haggard's earliest memories are of grinding labor and poverty in the migrant labor camps where he grew up. Typically, he was soon in trouble with the law. From the age of sixteen until his release in 1960 at the age of twenty-three, he was constantly in and out of reform school and prison. In San Quentin, where he served three years, he began his career as a song-writer. When Haggard writes and sings of his criminal and prison experience, he perceives himself as a law-breaking individual. Sometimes this is in a picaresque vein, as in "Huntsville," where he gives a witty view of himself as an inept rogue who got caught on "a caper I had planned for days." At other times, he pleads for forgiveness for the paroled convict, as in "Branded Man." Often he sees his crimes coming from his early poverty, but he still blames himself as an individual rather than the society that impoverished his family in the midst of wealth. Take, as a striking contrast to the Afro-American view, the song Haggard chose to open his famous concert in Muskogee, Oklahoma, "Mama Tried." The song describes his early poverty, lavishes admiration on the heroic endurance of his mother, and pictures himself as a boy who just went wrong:

> One and only rebel child
> From a family meek and mild,
> My Mama seemed to know what lay in store.
> Spite of all the Sunday learning,
> Toward the bad I kept on turning,
> Til Mama couldn't hold me any more.
>
> I turned twenty-one in prison,
> Doing life without parole.
> No one could steer me right
> But Mama tried, Mama tried,
> Mama tried to raise me better,
> But her pleading I denied.
> That leaves only me to blame,
> 'Cause Mama tried.[41]

There is then no inconsistency, from Haggard's view, in wrapping himself in the flag, as in his most nationalistic song, "The Fighting Side of Me": "When you're running down my country, hoss, / You're walking on the fighting side of me." This is not to accept the usual liberal caricature of Haggard as a raving reactionary. His art is basically a people's art. His themes are poverty, loneliness, love, alienation, and both the degradation and the dignity of poor and working people. Unlike Bunker, who accepts the role of isolated desperado and turns society's contempt for the convict into a fantasy of the lone criminal defying and besting society, Haggard reintegrates with the people from whom he came. Haggard speaks to the lives of today's Okies, as you can hear in the recorded tumultuous ovation of the people in Muskogee to "Mama Tried"—with the biggest cheers for the line, "Doing life without parole." His art is not racist; for example, in "Irma Jackson" he tells of a white man whose love for a Black woman is frustrated by society, and in "Uncle Lem" of a ninety-year-old ex-slave whose generosity exposes the petty values of the leading citizens in a small town. But unlike the white prisoners and prisoner-artists of today, his consciousness was never touched by the Afro-American movement, with its rejection of American nationalism and its exposure of the various kinds of slavery and crimes upon which America was built.

Ross Laursen, Chairman of the Folsom Creative Writers' Workshop for over eight years, comes from a social background very close to Haggard's—except that his mother was a Comanche—but he sees America in quite a different light, as in his short poem "Fourteen Year Old Boys Make the Easiest Targets":

> I eat Watergate
> with my breakfast
> each morning
> and wonder
> how many
> will die
> that day
> in America
> by a warning shot
> in the back[42]

In *Lock the Lock,* an autobiography in prose, verse, and pictures, Tommy Trantino, who spent eight years on death row and is now doing life, envisions America as a prison not just for Blacks but for poor whites like himself. Looking back, he sees his first prison as the school where he was conditioned into racism, anticommunism, and blind acceptance of authority:

i was in prison long ago and it was the first grade and i have to take a shit and even when you have to take a shit the law says you must

first raise your hand and ask the teacher for permission so i
obeyer of the lore of the lamb am therefore busy raising my hand to
the fuhrer who says yes thomas what is it? and i thomas say i have
to take a i mean may i go to the bathroom please? . . . but she says
NO and i say but mrs parsley judge sir ma'am i gotta go make
number two![43]

His isolation and loneliness are not perceived as merely individual but as a societal experience, part of an existence that is
literally cellular, prefiguring his ultimate cage. From the windows of his junior high school, he would look out

and smile at the women across the street looking out of their prison
tenements and sometimes we'd catch each other's eyes   but they
hardly ever smiled back and sometimes i would wave to them but
the teachers would always say VERBOTEN   people were being
kept apart and we were keeping ourselves apart and we were all
hurting like a motherfucker but wasnt no one telling (19)

The key figure embodying class unity in prison consciousness is
George Jackson, the leading theoretician of the prison movement.
And the key event is the Attica rebellion, which was in part a
response to the murder of Jackson. In that rebellion there was
interracial unity, which came about through all the participating
prisoners' applying Afro-American historical experience to their
own oppression.

On August 30, 1971, the white revolutionary who named himself Sam Melville (for Herman Melville) wrote a letter from Attica:

A lot of activity around George Jackson. . . . At the midday meal
(the large meal in prison), not a man ate or spoke—black, white,
brown, red. Many wore black armbands. . . . No one can remember
anything like it here before.

Of course we all realize the lying & distortion of the media but it
doesn't matter here. G.J. was beloved by inmates throughout the
country.[44]

Ten days later came the rebellion, and then the massacre, authorized by Nelson Rockefeller, in which Sam Melville was one of the forty-three men killed.

The extraordinary collection *Betcha Ain't: Poems from Attica* contains two striking poems by Black prisoners who present the primary contradiction as not between white and Black, or even between guards and prisoners, but between the forty-three murdered victims at Attica—thirty-two prisoners and eleven guards—on one side and the power incarnated in the man soon to be appointed vice-president on the other. "Was It Necessary?" by Sam Washington accumulates the questions raised by the massacre stanza by stanza:

> Was it really necessary?
> Did they really have to carry
> Rifles and shotguns?
>   Let's ask the gov',
>   Who's so full of love!

> Was it really necessary?
> Did they really have to carry
> Rifles and shotguns?
> Against sticks and knives!
> Was it worth 43 lives?
>   Let's ask the gov',
>   Who's so full of love!

> Was it really necessary?
> Did they really have to carry
> Rifles and shotguns?
> Shoot them with intent to kill!
> Shoot them even when they lay still!
>   Let's ask the gov',
>   Who's so full of love!

> Was it really necessary?
> Did they really have to carry
> Rifles and shotguns?
> While troopers were killing with hate and glee,
> Rock was safe in Albany!
>   Wasn't he?
>   Let's ask the gov',
>   Who's so full of love!

Was it really necessary?
Did they really have to carry
Rifles and shotguns?
Rock on T.V., says he didn't know,
While 43 are helping daisies to grow!!
   Does it sound like I'm angry?
   Damn right, my heart pains me!!
     Let me tell you something,
     Since it's time for me to split.
     Don't ask the governor nothing, Man,
     Cause he's full of it.
             Peace[45]

Washington maintains a tension between formal speech and Black street phrasing until the very end, when he lets go, dropping into the conventions of the "toast" (signaled by the conventional "Since it's time for me to split").

"Formula for Attica Repeats" by Mshaka (Willie Monroe) flows from the same underlying vision but relies on different poetic conventions. Its artistry is extraordinarily tight and penetrating, and its message is quite sweeping. For example, the economic predicament of the U.S. empire is compressed into two words— "aluminum paid"—while the equally debased coinage of its language materializes in the word "Kool." This is the full text (ellipses are in the original):

      ...... and when
the smoke cleared
they came aluminum paid
lovers
from Rock/The/Terrible,
refuser
of S.O.S. Collect Calls,
Executioner.

They came tearless
tremblers,
apologetic grin factories
that breathed Kool
smoke-rings
and state-prepared speeches.
They came

> like so many unfeeling fingers
> groping without touching
> the 43 dead men
> who listened . . .
> threatening to rise
> again. . . .[46]

Despite grave obstacles, it is in the prisons of America that unity among its domestic victims has at times reached a revolutionary level. Two white prisoners put it this way in a four-line poem in a smuggled letter:

> We're down for the change and
> it's coming down.
> Jackson lives in our heads
> Attica lives in our hearts.

Whether this points toward the future of the American prison and its literature remains to be seen.

Notes

Notes for Introduction

1. *The Path On the Rainbow* (New York: Boni & Liveright, 1918, 1934), p. v.

2. These Black poets were considered fairly standard. For example, Alfred Kreymborg's widely used *Lyric America: An Anthology of American Poetry, 1630–1930* (New York: Coward-McCann, 1930) contained selections from Paul Laurence Dunbar, James Weldon Johnson, Fenton Johnson, Claude McKay, Jean Toomer, Langston Hughes, Countee Cullen. Even anthologies of English and American poetry included some of them. For example, *The New Poetry: An Anthology of Twentieth-Century Verse in English,* edited by Harriet Monroe and Alice Corbin Henderson (New York: Macmillan, 1932), had selections from Countee Cullen, Langston Hughes, Fenton Johnson, and James Weldon Johnson. I am indebted to Carolyn Karcher for initiating this research into the standard early 1930s' anthologies.

3. These still greatly influential collections include: Cleanth Brooks, John Purser, and Robert Penn Warren, *An Approach to Literature,* 1936, enlarged and revised in 1952, with sections of poetry, fiction, biography, essays, and drama—all by white authors; Brooks and Warren *Understanding Poetry,* 1938, 1946, 1950, enlarged and revised in 1952—all white; Cleanth Brooks, *Modern Poetry and the Tradition,* 1939—all white; Brooks and Warren, *Understanding Fiction,* 1943, greatly enlarged, quite revised, but still pure white in 1959; Caroline Gordon and Allen Tate, *The House of Fiction,* 1950, revised but still pure white in 1960; and several similar anthologies.

4. These three examples are among those discussed in *Searching for America,* edited by Ernece B. Kelly (Urbana, Ill.: National Council of Teachers of English, 1972). This is an invaluable survey of Anglo-American ethnocentricity in the definition of American literature.

5. Ibid., pp. 8, 40, 47.

Notes for Chapter 1

1. *The South Vindicated from the Treason and Fanaticism of the Northern Abolitionists* (Philadelphia, 1836), pp. 69–70.

2. Simms, "The Morals of Slavery" (1837; 1852), in *The Pro-Slavery Argument as Maintained by the Most Distinguished Writers of the Southern States* (Philadelphia, 1853), p. 217.

3. "Old News," in *Hawthorne's The Snow-Image* (Boston: Houghton, Mifflin, 1895), pp. 156–57.

4. *Life of Franklin Pierce* (1852), in *The Complete Writings of Nathaniel Hawthorne* (Boston: Houghton, Mifflin, 1900), vol. 17, p. 164.

5. Ephraim Peabody, "Narratives of Fugitive Slaves," *Christian Examiner and Religious Miscellany* 47 (July 1849): 61.

6. Charles H. Nichols, *Many Thousand Gone: The Ex-Slaves' Account of Their Bondage and Freedom* (Bloomington and London: Indiana University Press, 1969), pp. xi–xiii.

7. Arna Bontemps, *Great Slave Narratives* (Boston: Beacon Press, 1969), p. vii.

8. Jean Fagan Yellin, *The Intricate Knot: Black Figures in American Literature, 1776–1863* (New York: New York University Press, 1972), p. 161.

9. Benjamin Quarles did a valuable introduction, mostly historical, for his 1960 Harvard University Press edition of the *Narrative.* In 1972, two extremely insightful but brief analyses appeared in critical books, Jean Yellin's *The Intricate Knot,* cited above, pp. 161–64, and Houston Baker's *Long Black Song: Essays in Black American Literature and Culture* (Charlottesville: University of Virginia Press), pp. 71–83.

10. These are: Nancy T. Clasby, "Frederick Douglass's *Narrative:* A Content Analysis," *CLAJ* 14 (1971): 242–50, and Albert E. Stone, "Identity and Art in Frederick Douglass's *Narrative,*" *CLAJ* 17 (1973): 192–213.

11. Baker, *Long Black Song,* pp. 75–76.

12. Stone, "Identity and Art in Frederick Douglass's *Narrative,*" 206–7.

13. George M. Fredrickson, *The Black Image in the White Mind: The Debate on Afro-American Character and Destiny, 1817–1914* (New York: Harper & Row, 1971), p. 43.

14. Quoted by Fredrickson, ibid., p. 49.

15. Ibid., p. 50. Fredrickson cites a number of other works prior to 1845 making the same biological case against the Negro: *The South Vindicated from the Treason and Fanaticism of the Northern Abolitionists* (cited above); James Kirke Paulding, *Slavery in the United States* (New York, 1836); J.H. Guenebault, *Natural History of the Negro Race* (Charleston, 1837); Reverend Josiah Priest, *Slavery, As It Relates to the Negro or African Race* (Albany, N.Y., 1843); Dr. Samuel A. Cartwright, *Essays, Being Inductions Drawn from the Baconian Philosophy* ... (Vidalia, La., 1843).

16. Ibid., p. 74. See also William Stanton, *The Leopard's Spots: Scientific Attitudes toward Race in America, 1815–1859* (Chicago: University of Chicago Press, Phoenix Books, 1966), p. 69 *et seq.*

17. Ibid., pp. 74–77. For an extremely valuable analysis of how Melville confronted and utilized this "science" see Carolyn L. Karcher, "Melville's 'The 'Gees': A Forgotten Satire on Scientific Racism," *American Quarterly* 27 (1975): 421–42.

18. P. 23 in the edition by Benjamin Quarles (Harvard University Press, 1960), which reproduces the text of the first edition, published in Boston, 1845; future references, indicated by page numbers in parentheses, are to this edition.

19. Copy of referee's report in my possession.

20. "On the Teaching of Literature in the Highest Academies of the Empire," *College English* 31 (1970): 549.

21. Clasby, 248.

22. Ibid., 249.

23. Frantz Fanon, *The Wretched of the Earth* (1961; New York: Grove Press, 1966), p. 27.

24. Clasby, 249.

25. Herman Melville, *Narrative of a Four Months' Residence* ... (London, 1846), p. 138.

26. Linda Brent, *Incidents in the Life of a Slave Girl* (Boston, 1861; reprint ed., New York: Harcourt Brace Jovanovich, 1973), pp. 38–39.

27. Brent, *Incidents,* p. 100. Subsequent page references will appear parenthetically in the text.

28. Henri Petter, *The Early American Novel* (Columbus, Oh.: Ohio State University Press, 1971), p. 29.

29. Ibid., p. 30.

30. *I'll Take My Stand: The South and the Agrarian Tradition* (1930; reprint ed., New York: Harper Torchbooks, 1962), p. 53.

31. Grady McWhiny, *Southerners and Other Americans* (New York: Basic Books, 1973), p. 188.

32. Davidson, *I'll Take My Stand,* p. 54.

33. Allen Tate, *Reactionary Essays on Poetry and Ideas* (New York, 1936), pp. 155–56.

Notes for Chapter 2

1. *Moby-Dick; Or, The Whale,* edited by Luther Mansfield and Howard Vincent (New York: Hendricks House, 1952), Ch. 14. Further references are by chapter to this edition.

2. Ibid., Ch. 26.

3. Linda Brent, *Incidents in the Life of a Slave Girl* (Boston, 1861; reprint ed. New York: Harcourt Brace Jovanovich, 1973), p. 172.

4. Ibid., p. 191.

5. *Narrative of a Four Months' Residence among the Natives of a Valley of the Marquesas Islands; Or, A Peep at Polynesian Life* (London, 1846), p. 1. Further references are by chapter to this edition.

6. Mao Tse-tung, "Talks at the Yenan Forum on Literature and Art" (1942), *Selected Works of Mao Tse-tung,* 4 vols. (Peking, 1965), vol. 3, p. 89.

7. Review of *Narrative of a Four Months' Residence* . . . in *The Spectator,* February 28, 1846.

8. Ibid.

9. Boston *Post,* November 20, 1851.

10. Review of *Moby-Dick* in *United States Magazine and Democratic Review,* January 1852.

11. For a demonstration of how Melville subtly demolishes Darwin's observations of the Galapagos Islands by showing that a common sailor would see and comprehend more than the famed scientist, see my article, "The Island Worlds of Darwin and Melville," *Centennial Review* 11 (1967): 353–70.

12. Nathaniel Hawthorne, *The Blithedale Romance* (Boston, 1852), Ch. 8.

13. "Bartleby, the Scrivener. A Story of Wall-Street," *Putnam's Monthly Magazine* 2 (November and December 1853).

14. "Benito Cereno," *Putnam's Monthly Magazine* 5 (October, November, December 1855).

15. *Israel Potter* was serialized in *Putnam's Monthly Magazine* 4–5 (July 1854–March 1855) and then published separately as a book in 1855. References are by chapter to the edition edited by Lewis Leary (New York: Sagamore Press, 1957).

16. *The Confidence-Man: His Masquerade,* edited by H. Bruce Franklin (Indianapolis: Bobbs-Merrill Co., 1967), Ch. 3. Further references are by chapter to this edition.

17. *Billy Budd, Sailor (An Inside Narrative),* edited by Harrison Hayford and Merton Sealts, Jr. (Chicago: Phoenix Books, The University of Chicago Press, 1962), pp. 43–44. This text prepared by Hayford and Sealts, and available in several editions, is the only version close to Melville's manuscript. All references are by page number to this edition.

Notes for Chapter 3

1. James Kennard, Jr., "Who Are Our National Poets?," *Knickerbocker Magazine* 26 (October 1845): 340.

2. Eileen Southern, *The Music of Black Americans: A History* (New York: W.W. Norton, 1971), p. 103.

3. Eugene Genovese, *Roll, Jordan, Roll: The World the Slaves Made* (New York: Random House, 1974), p. 250.

4. Kennard, "Our National Poets," p. 331.

5. See Alexander Saxton, "Blackface Minstrelsy and Jacksonian Ideology," *American Quarterly* 27 (March 1975): 3–28.

6. Henry Edward Krehbiel, *Afro-American Folksongs: A Study in Racial and National Music* (New York, 1914), p. v.

7. Ibid., p. 93.

8. Ibid., p. 94.

9. Ibid.

10. Donald Davidson, "A Mirror for Artists," *I'll Take My Stand* (1930; reprint ed., New York: Harper Torchbooks, 1962), p. 53.

11. Richard Foster Jones, *The Triumph of the English Language* (Stanford: Stanford University Press, 1953), p. 168. Jones provides a magnificent history of the triumph of the people's living language as it rushed on "past the demands of spelling, grammar, and lexicography to a rendezvous with the greatest literature England ever produced," causing at least one Elizabethan grammarian to lament that "the English became eloquent before they were grammatical" (p. 167).

12. Otto Jespersen, *Language, Its Nature, Development, and Origin* (London, 1933), p. 432.

13. Willard R. Trask, *The Unwritten Song: Poetry of the Primitive and Traditional Peoples of the World,* 2 vols. (New York: Macmillan, 1966–67), vol. 2, p. xxviii.

14. Jespersen, *Language,* p. 432.

15. This is a highly controversial area. The theory of the origin of poetry in labor was argued at length by Karl Bücher in *Arbeit und Rhythmus* (Leipzig, 1899). Bücher made a number of errors, and his work was subsequently subjected to heavy debunking. However, his theory was later supported by work in the physiology of language and linguistic theory, for example in Richard Paget's *Human Speech* (London, 1930) and Jespersen's work cited above, in literary criticism and the history of literature, with a line of development from Christopher Caudwell's *Illusion and Reality* (London and New York, 1937) into recent Marxist theory, in classical studies, notably by George Thomson's *Studies in Ancient Greek Society: The Prehistoric Aegean* (London, 1945, 1961), and with massive compilations from anthropology in *The Growth of Literature* by H.M. Chadwick and N.K. Chadwick (Cambridge, 1932–40, 3 vols.).

16. Trask, *The Unwritten Song,* vol. 1, pp. xiii, xxiii.

17. M.V. Portman, "Andamanese Music," *Journal of the Royal Asiatic Society* n.s. 20 (1888): 184. As quoted in Trask, vol. 1, p. xiii.

18. Knud Rasmussen, *Intellectual Culture of the Copper Eskimos* (Copenhagen, 1932), p. 130. As quoted in Trask, vol. 1, p. xiii.

19. R.F. Fortune, *Sorcerers of Dobu: The Social Anthropology of the Dobu Islanders of the Western Pacific,* (New York, 1932), p. 251. As quoted in Trask, vol. 1, p. xiv.

20. H. Munro Chadwick and N. Kershaw Chadwick, *The Growth of Literature,* 3 vols. (Cambridge, 1932–40), vol. 3, p. 659. See also George Thomson, *Studies in Ancient Greek Society: The Prehistoric Aegean* (New York: Citadel Press, 1965), p. 454.

21. Frederick R. Burton, *American Primitive Music* (New York, 1909), pp. 172–73.

22. R.H. Codrington, *The Melanesians: Studies in Their Anthropology and Folklore* (Oxford, 1891), p. 334. As quoted in Trask, vol. 1, p. x.

23. John Greenway, *Literature among the Primitives* (Hatboro, Pa.: Folklore Associates, 1964), p. 57. On the same page, Greenway offers the following as examples of true work songs: "the agricultural group labor songs and prison gang songs of the Negroes of the Southern United States or the capstan shanties of the wooden-ship sailormen."

24. Newman I. White, *American Negro Folk-Songs* (Cambridge, Mass.: Harvard University Press, 1928), p. 5.

25. *Notes of Travel, Volume II, The Complete Writings of Nathaniel Hawthorne* (Boston: Houghton, Mifflin, 1900), vol. 20, pp. 62–63.

26. J.J. Trux, "Negro Minstrelsy—Ancient and Modern," *Putnam's Monthly Magazine* 5 (January 1855): 72–79.

27. Thomas Wentworth Higginson, "Negro Spirituals," *Atlantic Monthly* 19 (June 1867): 684–94. This was republished with minor changes in Higginson's text and virtually none in the collected songs as a chapter in his *Army Life in a Black Regiment* (1869), available in a Beacon Press paperback. Songs quoted from Higginson can be found in either publication; quotations are from the original article.

28. William Francis Allen, Charles Pickard Ware, and Lucy McKim Garrison, *Slave Songs of the United States* (New York, 1867; reprint ed., New York: Peter Smith, 1951), p. xx.

29. William Wells Brown, *Clotel; Or, the President's Daughter: A Narrative of Slave Life in the United States* (London, 1853), Ch. 16.

30. Frederick Douglass, *My Bondage and My Freedom* (New York, 1855), Ch. 18.

31. *Clotel,* Ch. 13.

32. Dorothy Scarborough, *On the Trail of Negro Folk-Songs* (Cambridge, Mass.: Harvard University Press, 1925), p. 165. For some other versions in other parts of the South see White, *American Negro Folk-Songs,* p. 382.

33. Higginson, "Negro Spirituals," p. 692.

34. Douglass, *My Bondage and My Freedom,* Ch. 19.

35. William Wells Brown, *Narrative of William W. Brown, A Fugitive Slave. Written by Himself* (Boston, 1847), Ch. 6. Brown also reprints this as "Song of the Coffle Gang" in his collection of antislavery songs, *The Anti-Slavery Harp* (Boston, 1848), p. 30.

36. Genovese, *Roll, Jordan, Roll,* p. 249.

37. See, for example, LeRoi Jones (Imamu Amiri Baraka), *Blues People* (New

York: William Morrow, 1963); Ben Sidran, *Black Talk* (New York: Holt, Rinehart, 1972); and *Roll, Jordan, Roll.*

38. Southern, *The Music of Black Americans,* p. 93. For a critical discussion of the controversy concerning the relation between Black and white spirituals, see D.K. Wilgus, "The Negro-White Spirituals" in *Anglo-American Folksong Scholarship* (New Brunswick, N.J.: Rutgers University Press, 1959), pp. 344–64.

39. János Maróthy, *Music and the Bourgeois; Music and the Proletarian* (Budapest: Akadémiai Kiadó, 1974), p. 496.

40. Ibid., p. 498. For Melville's use of the shanty see Agnes D. Cannon, "Melville's Use of Sea Ballads and Songs," *Western Folklore* 23 (1964): 1–16, which ends by focusing on "Billy in the Darbies," and Robert J. Schwendinger, "The Language of the Sea: Relationships Between the Language of Herman Melville and Sea Shanties of the 19th Century," *Southern Folklore Quarterly* 37 (1973): 53–73.

41. Ibid., p. 318. A version of this song on Library of Congress Archives of American Folk Song, L27, A-5, includes the line, "I've picked the cotton and hoed the corn."

42. Ibid., p. 492.

43. Harold Courlander, *Negro Folk Music, U.S.A.* (New York: Columbia University Press, 1963), p. 43.

44. Bruce Jackson, *Wake Up Dead Man: Afro-American Worksongs from Texas Prisons* (Cambridge, Mass.: Harvard University Press, 1972), p. 195.

45. Louise Pound, *Poetic Origins and the Ballad* (1921; New York: Russell & Russell, 1962), pp. 91–92, 93, 158.

46. Ibid., p. 157.

47. John Dollard, *Caste and Class in a Southern Town* (1937; New York: Doubleday Anchor Books, 1957), p. 242.

48. Ibid., pp. 243–44.

49. Pound, *Poetic Origins,* p. 158.

50. Bruce Jackson transcribes and discusses this song in *Wake Up Dead Man,* pp. 99–101.

51. John G. Van Deusen, *The Black Man in White America* (Washington, D.C.: Associated Publishers, 1938), p. 124.

52. Ibid.

53. Pete Daniel, *The Shadow of Slavery: Peonage in the South, 1901–1969* (Urbana: University of Illinois Press, 1972), pp. 19–20. See also Richard Barry, "Slavery in the South To-Day," *Cosmopolitan Magazine* 42 (March 1907): 481–96.

54. Daniel, *Shadow of Slavery,* p. 11.

55. Mary F. Berry, "Do Black People Have a Constitutional Right to Life: A Consideration of Federal and State Concern about the Murder of Black People, 1877–1969," paper delivered to Southern Historical Association Convention, November 12, 1970, pp. 22–28. Cited by Daniel, p. 126.

56. Lawrence Gellert, *Negro Songs of Protest* (New York, 1936), p. 21.

57. Scarborough, *On the Trail of Negro Folk-Songs,* pp. 163–64. For some other versions, see White, *American Negro Folk-Songs,* pp. 204, 271, 360, 361.

58. Howard W. Odum and Guy B. Johnson, *Negro Workaday Songs* (New York: Negro Universities Press, 1926, 1969), pp. 78–79.

59. Paul Oliver, *The Meaning of the Blues* (New York: Collier Books, 1963), p. 242.

60. Daniel, *Shadow of Slavery,* p. 26.

61. Van Deusen, *Black Man in White America,* p. 131.

62. Oliver, *Meaning of the Blues,* p. 240.

63. Ibid.

64. Billie Holiday, *Lady Sings the Blues* (1956; New York: Lancer Books, 1969), p. 26.

65. Ibid.

66. Odum and Johnson, *Negro Workaday Songs,* p. 87.

67. For extensive documentation see: Daniel; Van Deusen; Walter Wilson, *Forced Labor in the United States* (New York, 1933); and Harry Haywood, *Negro Liberation* (New York: International Publishers, 1948).

68. Daniel, *Shadow of Slavery,* p. 26; Wilson, *Forced Labor,* p. 87.

69. Daniel, *Shadow of Slavery,* p. 29; "The New Slavery in the South—An Autobiography, By a Georgia Negro Peon," *The Independent* 56 (February 25,1904): 412.

70. Daniel, *Shadow of Slavery,* p. 114.

71. Ibid., p. 41.

72. *Crisis* 35 (January 1928): 5. The story of the flood is told in: Daniel, pp. 149–69; William Alexander Percy, *Lanterns on the Levee* (New York, 1953); Wilson, pp. 104–5; Oliver, pp. 262–68; *Crisis,* Jan., Feb., March 1928.

73. Hoover, responding to allegations that the conditions for these refugees were atrocious, requested that a select committee be chosen "to visit any of the negro concentration camps in Mississippi, Arkansas, or Louisiana." *(The New York Times,* May 28, 1927.)

74. Oliver, *Meaning of the Blues,* p. 267.

75. Jackson, *Wake Up Dead Man,* p. 2.

76. Ibid., p. 30.

77. *The Leadbelly Songbook,* ed. Moses Asch and Alan Lomax (New York: Oak Publications, 1962), p. 50.

78. Courlander, *Negro Folk Music,* p. 142.

79. *The Leadbelly Songbook,* p. 50.

80. Jackson, *Wake Up Dead Man,* p. 114.

81. Ibid., p. 118.

82. Van Deusen, *Black Man in White America,* p. 123.

83. White, *American Negro Folk-Songs,* p. 279.

84. Odum and Johnson, *Negro Workaday Songs,* p. 104.

85. White, *American Negro Folk-Songs,* pp. 257–58.

86. Ibid., p. 259.

87. Guy B. Johnson, *John Henry: Tracking Down a Negro Legend* (Chapel Hill: University of North Carolina Press, 1929), pp. 71–72.

88. John Greenway, *American Folksongs of Protest* (New York: Octagon Books, 1971), p. 107.

89. Courlander, *Negro Folk Music,* p. 110. See also White, *American Negro Folk-Songs,* pp. 260–62.

90. Johnson, *John Henry,* pp. 1, 3, 69.

91. William E. Barton, D.D., *Old Plantation Hymns* (Boston, 1899), p. 34.

92. Johnson, *John Henry,* p. 101.

93. Gellert, *Negro Songs of Protest,* p. 45.

Notes for Chapter 4

1. There is no comprehensive or even extended bibliography at all. The best single source for the earlier works by convicts is Augustus F. Kuhlman's standard bibliography, *A Guide to Material on Crime and Criminal Justice* (1929), with corrections and author index by Dorothy Campbell Culver (Montclair, N.J.: Patterson Smith, 1969), which includes some listings of literature by convicts and criminals, mostly personal narratives. Although Kuhlman does not rigorously distinguish between authentic autobiographical works and sensationalized narratives palmed off as "confessions" by notorious criminals, his listings certainly demonstrate that the genre of the criminal confession was quite widespread, a fact of great significance (see, for example, my discussion of the so-called *Confessions of Nat Turner* in the light of the confession genre, pp. 132–33). Other bibliographic sources are even more fragmentary. For a detailed discussion of previous bibliographic materials and the problems in locating the literature written by convicts, see my preface to the Appendix, "An Annotated Bibliography of Literature by American Convicts: 1800–1977" (pp. 291–93). Critical literature is virtually nonexistent, except for notable individual authors such as O. Henry, Jack London, Jim Tully, Agnes Smedley, Chester Himes, etc.

2. Daniel Defoe, *Moll Flanders,* edited by J. Paul Hunter (New York: Thomas Crowell, 1970), pp. 254–55.

3. A.G.L. Shaw, *Convicts and the Colonies* (London: Faber and Faber, 1966), p. 25.

4. Ibid., p. 35.

5. From a copy in the New York Public Library.

6. *A Narrative of the Life, Adventures, Travels and Sufferings of Henry Tufts ... in substance, as compiled from his own mouth* (Dover, N.H., 1807), from the final chapter, "Advice to the Young." As with the slave narratives, many convict narratives, from Tufts's through Malcolm X's, are transcribed from their oral telling.

7. Herman Melville, *The Confidence-Man,* edited by H. Bruce Franklin (Indianapolis: Bobbs-Merrill, 1967), pp. 5–6.

8. As quoted in *Imprisoned in America,* edited by Cynthia Owen Philip (New York: Harper & Row, 1973), pp. 56–59.

9. *The Confessions of Nat Turner ... As fully and voluntarily made to Thomas R. Gray* (Baltimore, 1831), in Herbert Aptheker, *Nat Turner's Slave Rebellion* (New York: Grove Press, 1968), p. 129. Subsequent page references appear parenthetically in the text.

10. "How I Became a Socialist," in *The War of the Classes* (New York, 1905), p. 278.

11. Ibid., p. 276.

12. "The Tramp," in *The War of the Classes,* pp. 79–80.

13. "Pinched: A Prison Experience," *Cosmopolitan* 43 (July 1907): 270.

14. "The New Slavery in the South—An Autobiography, By a Georgia Negro Peon," *The Independent* 56 (February 25, 1904): 409. Subsequent page references appear parenthetically in the text.

15. Donald Lowrie, *My Life in Prison* (New York, 1912), p. 420.

16. Ernest Booth, "Ladies in Durance Vile," *American Mercury* 23 (April 1931): 402.

17. Ernest Booth, *With Sirens Screaming* (Garden City, N.Y., 1945), p. 280.

18. Jim Tully, *Beggars of Life* (New York, 1924), pp. 308–9.

19. Jim Tully, *Shadows of Men* (Garden City, N.Y., 1930), pp. 12–13.

20. Herman K. Spector, "What Men Write in Prison," *Tomorrow* 5 (December 1945): 53.

21. Miriam Allen De Ford, "Shall Convicts Write Books?," *Nation* 131 (November 5, 1930): 496.

22. Walter Wilson, *Forced Labor in the United States* (New York, 1933), p. 37.

23. Robert E. Burns, *I Am a Fugitive from a Georgia Chain Gang!* (New York, 1932; reprinted by Gale Research Company, Detroit, 1972), p. 62.

24. Black, *You Can't Win,* pp. 42–43.

25. Tully, *Shadows of Men,* pp. 52–53. For the version in *Clotel,* see p. 89.

26. Quoted in Olive Woolley Burt, *American Murder Ballads and Their Stories* (New York: Oxford University Press, 1968), pp. 212–13.

27. Edna O'Brien, *So I Went to Prison* (New York, 1938), p. 20.

28. *Female Convict, As told to Vincent Burns* (New York, 1934), p. 12. Vincent

Burns, minister and brother of Robert E. Burns, has, as far as I can tell, made no qualitative changes in the text and, judging from his own writings, I believe he has had no particular influence on its style.

29. Roger Benton, *Where Do I Go from Here? The Life Story of a Forger, As told to Robert O. Ballou* (New York, 1936), p. 97.

Notes for Chapter 5

1. *False Starts: A Memoir of San Quentin and Other Prisons* (Boston: Little, Brown, 1976), p. 170. Further citations appear parenthetically in the text.

2. *Felony Tank* (New York: Pocket Books, 1976), p. 73. Further citations, appearing parenthetically in the text, are to this edition, which is substantially revised from the first edition, published by Fawcett as a Gold Medal Original in 1961.

3. Braly has indicated to me in conversation that the 1961 ending was tacked on for purely commercial reasons.

4. *Shake Him Till He Rattles* (New York: Pocket Books, 1976), p. 9. Further citations, appearing parenthetically in the text, are to this edition, which is slightly revised from the first edition, published by Fawcett as a Gold Medal Original in 1963.

5. *It's Cold Out There* (New York: Pocket Books, 1976), p. 26. Further citations, appearing parenthetically in the text, are to this edition, which is slightly revised from the first edition, published by Fawcett as a Gold Medal Original in 1966.

6. *On the Yard* (Greenwich, Conn.: Fawcett Publications, 1968), p. 258. This is an unrevised reprint of the much scarcer hardcover first edition published by Little, Brown in 1967. Further citations appear parenthetically.

7. Chester Himes, *The Quality of Hurt: The Autobiography of Chester Himes, Volume I* (Garden City, N.Y.: Doubleday, 1972), p. 125.

8. William S. Lynch, review of *If He Hollers Let Him Go, Saturday Review* (November 17, 1945), pp. 53–54.

9. W. R. Burnett, review of *Cast the First Stone, Saturday Review* (January 17, 1953), p. 15.

10. Gilbert Millstein, review of *Cast the First Stone, New York Times Book Review* (January 18, 1953), p. 24.

11. *The Quality of Hurt,* pp. 136, 285.

12. Ibid., p. 60.

13. James Lundquist, *Chester Himes* (New York: Frederick Ungar, 1976), p. 74.

14. *The Quality of Hurt,* p. 117.

15. Chester Himes, *My Life of Absurdity: The Autobiography of Chester Himes, Volume II* (Garden City, N.Y.: Doubleday, 1976), p. 125.

16. *The Quality of Hurt,* p. 61.

17. *Prison Mass, Abbott's Monthly and Illustrated News* 6 (March 1933): 36, 37,

61–64; (April 1933): 20, 21, 48–56; (May 1933): 37, 61, 62. References are given parenthetically by month and page.

18. "I Don't Want to Die," *Abbott's Monthly* 6 (October 1933): 21.

19. "Crazy in the Stir," *Esquire* 2 (August 1934): 114.

20. "To What Red Hell?," *Esquire* 2 (October 1934): 100.

21. *Cast the First Stone* (New York: Signet, 1972), p. 133.

22. Raymond Nelson, "Domestic Harlem: The Detective Fiction of Chester Himes," *Virginia Quarterly Review* 48 (1972): 276.

23. Edward Margolies, "The Thrillers of Chester Himes," *Studies in Black Literature* 1 (1970): 10.

24. *My Life of Absurdity,* pp. 101–6.

25. "He Knew," *Abbott's Weekly and Illustrated News* 1 (December 2, 1933): 15.

26. *For Love of Imabelle* (New York: Signet, 1974), pp. 81–86.

27. *Cotton Comes to Harlem* (New York: Putnam's, 1965), pp. 201–2.

28. *My Life of Absurdity,* p. 292.

29. *Hot Day, Hot Night* (reissue of *Blind Man With a Pistol*) (New York: Signet, 1975), pp. 167–68.

30. *My Life of Absurdity,* p. 360.

31. Ibid., p. 363.

32. "Prediction," *Black on Black* (Garden City, N.Y.: Doubleday, 1973), p. 281.

Notes for Chapter 6

1. Stephen Henderson, *Understanding the New Black Poetry: Black Speech and Black Music as Poetic References* (New York: William Morrow, 1973), p. 20.

2. *The Autobiography of Malcolm X* (New York: Grove Press, 1965, paperback, 1966), p. 3. Subsequent page references are given parenthetically.

3. Etheridge Knight, *Poems from Prison* (Detroit: Broadside Press, 1968), p. 28.

4. Bobby Seale, *Seize the Time* (New York: Random House, 1970), p. 3.

5. Eldridge Cleaver, *Soul on Ice* (New York: Ramparts Books, McGraw-Hill, 1968), p. 58.

6. *Who Took the Weight? Black Voices from Norfolk Prison* (Boston: Little, Brown, 1972), p. 49.

7. *Uniform Crime Reports for the United States—1975* (Washington, D.C.: Federal Bureau of Investigation, U.S. Department of Justice, 1976), p. 179.

8. John Sinclair and Robert Levin, *Music & Politics* (New York and Cleveland: World Publishing, 1971), p. 7.

9. Knight, *Poems from Prison,* back cover. Knight's early history is commonplace. One of Hurricane Carter's childhood friends, "like many other thousands of soldiers" wounded in Korea, "was fed a steady diet of alkaloid morphine to numb his pain." No effort was made either to take him off the drug or to remove "the chunks of shrapnel still lodged in his body": "Uncle Sam had hooked him on dope." Carter's friend did not end up being a writer; he was electrocuted by the state of New Jersey. (*The Sixteenth Round,* New York: Warner Books Edition, 1975, p. 226.) Somewhat more fortunate was the poet William Wantling, who had the same experience with government-administered narcotics in Korea. See p. 262.

10. We should know a few facts about Reddy. In 1968, a barn burned in Charlotte, North Carolina. Three years later, Robert Mardian, then head of the U.S. Justice Department's Internal Security Division, later a convicted felon, supervised a deal whereby two ex-convicts would each be paid $4,000 in cash by the U.S. Government, plus having all the many charges pending against them dropped, in return for testifying that the barn had been burned by Reddy and two other Black political activists. (Mardian, whose lawyer in the Watergate conspiracy trial described him as "pure as the driven snow," was then Nixon's leading hatchet man against the left. He made similar deals to procure false testimony against Black, Chicano, Indian, and white activists throughout the country, myself included.) This frameup left T.J. Reddy serving twenty years, a sentence that even *The Washington Post* and *The New York Times* called "astonishing."

11. T.J. Reddy, *Less Than a Score, But a Point* (New York: Vintage, 1974), pp. 13–14.

12. Knight, *Poems from Prison,* p. 18.

13. See above, p. 143.

14. Ellsworth R. Johnson, "Alcatraz," *Freedomways* 6 (Summer 1966): 230–31.

15. Carter, *The Sixteenth Round,* p. 210.

16. On *Archive of Folk Music,* FS-202.

17. *The Last Stop: Writings from Comstock Prison* (Greenfield Center, N.Y.: The Greenfield Review Press, 1974), p. 56.

18. *Narrative of the Life of Frederick Douglass* (Cambridge: Harvard University Press, 1973), p. 133.

19. Jessica Mitford, *Kind and Usual Punishment: The Prison Business* (New York: Vintage, 1974), p. 215.

20. Ibid., pp. 209–10.

21. Of the people in jail, 57.4 percent are legally innocent (they just cannot afford bail), and of the people convicted each year, between 84 and 90 percent have accepted a bargained plea (mostly because they cannot afford a trial). See *Sourcebook of Criminal Justice Statistics—1975* (Albany, N.Y.: U.S. Department of Justice, Criminal Justice Research Center, 1976), pp. 587, 614. Of those who have formal charges brought against them by the police, only 16.5 percent are acquitted or dismissed (*Uniform Crime Reports—1975,* p. 174). See also Mitford, *Kind and Usual Punishment,* pp. 19, 84.

22. *Look for Me in the Whirlwind* (New York: Random House, 1971), p. v.

23. *Captive Voices: An Anthology from Folsom Prison* (Paradise, Calif.: Dustbooks, 1975), pp. 198–99.

24. *The Last Stop*, pp. 58–59.

25. *Who Took the Weight?*, pp. 57–58.

26. Knight, *Poems from Prison*, pp. 11–12.

27. Ibid., p. 14.

28. Etheridge Knight, *Black Voices from Prison* (New York: Pathfinder Press, 1964), p. 7.

29. George Harsh, *Lonesome Road* (New York: W.W. Norton, 1971), p. 8.

30. William Wantling, *The Source* (El Cerrito, Calif.: Dustbooks, 1966), p. 3.

31. William Wantling, *San Quentin's Stranger* (Dunedin, New Zealand: Caveman Press, 1973), p. 56. Wantling has a much larger audience in Great Britain and the Commonwealth than in the United States.

32. Ibid., p. 14.

33. Ibid., pp. 17–18.

34. Ibid., p. 21.

35. Ibid., p. 32.

36. Edward Bunker, "War Behind Walls," *Harper's Magazine* (February 1972): 42.

37. Ibid., p. 47.

38. Ibid., p. 42.

39. *Guardian* 28 (June 30, 1976): 3.

40. Edward Bunker, *No Beast So Fierce* (New York: Manor Books, 1975), p. 29. Originally published in hardback, New York: W.W. Norton, 1973. Subsequent page references are given parenthetically.

41. On *Okie from Muskogee,* Capitol ST-384.

42. *Captive Voices*, p. 117. Laursen was finally paroled from Folsom in 1975, the same year that his splendid collection of poetry, *Sweet Tomorrow*, was published (by Peace & Pieces Foundation, P.O. Box 99394, San Francisco).

43. *Lock the Lock* (New York: Bantam, 1975), p. 4. Originally published in hardback, New York: Knopf, 1973.

44. Samuel Melville, *Letters from Attica* (New York: William Morrow, 1972), p. 172.

45. *Betcha Ain't: Poems from Attica*, ed. Celes Tisdale (Detroit: Broadside Press, 1974), pp. 43–44.

46. Ibid., p. 27.

Index